Emil Staiger

Basic Concepts of Poetics

(Grundbegriffe der Poetik)

Translated by
Janette C. Hudson and Luanne T. Frank

Edited by
Marianne Burkhard and Luanne T. Frank

With an Introduction by
Luanne T. Frank

The Pennsylvania State University Press
University Park, Pennsylvania

Publication of this work was supported by the Swiss Foundation Pro Helvetia and received the assistance of the Swiss American Historical Society. The copyright has been granted by the Estate of Emil Staiger.

Library of Congress Cataloging-in-Publication Data

Staiger, Emil, 1908–
   [Grundbegriffe der Poetik. English]
   Basic concepts of poetics / Emil Staiger; translated by Janette
C. Hudson and Luanne T. Frank: edited by Marianne Burkhard and
Luanne T. Frank.

     p. cm.
   Translation of: Grundbegriffe der Poetik.
   Includes bibliographical references (p.
   ISBN 0-271-00674-9
   1. Poetics. I. Burkhard, Marianne. II. Title.
PN1042.S7613 1991
808.1—dc20   89–71034

Contents

Preface

Translating is an act of mediation, not just between languages but also between cultures and modes of thought. The translation of Emil Staiger's *Grundbegriffe der Poetik* (Basic Concepts of Poetics) is no exception and hopes to fulfill several mediatory tasks.

The first is cultural. To be sure, a translation of Staiger's work mediates between German and English. At the same time, however, it reaches a wider realm because the author chooses his examples from various European literary traditions, thus engaging the expert in national literatures as well as the comparatist. And Staiger does even more. His *Poetics* explores fundamental patterns of literary creativity and thereby invites a dialogue with those who are immersed in the study of non-Western literary traditions and whose lingua franca is English.

The second mediation is between audiences. Emil Staiger always endeavored to write not only for fellow scholars but for all those who love literary works and are consoled by them. Choosing an inductive method, he gives examples that are enjoyable and offers a text that remains accessible to all. The general reader may therefore want to skip the introduction and delve right into Staiger's discussion. The specialist, however, might welcome the introductory essay, which strives to clarify the critical context within which Staiger's *Poetics* must be set if it is to be satisfactorily understood.

The third mediation is historical. In her introduction, Luanne T. Frank mediates between modes of literary criticism current in the 1940s and those of the 1980s, as well as between those practiced by European and those embraced by American scholars. From an Anglo-

American perspective, Frank first situates Staiger's work in relation to the history of genre criticism, but in defining Staiger's goals and merits, she formulates a much broader response to him, informed by the phenomenological and hermeneutical thought on which he drew. This is a response long overdue in Europe and most welcome in the United States.

The Swiss American Historical Society, itself devoted to mediating between Swiss and American traditions, is proud to include an English translation of Emil Staiger's *Grundbegriffe der Poetik* in its publication program in the hope of making it available to as wide an audience as possible.

In presenting this translation, the Swiss American Historical Society gratefully acknowledges the generous support granted by the Foundation Pro Helvetia.

Marianne Burkhard

Introduction:
Staiger's *Basic Concepts of Poetics* and Its Literary-Critical Contexts

Luanne Frank

I

We can view the history of criticism as a record of evolution, or as a record of "chaos marked by sudden revolution."[1] We can argue that the essential task of the critic is to contribute to change in his or her discipline,[2] or that it is not to contribute to change at all but rather to interrupt.[3] We can even argue that since "interruption" implies the eventual resumption of business as usual, the real task of the critic is to *disrupt* critical discourse. Whatever our position, it opens to us the possibility of recognizing Swiss scholar Emil Staiger as a critic par excellence, one who engages in disruptions, in profound interruptions whose purpose is to bring about change, in each of his chief critical works. Progressively, these books develop a critical theory new for his time and important for ours. The best known are *Time as Poetic Imagination* (*Die Zeit als Einbildungskraft des Dichters*) (1939), *Basic Concepts of Poetics* (*Grundbegriffe der Poetik*) (1946; henceforth, *Poetics*), *Goethe* (three volumes, 1952–59), *The Art of Interpretation* (*Die Kunst der Interpretation*) (1955), and *Friedrich Schiller* (1967).

Among them, the *Poetics* is probably the most radical, the most disruptive, the most change-laden, for it constructs a revolutionary new poetics and erects it alongside the old. Moreover, it does so with an indifference to the old that is scalding in its majesty and puzzling

---

1. George Watson (cf. *The Literary Critics* [Harmondsworth, Middlesex, 1962, 10–11]), cited by René Wellek, "Poetics, Interpretation, and Criticism," in *The Attack on Literature and Other Essays* (Chapel Hill: University of North Carolina Press, 1982), 33.

2. David Couzens Hoy, *The Critical Circle* (Berkeley: University of California Press, 1976), 160.

3. Watson, *The Literary Critics*, 10–11.

to the reader accustomed to altercation, to controversy, and to the dialectic as the more typical modes in which one criticism typically takes account of another. But Staiger discredits the old poetics implicitly rather than explicitly. He discloses its false grounding and hence its irrelevance not by arguing against it but rather by setting it aside and constructing it and its foundations anew—foundations that it has always lacked. Thus does he call into question the legitimacy of that most distinguished of Western literary-critical paradigms, the genre theory that traces its provenance and its prestige to Aristotle. After finding renewed sanction in the Renaissance, this theory became, in the eighteenth century, part of critics' indispensable theoretical equipment—a sort of literary sine qua non—and this it has remained.

As the agent of this privileged theory's quiet undoing, the *Poetics* would seem to have had its place at the forefront of Staiger's works already explained. But the surprising fact is that its anti-Aristotelianism and its revolutionary intent appear to have had almost nothing to do with its popularity. This seems to rest, if not on the *Poetics'* supposed conformity to tradition, at least on its close-enough congruence with it. The extent of its antitraditional stance and of its destructive intent appear to have been resolutely overlooked. It has been far from clear to Staiger's readers, for example, that the *Poetics* is intended as an interruption, and as a disruption, of critical discourse, rather than as merely a contribution to it. It has been far from clear that it is intended as an abrupt and radical calling into question of what has gone before. Thus this literary-critical landmark is not only Staiger's best known and most read work, it is also probably his most misunderstood.

The *Poetics* was easily susceptible to misunderstanding at the outset because it explores literary-critical territory that was open only to the most intrepid critics when it appeared in 1946. It remained misunderstood because no substantial audience familiar, or in accord, with its enabling assumptions developed for it. The most vocal and most influential of its existing audiences, the postwar Germanists schooled in an "immanent" criticism, so-called—part Formalistic, part Neo-Kantian New Critical—brought to it a body of literary-critical presuppositions that could accommodate neither the nature nor the range of the *Poetics'* concerns. This audience had, in fact, no hope of understanding them, or so it seems in retrospect. I am speaking here of both the American and the European Germanists whose critical practice is everywhere dominated in the postwar period—even and particularly in Germany,[4] the homeland of *Geistesgeschichte*—by Formalistic and

4. Wlad Godzich, "Introduction," in Hans Robert Jauss, *Aesthetic Experience and Literary Hermeneutics* (Minneapolis: University of Minnesota Press, 1982), viii.

New Critical ideas.[5] Like any other, this audience was able to see in the object of its attention only what it sought, only what it had prepared itself to see. Thus the form-oriented "absolutist" critics of the fifties and sixties, and even their descendants of the seventies, saw Staiger more as one of themselves than as a critic of a different order. They judged his work by their own models of criticism, rather than his, and tried to force the fluid possibilities for understanding yielded by his insights into their own more rigid categories. The result was that his work remained for them at best only fragmentarily assimilated, and much misread, a fact of which they remained interestingly unaware.[6]

They objected to those practices of Staiger's that they could readily identify as running explicitly counter to their own, or that extended beyond their own critical parameters,[7] and they apprehended him only where his views matched, or could be made to seem to match, theirs. But this left much of Staiger's most important and original thinking beyond their range and thus out of their consideration. In a story by now all too familiar in other connections, the New Critics suppressed as irrelevant, misguided, or worse those styles of criticism

5. The term "New Critics" here refers to and includes those critics and scholar-critics whose methodology is that of the New Criticism and whose work is inspired by its principles and limited by its constraints. It does not refer merely to the small group of theoreticians (Richards, Empson, Wimsatt, Beardsley, Brooks, and others) whose work established the movement in the United States and Great Britain and guided it from the 1920s through the 1950s. I shall often couple New Criticism and Formalism in my comments and will not attempt to distinguish between them for the purposes of this study. Retaining both terms, however, is meant to indicate a difference between them. Both, of course, try to displace content in literary analysis and to treat a work's form in ways corresponding to empirical research, and both try to understand generic form's relation to the more minute and detailed structures that close analysis reveals. See especially Ewa M. Thompson, *Russian Formalism and Anglo-American New Criticism* (The Hague: Mouton, 1971).

6. Theirs was a misreading different in kind from the sort of expansive, creative misreading that, for example, the numerous studies of a scholar like Harold Bloom have both traced and participated in. It was more properly a constricting of both Staiger and his reader-theorists than a releasing of potential either in his theory or to the reader-theorists' insights, and thus had the effect of a stranglehold on both.

7. See, for example, Elizabeth Wilkinson, "Review of Emil Staiger, *Grundbegriffe der Poetik*," *Modern Language Review* 44 (1949):433–37; and Peter Salm, "Emil Staiger," in *Three Modes of Criticism: The Literary Theories of Scherer, Walzel, and Staiger* (Cleveland, Ohio: Press of Case Western Reserve University, 1968), 79–117. A recent example of a reference to Staiger as a sort of paragon of German New Criticism without an acknowledgement of his divergence from it occurs in Peter Hohendahl's comment: "Adorno's claim to *Immanenz* should not be interpreted as a German version of New Criticism, the equivalent of Emil Staiger for instance." "Autonomy of Art: Looking Back at Adorno's *Ästhetische Theorie*," *German Quarterly* 54 (March 1981):140.

that could have provided congenial, and legitimate, readings of Staiger, namely Aristotelianism on the one hand and the criticism deriving from phenomenology and phenomenological hermeneutics on the other. They domesticated Staiger sufficiently to be able to make of him, if not precisely one of their own, at least a close relative, one who was intermittently erring, but acceptable. For their part, the genre critics recognized Aristotelian theory as a legitimate and useful means of approaching Staiger, but failed to apprehend the extent of his breaks with Aristotelianism. They thus inevitably also failed to note his indications of how these breaks could become fruitful departures for a completely new comprehension of genre. The new conception would stand in polar opposition to the old. It could thus be construed as a repudiation of it. More broadly and sympathetically viewed, it could be understood as one of its conditions of possibility—as a necessary grounding for it.

The genre critics failed to see either of these possibilities in Staiger's work. They failed to see that it represents an innovator's bold turn *from* traditional genre criticism as it was conventionally understood and practiced rather than a mere renovator's reembrace of it. They instead emphasized isomorphisms between his and the older theory, almost automatically sorted him into a critical sector marked "traditional genre," and left him there, another of a multitude of post-Aristotelian tinkerers with a precursor theory whose authority had supposedly not met with crucial challenge.[8] The approach of the New Critics and the Formalists was similar. They failed to distinguish between their own orientation to the text and Staiger's quite different one. Formalists, New Critics, and genre critics appear never to have recognized the goal Staiger was pursuing, and, unmistakably, they never recognized the extent of the challenge that he posed for them and for criticism after them. It is only now that developments in Continental criticism provide a context within which this challenge can become widely recognizable, only now that it shows promise of being met.

Staiger, a prominent critic among the German-speaking peoples after World War II, was one of the most productive and original

---

8. See, for example, Paul Hernadi, *Beyond Genre: New Directions in Literary Classification* (Ithaca, N.Y.: Cornell University Press, 1972), 23–34. Hernadi adopts Meyer H. Abrams's (*The Mirror and the Lamp*, 1953) four basic approaches to genre—"expressive," "pragmatic," "structural," and "mimetic"—and their correlation with "the author, the reader, the verbal medium, [and] the evoked world" as his classificatory system. Hernadi classifies Staiger with "expressive" genre critics.

interpreters of their literatures. His works were especially familiar in the scholarly communities of Germanists on both sides of the Atlantic. They are still read in these circles, where his *Poetics* and his studies of Goethe are looked upon as classics of sorts. But there are further indications of the importance of Staiger's work in general, and of the *Poetics* in particular. He appears as one of the principal subjects of Peter Salm's *Three Modes of Criticism: The Literary Theories of Scherer, Walzel, and Staiger* (see footnote 7, above). In its Staiger section, that study focuses exclusively on the *Poetics*, suggesting that this work is the heart of his criticism. Moreover, practicing critics—both Germanistic in their emphasis and not exclusively so—continue to cite Staiger.[9]

Despite his stature and the staying power of his work, however, Staiger has received no readings adequate to his view of what he has attempted, none adequate to his achievement. Phenomenology's importance for Staiger's work appears not to have been studied. One summary links him with the Husserlian inclinations of the Geneva School,[10] but the single major study of this school's work omits mention of him altogether.[11] Heidegger's influence on Staiger has been recognized, but, with a single exception, critics have misunderstood it and regarded it unsympathetically (we review their assessments in section VIII below). Alexander Gelley's comprehensive article discussing the Heideggerian characteristics of Staiger's work in general marks the exception here, and it should be emphasized, since Gelley has disclosed Staiger's Heideggerian aims with particular sensitivity to both men's points of view.[12] Since Gelley's article does not consider the *Poetics*, however, this book especially remains to be sympathetically elucidated in its Heideggerian connection. Gelley himself emphasizes the need for an examination of its Heideggerian concerns.

Staiger himself long contended that he was not understood, and published responses to his work corroborate his claim. One can explain this simply enough: Staiger wrote substantially ahead of his time. His work was addressed to an audience of speculative critics, and such an audience did not yet exist. One can, it is true, point to

9. Staiger's name sustains itself with regular entries in the *Arts and Humanities Citation Index*.

10. Robert R. Magliola, *Phenomenology and Literature: An Introduction* (West Lafayette, Ind.: Purdue University Press, 1977), 25.

11. Sarah Lawall, *Critics of Consciousness: The Existential Structures of Literature* (Cambridge, Mass.: Harvard University Press, 1968).

12. Alexander Gelley, "Staiger, Heidegger, and the Task of Criticism," *Modern Language Quarterly* 23 (1962):195–216.

Husserl and Kant in the direct line of antecedents to Formalism and the New Criticism, but, when Staiger wrote, philosophy in general was unwelcome in critical circles, and speculative philosophy in particular. Criticism's philosophical base was often lost sight of: Philosophy was "foreign" to the aesthetic object. Speculative, relativistic, so-called heretical philosophy in the line of Hegel was anathema. Thus it is no accident that the first popularizations of Heidegger's thought addressed the life world rather than the presumably more rarified world of art. Existentialism, that is, though various authors and literary characters subscribed to it, was clearly a theory of life rather than a theory of art, a theory of existence rather than a theory of form. Even where admitted as a means of literary understanding it was not linked to form, and its main inroads into "Germanistik" came later than Staiger's theorizing. Moreover, Staiger's *Poetics* itself gave little indication of how it might best be understood. Its footnote apparatus concerned itself primarily with traditional genre theory. The *Poetics* did not reveal much of its philosophical indebtedness or of its philosophical leanings, except, perhaps, to the rare formalist who had held Heidegger to his bosom. Such a reader might have heard a key phrase from Heidegger's *Being and Time* echo in Staiger's title. But if there were such readers, none came forward in print. The echo has, I believe, never been mentioned, and as we shall see it is of some consequence.

Thus, among the Germanists who were Staiger's principal readers, philosophical speculation was a legitimate route neither to the systematization nor to the understanding of literature. Lacking a close acquaintance with contemporary philosophy—in this case phenomenology—Staiger's audience lacked the means to recognize that his reluctance to theorize was itself a form of theory. They also did not have the means to recognize that his *Poetics* was itself in fact the unfolding of more than one explicit philosophical theory in the course of a particularized praxis. His audience's task was of course made no easier by what must have seemed at the time the almost excessively literary ambitions of the *Poetics*, which displays itself with a degree and quality of literariness equaling, and often surpassing, that of the works it treats. (This quality makes the *Poetics* a challenge without significant rival in the European and Anglo-American critical literature until the onslaught of Derridean discourse in the late sixties and in the seventies.)

An audience that can appreciate both the literariness of criticism and its philosophical character—and thus Staiger's work—however, now exists in substantial numbers, its emergence corroborated by numerous articles and its appearance observed, accounted for, and thematized in such a work as Elizabeth Bruss's *Beautiful Theories*.[13] It is in large part an audience associated with the Continental criticism that grounds itself most notably in the thought of Husserl and Heidegger, the primary philosophical bases of Staiger's own work.

This new audience began to form—in the United States, at least—early in the seventies, after the appearance of *The Languages of Criticism and the Sciences of Man*, edited by Richard Macksey and Eugenio Donato (1969).[14] But Staiger had published the first of his three chief theoretical works a full thirty years earlier: *Time as Poetic Imagination* appeared in 1939, *Poetics* in 1946, and *The Art of Interpretation* in 1953. These years marked a time of High Formalism in Anglo-American and German critical circles. Thus, the period of Staiger's greatest theoretical productivity was also the period of Formalism's viselike hold on the critical consciousness of his readers, years in which criticism closed out relativism of all kinds, from the mild to the anarchical. Staiger would have been situated among the relativists immediately had he not been misconceived as a member of the accepted "schools" of criticism.

Staiger's interests and those of the Formalists may have appeared to coincide because of the ultimately phenomenological grounding of both, but where Staiger went Formalism could not follow. Pursuing Husserl's lead in part, and in part Heidegger's, Staiger attempted to penetrate the recesses of the artistic consciousness in order to understand and describe the author's pretextual expressive impulse. Formalism remained with the text. Those aspects of Staiger's work that seemed concerned with the purely textual the Formalists lauded. What went beyond questions of the text itself into questions of the conditions of its genesis in the artistic consciousness, (and further, into an understanding of texts not as absolutes, as aesthetic objects, but as thoroughly contingent linguistic precipitations of styles of being in the world), the Formalists objected to or ignored. Staiger could seem to provide a secure foothold for Formalist readers. His practice could seem to match theirs since his work was anchored in the text. He began with the text, gleaning specific insights from it. But "the text" understood as the Formalists' well-known "aesthetic object" is not his focus in any of his works, any more than, as we shall see, genre proper, as the "objectively verifiable" form taken *by* a text, is his focus in the *Poetics*. Staiger had already situated himself in a space beyond Formalism's "text" in his earliest theoretical works. In the

13. Elizabeth Bruss, *Beautiful Theories* (Baltimore, Md.: Johns Hopkins University Press, 1982).
14. Baltimore, Md.: Johns Hopkins University Press, 1969.

Poetics he goes beyond genre, at least as it is understood in a traditional sense. His success in grounding genre in an uncharted territory beyond its surface forms makes the *Poetics* a trailblazing critical achievement. It can be considered Staiger's most important theoretical one.

II

The primary impulse behind the *Poetics* is Staiger's desire to revolutionize the understanding of all of literature. He would do so by disrupting and changing the most fundamental of critical practices, that of genre criticism, and do this in turn by revolutionizing the understanding of genre. This he would accomplish by bringing about a crisis in the understanding of this criticism's basic concepts. He would reground and radically revise them, revealing in this way their traditional insufficiency. By broadening and deepening our understanding of these concepts, Staiger would hope to change our approach to genre profoundly.

Staiger's familiarity with genre criticism is exhaustive in its thoroughness, yet this criticism's characteristic discoveries he finds narrow, constricting, predictable, sterile. In the preface to the second edition of the *Poetics*, he will call the yield of traditional poetics "a matter of indifference." But because he is aware that what he is doing inhabits a different critical universe from that of the Aristotelians, Staiger does not attempt a noisy displacement of their theories by his own, nor does he produce an approach to genre, and to his related concerns, that is revolutionary in an explosive sense.

One must still argue, however, that his work is revolutionary in that, abruptly and almost altogether, it abandons the methodologies of classical criticism—those that emphasize concrete formal distinctions between literary kinds, and between the literary elements that constitute them. Staiger does not emphasize isolating, identifying, and describing literary types and forms as conclusive events in the process of understanding them. He concentrates, rather, on exploring the conditions of possibility in human consciousness out of which distinguishable literary forms and types arise—investigates the historicity of situations of consciousness that translate, when rendered in language, into distinguishable literary qualities. The special relevance of Staiger's work today lies in his conviction of the importance of describing this sometimes preconceptual, always pretextual substratum of poetic language and of genre. His pretextual concern is less with the prelinguistic, however, than with identifiable, describable experiential structures existing prior to the inscribed text. His concern is apprehending what amounts to an "archaeology" of language and of genre, in Michel Foucault's understanding of this term. Staiger would acquaint us with the conditions of possibility that enable identifiable literary qualities.

Staiger wishes to change critical practice by radically extending the boundaries of the territory to which genre criticism has traditionally laid claim and also by mapping the new territory. This he wishes to accomplish with a new instrument of great potential power, precision, delicacy, and scope—one that is able to penetrate the site of the hollow ruin labeled "genre study" to its bottommost layer, and in doing so uncover that foundation of the edifice of literary art and poetic language to which traditional genre considerations are only tenuously attached if they are attached at all. This latter Staiger doubts—initially, at least. Through such excavations, the focus of the question of genre will automatically shift from an overriding concern with literary art's end product, understood as form, to an interest in the form-generating modes of the poetic impulse. This concern should produce an organic type of explanation of the sort that constitutes understanding.

Rather than focusing exclusively on the forms-as-such assumed by the work itself, and rather than permitting this focus to mark the limit of the critic's major concern, Staiger would lay open for exploration those states of consciousness, awareness, and understanding that are entered into by an author before she or he chooses a particular genre as the "vessel" of her or his expression. According to Staiger, these states in fact determine that choice—they are the determiners of genre, the conditions of the genres' possibility. We will examine these points again later (sections VI, VII, and X below).

III

Why does Staiger not orient his reader to his intent? The long-standing misapprehension of his work is attributable in part to his own failure in this connection. Why does he choose not to construct a context of explanatory comments that would reveal and explain his work in clear-cut opposition to traditional theory?

Since Staiger chooses the quintessentially phenomenological method of reading a given text with as few preconceptions as possible (and certainly without an ungainly theoretical superstructure that pulls the text into its own forms), he denies himself the luxury of equipping the reader of the *Poetics* with a method, with a prior system of thought that would guide understanding. For him to provide such a "key" to his work would run contrary to exactly the sort of criticism he is attempting to develop there. He is implicitly arguing for a preconceptionless, inductive criticism that eschews traditional applications of the traditional preconceptions dominating traditional genre criticism. If his own work is to exemplify preconceptionless method, he must allow his commentary (his "practice") itself to be its own reason for being.

A second reason for Staiger's failure to explain his unconventional methodology in the *Poetics* would be an understandable reluctance to rehearse the contents of Heidegger's *Being and Time*, which could already be familiar to his readers. Another possible reason would be an assumption that they would already be familiar with his earlier work, *Time as Poetic Imagination*, which, in its own right, is a tour de force of the application of Heideggerian temporal categories to the work of literary art.

After widespread misunderstanding greets the *Poetics'* first edition, however, Staiger does provide a preface and a postscript for the second, where he offers contained suggestions for approaching, evaluating, and extending his work. Perhaps predictably, however, he reserves the most telling of his comments for the postscript, leaving the still uninitiated reader to make what she or he can of the text without preliminary authorial guidance. But even in the postscript Staiger's comments remain improbably brief, schematic, and reticent, especially when one considers the ambitiousness of his program, its revolutionary character, and its potential importance. He continues to refrain from any but minimal interpretation of his intentions in their implicitly adversary relation to tradition.

Even supposing that Staiger's readers were theoretically inclined, however—less, that is, than insistently "immanent" in their orientation—it is not difficult to understand why his few direct, even well-chosen comments accompanying the second edition were ineffectual in putting his audience in touch with his intentions. In their brevity and relative lack of force his observations are patently inadequate instruments for weaning a literary-critical public from habits of thought with over two thousand years of specific tradition behind them. The Aristotelian convention Staiger is departing from remains a powerful part of the critical equipment of his readers—too powerful for his abbreviated counterargument to have an appreciable effect. This tradition in fact makes a satellite out of Staiger's theory, as is amply demonstrated by references that identify him as a genre theorist without pointing to the radical nature of his perspective. In order to see its revolutionary character clearly, the reader still requires the rationale for the *Poetics* that Staiger never wrote.

IV

The *Poetics* is of sufficient importance to justify examining it in connection with the bodies of literary-critical practice it most discernibly relates to: those from which it most directly diverges, as well as those it most closely derives from and carries forward. These are the Aristotelian, on the one hand, and the phenomenological (Husserlian) and phenomenological-hermeneutic (Heideggerian), on the other. Before setting out to elucidate Staiger in these contexts, a word of warning, however. Staiger bursts the bonds of any and all the critical approaches he appropriates. He borrows one set of insights from a given system and contradicts another set from the same system. He aligns himself with one aspect of a system only to oppose another. He is an iconoclast without necessarily making iconoclasm his aim. Staiger is an Aristotelian and a non-Aristotelian at the same time; he is a Formalist/non-Formalist, a Husserlian/non-Husserlian, and a Heideggerian/non-Heideggerian as well, simultaneously. But this need not deter us.

In what follows we will omit pursuing an understanding of Staiger in relation to Formalist precepts. Rather, we will look briefly at his relation to Aristotelian and phenomenological practice, and then examine more fully his relation to the insights of phenomenological hermeneutics. For it is in connection with the latter that Staiger develops his own critical voice in the *Poetics*. Moreover, this is the aspect of his work that remains least commented upon.

V

In arguing that Staiger's work in the *Poetics* departs so markedly *from* traditional genre theory as to make it no longer properly identifiable *as* such a theory, I do not wish to imply that his work cannot be related—successfully and productively related—*to* such a theory. As we will note in section XI below, Staiger himself eventually sees the possibility of relating it thus. I am convinced, however, that if such a connection is to be understood, the dissimilarity between Staiger's work and traditional theory must first be clarified.

Before explaining how Staiger moves beyond Aristotle and traditional concepts of genre, let us note that there is a significant sense in which critics who place him in an Aristotelian context—and who find his work valuable or wanting in terms of that tradition—are not altogether in error, for it is clear that Staiger himself chooses to be found there. Despite his indifference to traditional genre theory itself, he chooses to remain within the world of commentary that recognizes genrelike distinctions, however little his own concerns include adding to them in their conventional form. One can confidently make such a statement not so much because Staiger refrains from mounting an argument expressly invalidating genre critics' precepts (he supplants them without argument) as because he retains terms and categories close to the primary terms and divisions of the Aristotelian tradition. From the conventional use of the nouns "lyric," "epic," and "drama" as references to the classical genres, for example, he shifts only to their adjectival derivatives "lyrical," "epic(al)," and "dramatic" as labels for the foci of his critical concerns—in this case literary qualities rather than the literary forms of the genre theorists. Heideggerian that he is, Staiger can scarcely fail to be aware that an attempt to overthrow the tradition would necessitate a new critical language.

And so, although Staiger sidesteps traditional theory's starting point, sets aside its basic assumptions, eschews its modus operandi, and regards with profound indifference the infinity of repetitively corroborative evidence that traditional genre practice has led to, he nonetheless clearly chooses to make traditional theory one of the parameters of meaning in his own work. Thus, one of the meanings of his *Poetics* will be precisely that relation his work bears to the tradition that comes before it. But it is especially necessary to recall at this juncture that this is a relation more of dissimilarity than of similarity. Hence, understanding Staiger in his Aristotelian context requires attention less to his moments of conformity to the norm than to his movement contrary to it.

Since Staiger chooses the insights of traditional genre criticism as a prerequisite for understanding his work, it is appropriate to look for a moment at the zone of operations typical of this tradition. I should thus like to situate genre study briefly in the general range of critical practice. I shall assume that every examination of a literary work develops as a means for making it accessible to its readers and assimilable by them—that each such study exists to broaden and deepen understanding of the work. Typically, accessibility is sought through examination of a work's content or of its form, through meaning or through structure, the two often being considered mutually exclusive, so that critics who concern themselves with form and those who concern themselves with content place themselves in opposition to one another.

Whether the critic studies content or form, however, whether she or he believes that the two are the same or different, each seeks a perception of the work that for her or him is meaning*ful*, or significant. The meaningfulness or significance she or he seeks will be seen to consist of the perception of a relation between the work in question (between some aspect, element, or feature of it) and something else— a familiar system of thought, or forms appropriate to the elucidation or analysis of the work in question but not identical to it. Fastidiously text-centered critics will seek to limit the field in which they perceive such relations as closely as possible to the work itself. They will largely choose to ignore the issue of the relational dependence or the radical historicity of their critical perceptions. They assume that to deal with anything beyond the confines of the work is to deal with "extraliterary" factors. Less restrictive theorists will extend their collective gaze as far as language, history, social practice, and intellectual disciplines permit, thus opening all possible systems of human knowing to the purview of literary criticism. Let the diagram that follows illustrate the potential field of operations of the thoroughly eclectic literary critic. The diagram consists of five columns here, but one can produce out of it the traditional three moments of literary criticism—production, text, and reception—by collapsing the two columns on the left into a single one and doing the same with the two on the right:

Author's social-historical ma-trix (or tradi-tion out of which author works)	Author	Text	Reader	Reader's social-historical ma-trix (or tradition out of which reader reads)

The eclectic critic can draw relations between any facet of the column representing the work itself and any facet of any other column. The Formalist or New Critic, on the other hand, ostensibly restricts herself or himself to the central column alone, creating meaning by relating aspects of only those systems that can be said to inhabit it.

The perceptions of the genre critic are similarly, though perhaps not so severely, limited. For her or him meaningfulness or significance consists of that relation that exists, or can be perceived to exist, between the particular form displayed by the text in question and similar, previously existing forms. To the extent that concern with such forms describes its major preoccupation, genre theory is quintessentially Formalistic, a criticism that concentrates on the shape taken by a particular work and on the type of content this shape typically embraces rather than on that content itself. (It is of course true that broader considerations of content have sometimes served as noticeable features of this criticism from Aristotle through the present.) Genre theory's range may not seem narrow to the genre critic himself, since it includes myriad forms to be traced from antiquity to the present through a plethora of permutations. But its concern, Staiger might argue, comes after the fact, and only by virtue of looking backward across centuries of now petrified forms: Its concern only begins after the advent of the finished text. It arises with recognition of this text's resemblance to others, a resemblance in which "type" is born. Thus in a sense genre theory could be said to be chasing its own tail.

Genre criticism of the traditional sort, Staiger would hold, is locked into a pattern of discovery in which it finds only endless permutations of or deviations from what it has already found. It is locked into a pattern of discovery best labeled "the accumulation of data." Moreover, its essentially nonrelational stance condemns it to be unable to explain anything. This is one of the meanings of "irrelevant" that Staiger early applies to it.

VI

Staiger sees genre criticism as irrelevant in that it fails to understand itself. For him this is to say that it fails to link the forms it isolates, identifies, and describes with the modes of being (in this case authorial) that give rise to these forms. Genre criticism, according to Staiger, does not ground its forms in human experience. They float, as it were, untethered; they are seen and known but not explained. Therefore he bypasses the function of classification by form that has been so long and meticulously fulfilled by the genre critic. He takes as his own project to demonstrate that what the tradition has so doggedly classified as discrete, apparently *a priori*, forms derives from peculiarly interrelated and anything but *a priori* ways of being in the world. These ways are isolable, describable, explainable. Moreover, they are not dead, but altogether quick. They are styles, or attitudes, of con-

sciousness, understanding, and awareness. In their linguistic precipitations as literary texts, he argues, they typically assume the formal
characteristics that critics are later able to isolate and classify as those
of the lyric, the epic, and the drama. Thus it is to the labels for these
styles of consciousness—and not to their linguistic precipitations (the
genres themselves)—that Staiger would give the name "basic concepts." It is not Staiger's goal at all to further define and demarcate
the traditional genres as such—that is, in and for themselves—or to
discover and describe new genres. Genre criticism's greatest short-
coming, Staiger would insist, is that it has described and classified
everything and understood nothing.

I am not arguing that Staiger's project is not itself a classificatory
one. It does categorize. But what it categorizes are not literary forms
but ways of being that give rise to and constitute them. Staiger examines and describes examples of the genres from the traditional literature, but for him such descriptions are not ends in themselves. They
are rather means of coming to an awareness and an understanding of
what the style of consciousness, what the mode of being might be that
precedes the emergence of each from the pen of its author. Staiger is
concerned with the existential authorial experience in which a given
work is grounded and that results in its identifiability as an example
of lyric, epic, or dramatic style. The sources of genre distinctions lie,
according to Staiger, in distinctions between modes of being in the
world. Moreover, the way of being that a given work expresses and
in fact embodies defines important areas of its meaning for its author
and for its reader. Staiger suggests that a way of being attuned to the
author's way of being serves the reader, or critic, as a satisfactory
means of entering into the work and hence of "understanding" it—
understanding it not "objectively," however, but from a point of view
significantly determined by the work. We use the term "objectively"
here in its Heideggerian sense of deriving from a system not developed
in terms fitting the entity in question and thus alien to it.

VII

Although a conceptual understanding of the modes of being informing
the expressive impulses behind given works is not a prerequisite for
a satisfactory participatory experience in the works themselves, it is
useful for the critic seeking to arrive at a comprehensive understanding
of them. In Staiger's view a comprehension of the modes serves as a

conceptual link between the formal features of a given work (traditional foci of the genre critic) and the pretextual experience of the
author—that from which his expressive impulse derives (an experience not heretofore addressed). The modes can thus be considered a
spacious interface between the surface features analyzed as "forms"
by the genre critic and the authorial experience that precipitates itself
in language and becomes retrievable as immanent content and prepo-
etic structure. I use the phrase "immanent content" to refer to constitutive content, distinguishing it from the surface content of the work,
or what the work is ostensibly "about." "Immanent" is thus understood here in the phenomenological sense of constitutive *of* the text—
the way of being that prompts it into existence and is objectified by
it—rather than in the New Critical sense of limited to the text, or
circumscribed by the text. We will return to this point at the end of
the present section.

It is important here to focus for a moment on another distinction,
which I have maintained unthematized in the foregoing paragraphs.
This is the distinction between the "style" or "mode" of experience of
the authorial consciousness and the experience itself. It is crucial
to distinguish the critical attempt to delineate an author's style of
experience or mode of consciousness from the critical attempt to re-
create that experience or moment of consciousness itself. By maintaining this distinction we are able to come close to the heart of one
of Staiger's major contributions in the *Poetics*. His chief goal is to
isolate, delineate, describe, and thus understand the mode of experience characteristic of the authorial consciousness of given works and
types of works. It is important to point out in this connection that
Staiger inhabits a position distinct from the Diltheyan one, which as
one of its goals sought participation *in* the author's actual creative-
experiential moment, albeit after the fact. Without the distinction
between mode of experience and experience itself one would be
tempted to identify Staiger's aims with Dilthey's. Staiger seeks the
expressive moment's existential conditions of possibility. He seeks
those of the moment's qualities that render its yield genre-classifiable.

In focusing on the mode of authorial experience, Staiger opens up
a space for critical understanding between the so-called pure and often
eminently classifiable forms of the genres and the actual, concrete,
unique, idiosyncratic, and heretofore unclassifiable experiences that
precede them and of which they are the selected rendering in language. He opens up for critical consideration the space in which the
precipitation of the experience into language either apparently, or in

fact, takes place. By focusing on modes of consciousness Staiger brings to light an area of potential understanding inaccessible both to criticism in general before he wrote and to the criticism dominant in his time. Only Heidegger had earlier investigated this area of potential understanding, and he only tentatively. Staiger explores the space that colors the expressive impulse, the space in which the impulse takes on its lyric, epic, or dramatic character and finally its form. The conceptual arena carved out by the phrase "mode of experience" is the place of an embrace between experience and form.

In order to see clearly what Staiger is attempting in this connection in the *Poetics* it will be helpful to look for a moment in a general way at the phenomenological criticism practiced by the group of critics labeled the Geneva School (Georges Poulet, Maurice Blanchot, Gaston Bachelard, Jean Rousset, Jean-Pierre Richard), and those influenced by them (Hillis Miller, Paul Brotkorb, and others). Staiger has been correctly associated with this school, but the nature of his indebtedness to and of his difference from it have not been investigated.

The phenomenological critic is generally unconcerned with the topics that interest either the genre critics and the formalists-structuralists on the one hand or the so-called ideological critics on the other. The phenomenological critic focuses not on such topics as structure, plot development, event line, and character development, or on readings that deliver the meaning of the literary work over to preexisting bodies of conceptual knowledge, such as Freudian or Jungian psychology, Marxist philosophy, anthropology, or history of ideas. The phenomenological critic is concerned with a single, infinitely complex development—that of the consciousness formed by and recording the literary work. For this critic, the features focused on by the Formalists and New Critics are surface features and those of the thematic critics are extrinsic to the work.

The phenomenological critics' concern with the development of the recording consciousness is a direct consequence of phenomenology's understanding of the nature of consciousness. These critics, unlike the thinkers of philosophical movements preceding theirs (namely, idealism and empiricism) consider consciousness an intentional act, a real interaction of the subject with the outside. In the idealist movement, the trend "is to eliminate the world as a source of knowledge" (Magliola, 4) by maintaining that the subject actively projects the object (subjectivity is constitutive of objectivity). The empiricist movement, on the other hand, stresses the passivity of consciousness ("there is a reflecting image . . . lodged in the knower" that is "imprinted by physical reality":

this " 'double' of reality-in-itself becomes the immediate object of knowledge" [Magliola, 4]).[15] For the phenomenologist-critic, literature is the precipitation in recorded language of the act-that-is-conscious-ness. Literature is not necessarily a total picture of consciousness, which exists and records itself in and through language, a consciousness con-stituted of linguistic forms; it is, on the contrary, a highly selective ver-sion of it. But literature is nonetheless a record of a configuration typical of this consciousness, which again and again realizes itself in character-istic patterns of expression that are the marks, or traces, or tracks of specifically identifiable—because often repeated—ways, or habits, of being.

It is the task of the phenomenologist as literary critic to isolate and describe, then postulate the nature of, this consciousness, to reveal its patterns of experience, its concerns, its ways of being in the world. Plot, character, event line, subject matter, and ostensible theme are merely the vehicles by which this consciousness develops and reveals itself. The concern of the phenomenologist-critic is to lay bare and elucidate the development and revelation of that experience—those acts of consciousness on whose basis the work is constituted as it is. These are the acts of consciousness generated in the work and by means of the work, acts of consciousness integral to the work, imma-nent in the work. Thus the phenomenologist's understanding of the term "immanent" referred to above as constitutive of the text.

Staiger sets himself a task that is particularly interesting when viewed against the assumptions and practices of phenomenological criticism. It could in fact be argued that phenomenological criticism is what Staiger is practicing in the *Poetics*. But if he is doing so, he is doing so with a difference that must be emphasized, one that is great enough to set him apart from phenomenology. He is doing *for entire genre kinds* something related to—though still distinct from—what the phenomenological critic does with the oeuvre of a single author. He is tracing the repeated precipitation of distinguishable modes of con-sciousness in a given genre. This repetition is the criterion for the typicality of that mode for the given genre. He is unearthing experien-tial styles, patternings or structures of being that works in the genre typically embody. Thus, like the phenomenological critic he is not concerned first of all with the surface features of the text. But whereas the phenomenological critic traces the specifically identifiable styles of being that characterize stages in the development of a single recording

15. I am also indebted to Lawall for her account of the work of the Geneva School (p. 18).

consciousness in a given oeuvre, Staiger seeks similar, or comparable, qualities that characterize genre styles. Unlike the phenomenologist-critic, he does not seek a pattern of development.

VIII

Yet it is only when we come to understand Staiger's work in the context of its Heideggerian provenance, that is, in the context of Heidegger's hermeneutic phenomenology, that the range, depth, originality, and revolutionary character of Staiger's achievement in the *Poetics* become altogether clear. It is only then that the Staiger of the *Poetics* comes into his own as a critic. Only an acquaintance with Heidegger's work provides sufficiently numerous points of contact with Staiger's to reveal the latter's complexity, systematicity, and originality. Heidegger's insistence that every discipline of knowing renovate its understanding of its basic concepts; his regrounding of Western philosophy's concept of Being in concrete experience, coupled with his investigation of Being's meaning; and his understanding of understanding and of the temporality that constitutes it—these mark the most prominent of these points of contact. They provide models and points of departure for Staiger's literary-critical practice and give us means of observing Staiger's dependence on, adaptations of, derivations from, supplementations to, and movement beyond what has preceded him. Heidegger's work marks the last outpost of conceptualization, as it were, on Staiger's journey to his own identity as a critic. What he takes from that outpost and what he does with it, where he goes after he leaves it, are all important to our conception of the *Poetics*. All are necessary means of revealing Staiger's intentions in the *Poetics* and the nature and extent of his achievement there.

Abbreviated references to a relation between Heidegger's thought and Staiger's are commonplaces of the scanty literature dealing with Staiger, but we still lack identifications of even some of the most rudimentary of his Heideggerian insights, not to mention a sustained clarification of them. This is so both in general and in connection with specific titles—with the *Poetics* in particular. Peter Salm offers occasional fragmentary glimpses of Heideggerian perspectives in the *Poetics*, but Salm's own perspectives are New Critical. He imposes these on the *Poetics* and sets up a dissonance between them and Staiger's Heideggerian views that is resolved heavily in favor of Formalism. One can scarcely say that Salm has accorded even perfunctory recognition to the true (that is, the Heideggerian) characteristics of

Staiger's criticism. He argues, for example, that Staiger's adaptation of Heideggerian temporal structures to lyric, epic, and dramatic style constitutes unsuccessful literary criticism. Staiger, he insists, has arrived at an "insuperable impasse" in the *Poetics*. Salm fails to acknowledge the morass in which genre criticism in general had been mired when Staiger turned his attentions to it with the intention of providing it with concrete experiential foundations. To read Staiger and Heidegger together understandingly (that is, from their own points of view) would lead to conclusions other than Salm's.

Paul Hernadi sponsors Staiger's renovated understanding of genre styles, insofar as this understanding is able to stand on its own. He regards as "highly doubtful," however, the correspondences Staiger draws between Heidegger's ontological analyses of care and the primary genre styles (33). It goes without saying that New Critical assumptions about the necessary self-sufficiency of a work of art *and* of its criticism determine this assessment. But Hernadi appears not to recognize the extent to which Staiger's presentation of the stylistic characteristics of the genres rests on Heidegger's analyses of the primary temporalities.

Magliola (25) writes that in the *Poetics* Staiger "imposes on genre study (in a priori fashion) the three temporal ecstasies suggested by Heidegger's *Sein und Zeit*," but that in the later works *The Art of Interpretation* (*Die Kunst der Interpretation*) (1951) and Stylistic Change (*Stilwandel*) (1963) the critic operates "purely in the Geneva [that is, in the phenomenological] tradition." In making these statements, Magliola indicates his preference for phenomenology as a literary-critical method and presumably for the assumption that it refrains from imposing structures of thought on the literary phenomena it treats. Whether or not one would see any literary structure without a prior matching framework is of course open to question, as is whether the matching activity is correctly understandable as an imposition. Thus one must ask whether "impose" is a satisfactory word for Staiger's activity in the *Poetics*. Certainly he would not see it as such. The answer to whether or not Staiger imposes the Heideggerian temporalities on the genres will be a function of one's perspective. In Staiger's view Heidegger's temporalities provide the long-missing link between concrete existence and literary form. For him, there is no question of impositions of any sort. As Staiger sees it, Heidegger has uncovered structures that the theory of literature has long been in need of to ground and validate its insights. With Heidegger's temporalities, the genres are no longer suspended, as it were, from skyhooks.

L. L. Duroche undertakes the most extensive review to date (I would in fact argue that it is the only one) of the relation between Heidegger's temporalities and Staiger's genre styles, but he contends that the connection between them "is often quite tenuous,"[16] that "Staiger himself seems unsure . . . of the nature of the link" between them and even of the real purpose of the *Poetics* (132), that "the genre theory Staiger evolves is never seriously applied"(133), and finally, that the *Poetics* "represents a blind alley in contemporary critical theory"(134). This may have been so when Duroche wrote. But this was before the contemporary renaissance of Heidegger studies (traceable in part from Lacan through Foucault and Derrida) and the widespread application of his insights to literary concerns. Thus the blindness of which Duroche speaks may be attributable more to Staiger's earlier readers than to his work's potential for extending the insights of genre criticism.

For a presentation of Staiger that focuses on his Heideggerian approach, understands his work from the point of view from which it is written, and recognizes it as having yielded positive achievements, we must depend exclusively on Alexander Gelley's earlier consideration of critical issues important for an understanding of Staiger's practice in all his criticism, his Goethe studies in particular. Such is Gelley's insightfulness that one would have welcomed further fruits of his understanding in this connection. His preferences here, however, lead him around the *Poetics*. It is only in a footnote, to which I shall refer below, that he calls for a thoughtful (a Heideggerian) reconsideration of that work.

IX

To attempt to "explain" the *Poetics* causally out of Heidegger would be alien to the spirit in which both he and Staiger worked, inasmuch as almost the entirety of their respective philosophical and literary-critical effort was dedicated to the use of means other than causal explanation and its logic as routes to satisfactory understanding. Be that as it may, it is almost impossible not to see Heidegger's insistence that a discipline comprehend its basic concepts in a fundamental way as *the* condition of possibility for Staiger's *Poetics*. Heidegger argues that a thoroughgoing investigation of these concepts is the only satis-

16. L. L. Duroche, *Aspects of Criticism: Literary Study in Present-Day Germany* (The Hague: Mouton, 1967), 118.

factory foundation for a discipline's understanding of its own knowledge and its own nature as a discipline. This argument is essential to
a clear understanding of what Staiger is undertaking in the *Poetics*,
and the relation between the two should be emphasized. The very
title of Staiger's work, not to say its meaning, derives from Heidegger's
focus on the topic of basic concepts at the outset of *Being and Time*.[17]
So thick has been the pall of misapprehension and misunderstanding
engulfing Staiger's work in the *Poetics* that not even this most elementary and most significant fact has been noted. Without it one has, as
it were, nowhere to come from in order to read the *Poetics* except the
sets of unexamined assumptions it struggles against. To read it in their
terms is to misread it.

Familiarity with Heidegger's views on the necessity of a discipline's
clear understanding of its foundation serves as the only adequate
grounding for Staiger's concern with genre criticism's basic concepts
in his work. Familiarity with Heidegger's views on this question also
makes clear that when Staiger asserts that genre criticism does not
understand itself, he does not necessarily mean that its discoveries
are either unimportant or invalid, though he calls them matters of
indifference. He means, rather, that the study of genre pursues its
concerns without an adequate conception of the meaning of its basic
concepts, and that the body of knowledge it consists of is thus not
anchored in a consciousness of the nature of its foundational experiences. "Pure information," something unanchored in experience or
unaware of its anchoring, is for Staiger a matter of indifference. Mere
amplification of the yield of the basic concepts, mere accumulation of
information whose nature is already guaranteed *by* the basic concepts,
is of no real interest.

Heidegger points out in *Being and Time* that such is the case with the
knowledges of his period, both the "pure" sciences and the sciences of
man. Only with an understanding of the meaning of their own basic
concepts, forged through radically revising ways of thinking about
them, would the sciences be deserving of the label "scientific." For
Heidegger the measure of a discipline's stature *as* a discipline is precisely its capacity to undergo whatever crisis becomes necessary as it
grounds its understanding of its basic concepts. It is in this connection
that he observes that "the level which a science has reached is determined by how far it is capable of a crisis in its basic concepts" (29). A
given discipline's capacity for crisis in his sense would be its capacity

17. Martin Heidegger, *Being and Time*, trans. John Macquarrie and Edward Robinson
(New York: Harper and Row, 1962), 28–31.

to see the extent to which it had heretofore operated in a condition of conceptual misunderstanding and thus insufficiency. (Heidegger's own project is an investigation and an analysis of the most basic concept of Western philosophy, that of Being, whose meaning has been closed off for two thousand years. His work bristles with suggestions of how all human knowing is rooted in this concept. His revolutionary thought is thus a challenge to all disciplines, those that make up the pure sciences and the sciences of man.)

It is a capacity for crisis of precisely the sort Heidegger speaks about that Staiger envisions as he reviews the practice of genre study, crisis of this sort that he attempts to bring about with his *Poetics*. Inducing crisis, however, does not necessarily mean a jettisoning of the conceptual system traditional to the field. On the contrary: Heidegger makes very clear that the concepts that a given discipline has operated with up to the time it undertakes to review its basic concepts mark the indispensable starting points for a reconsideration (28–31). They mark long-validated conceptual points of entry into it—they in fact serve to legitimate it. It is probably for this reason that Staiger uses approximations of the traditional terms of genre study and attempts to move back from them to a consideration of their origins and meaning.

X

I have acknowledged that an attempt to explain the *Poetics* causally out of Heidegger would be alien to the spirit in which both Heidegger and Staiger worked. Certainly both set aside such explanation and its ruler-line logic as ways of knowing, preferring in their stead phenomenological description and the logic of the hermeneutic circle. But Heidegger's understanding of the temporal structure of human Being as elucidated in *Being and Time* does provide the conceptual groundwork for Staiger's literary criticism. It thus also serves as an indispensable means of understanding it.

Eventually, Staiger himself accounts explicitly for his indebtedness to Heidegger. He attributes to Heidegger the fundamental insights into the temporal nature of existence—in its character as understanding *via language*—that inform his own approach to literature and that are its most outstanding feature. Writing in 1959 in celebration of Heidegger's seventieth birthday, Staiger points to the evolution of his own approach under the aegis of Heidegger's philosophy. Staiger had read *Being and Time* as a student in 1928 (Gelley, 198) and he remarks on his early recognition that "by illuminating [the nature, function, and significance] of primordial time, Heidegger had laid a reliable foundation" for what are now called the sciences of man, and "had thus achieved what Wilhelm Dilthey had attempted but failed to do."[18] Staiger comments further on how this recognition brought him to understand the goal of his own criticism as the "interpretation of literary works with a perpetual view to their hidden temporal structure."[19]

In *Time as Poetic Imagination* (*Die Zeit als Einbildungskraft des Dichters*) (1939), Staiger explores the nature of the experiences of time that suffuse and inform the individual works and hence the oeuvres of three different authors (Brentano, Goethe, and Keller). By the time of the *Poetics* (1946), he has dramatically altered his perspective and moved on. Here he attempts to understand not only individual works and oeuvres from the point of view of their hidden time structures, but also to understand *entire genre kinds* in this way. After the *Poetics* he returns from examining the genres and again sets about scrutinizing individual works and individual authors. He does so with a profound difference, however. He has discovered, he writes,

> that the change of time relationships on which the manifoldness of the creative individual rests can scarcely be adequately grasped in scientific terminology. It therefore seemed to me proper not to speak directly about time any longer, but to indicate its unified rule only in the background. It is enough that the reader feel that everything that is said about a work of literature conform to the temporal succession even if he does not dare elaborate it in abstract terms.[20]

It is clear from this statement that in his work postdating the *Poetics* Staiger is excavating beneath the foundations laid in the *Poetics* and

18. "*[Heidegger habe] durch die Erhellung der ursprünglichen Zeit ein zuverlässiges Fundament der Geistes wissenschaften gelegt und also geleistet, was Wilhelm Dilthey noch schuldig geblieben war*" (*Neue Zürcher Zeitung*, 26 September 1959). I am indebted to Gelley, 199, for this and the following citation in the text proper.

19. "*Interpretation poetischer Werke in ständigem Hinblick auf ihre verborgene temporale Struktur.*"

20. " . . . *dass der Wandel der Zeitverhältnisse, auf dem die Mannigfaltigkeit der schöpferischen Individualitäten beruht, in wissenschaftlicher Terminologie kaum adäquat erfasst werden kann. Es schien mir deshalb richtig, nicht mehr unmittelbar von der Zeit zu sprechen, sondern ihr einheitliches Walten nur im Hintergrund anzudeuten. Es genügt, wenn der Leser spürt, dass alles, was über eine Dichtung ausgesagt wird, im Gefüge der Zeit übereinstimmt, auch wenn er sich hütet dieses Gefüge in Abstraktionen herauszuarbeiten.*" (Quoted in Gelley, 199.)

beneath the systematizations of Being and its temporalizations worked out by Heidegger in *Being and Time*. Staiger moves from consideration of kinds of literary qualities to considerations of linguistic objectifications of these kinds so unique and multiplicitous that to belabor their temporal categories is almost to misrepresent them. Still, however, he refers to time's "unified rule" and emphasizes that *everything* he says "conforms to the temporal succession"—that is, to the hidden time structures he has elaborated in the *Poetics*.

What, exactly, Staiger means by hidden temporal structures is thus crucial to an understanding of his approach and his achievement in the *Poetics* and in his later criticism. What he emphatically does not mean is what is referred to as the chronological situatedness of the events narrated, pondered, or suggested by a given work—its time frame, in short. (Heidegger insists that the primordial time structures are not temporalities "in" or "within" which Being or events take place; they are rather the *ways* Being takes place.) Moreover, Staiger is not referring to the meanderings of plot, to the one-thing-after-the-other-ness of events at a work's surface level, but rather to that experience of time that suffuses the work because it is objectified by it. The work is of course inevitably suffused by that temporalization of existence that it itself is a linguistic objectification of. In order to apprehend what Staiger means by hidden temporal structures it is necessary to review Heidegger in brief summary, since his theory of the temporal structure of Being, and of its three constituent "ecstasies," or "raptures," provides an explanation. Heidegger's theory is one of the foundational structures of thought that makes Staiger's criticism possible. A summary of it will be a useful supplement both to the perfunctory references to Heidegger's time structures that the scholarly commentaries on Staiger set down and to Staiger himself. For at no point in his introductory or postscriptural remarks in the *Poetics* does Staiger himself attempt to explain the Heideggerian system in its relation to his own. This is so despite the fact that, beyond any question, Heidegger's work is the sine qua non for a satisfactory understanding of what Staiger intends and accomplishes.

Heidegger has reviewed the history of philosophy in the West from the time of Greek antiquity through that of the writings of Dilthey and Husserl and notes that the way of knowing it sanctions and fosters has no adequate grounding. He observes that the processes of Being that presumably yield the way of knowing dominant in the West, and indeed the form of that knowing itself, have gone unexamined, have been taken for granted (21–24). The meaning of the phenomenon of Being that the West's knowing grows out of and depends on has been overlooked. Thus we know, but we do not know the basis of our knowing. We have no grounds on which even to begin to comprehend its nature.

Heidegger thus undertakes a radical critique of the philosophical tradition of the West, coming to understand its essentially metaphysical emphasis as a primary source of its failure to apprehend the nature of Being and thus the nature of its knowing. As a result, he chooses to derive his own thought from the pre-Socratics, whom the West had veered from in the works of Plato. He returns to this tradition in an attempt to construct a suitable practice of knowing on its foundations, one that will be a direct result of an understanding of the nature of Being. In attempting to come to an understanding of the nature of Being, Heidegger recognizes that it is constituted by processes of hermeneutics, or acts of understanding. Although I will elaborate these points below, it will be useful to note here that such acts of understanding are in their turn constituted of—that is, made possible by —time, or temporality, and that this temporality manifests itself in the primary temporal modes. Heidegger refers to this as temporality temporalizing itself.

To clarify how Heidegger's "Being" would itself need to be understood in order for it to be able to accommodate "acts of understanding" as its constituent elements, we can look more closely at the possible meanings of the term. There is a difficulty at the outset in shedding adequate light on Heidegger's precise meaning, since the language he has inherited, and in which he is forced to write, namely, the language of the metaphysical tradition, lacks the necessary words and above all the grammar for an adequate apprehension and representation of his insights. Heretofore blind to the insights at which Heidegger is the first to arrive, this language has not evolved forms that can speak them or represent them, and thus yield a close understanding of them.

Acknowledging the variety of published opinions on the meaning of Heidegger's "Being," many of which conflict among themselves and some of which were repudiated in his lifetime by Heidegger himself,[21] it still appears safe to say that the Being, or *Sein des Seienden*, that Heidegger explores refers not to the phenomenon of existence itself, as in the existence of entities, or even to the nature of entities themselves, but is essentially revelation. According to John N. Deely,

---

21. See Herbert Spiegelberg, *The Phenomenological Movement*, 2d ed. (The Hague: Nijhoff, 1965), 288ff.

it is "bound up intrinsically and essentially with the revelation of beings in human awareness."[22]

With this interpretation in hand, it is crucial to point out that the acts by which beings become revealed in human awareness are hermeneutic acts, and that these acts are in large part linguistic. Recognition of this permits Heidegger (and Staiger after him) to see in the act of bringing-into-Being-via-the-word, and most specifically in the creation of the literary work of art, the quintessential act of Being. In exploring the nature and importance of the linguistic act of unconcealment, *Being and Time* and the works that follow it become events of profound importance for literary criticism, linking it with philosophy in a near isomorphism in which both heretofore presumably separate ways of knowing become aspects of a single exploration of the understanding of understanding. Both become modes of studying the process of unconcealment via language by which Being comes to be.

Seeing in the literary work the quintessential act of Being, Heidegger regards poets as those most dedicatedly occupied with Being's creation, and he thereupon sets in motion a revaluation of the role of writer as profound as the ones he inaugurates for the roles of literary critic and philosopher. He sees in the writer the guarantor, the perpetuator, of Being by virtue of his role in bringing the world into unconcealment through creation in language (new texts) and of language (new usages, new concepts, new words).

Staiger, who shares Heidegger's view, thus commits himself to the type of interpretation we have seen him describe, arguing that the proper function of the literary critic in relation to the literary work of art is no longer either a categorizing or an explaining one. It is, rather, participatory: He sees the literary critic as one among many successive participants *in* the linguistic act of unconcealing initiated by the poet. Rather than comment on or explain a work's meaning *apart* from the words in which it is couched, it is the critic's proper role to reveal *through* these words specific dimensions of their meaning essential to a full understanding but perhaps not immediately apparent to readers.

Since Staiger understands via Heidegger that the linguistic acts of unconcealment material to literature are themselves constituted of temporality, he chooses to elucidate literary works from the point of view of their constituent temporal structures. According to Heidegger,

22. John N. Deely, *The Tradition via Heidegger: An Essay on the Meaning of Being in the Philosophy of Martin Heidegger* (The Hauge: Nijhoff, 1971), 24.

hermeneutic acts, or acts of understanding or unconcealing, are temporality's temporalizations of itself. The temporality that constitutes understanding, moreover, temporalizes itself in three primary modes—future, past, and present—that are theoretically separable, even theoretically discrete. Yet they do not in fact occur in pure form, as separate and distinct from one another. Each occurs in a form in which all three are simultaneously present, one being dominant and the others recessive, as it were. To these modes Heidegger gives the name ecstasies or raptures.

Operating in this Heideggerian context, Staiger sees that a particular "temporalization of temporality" lies behind every work of art. Whatever the more minutely discrete temporalities may be that are participated in by a poet in a creative linguistic act, Staiger sees that any given work characteristically embodies one or the other of the three primary temporal modes. He then expands this insight into the awareness that the same is true of the genres: Each genre represents a privileging of a particular temporal mode. He thus comes to see an equivalence between Heidegger's primary ecstasies—futurity, pastness (or having-been), and presentness—and the genres of drama, lyric, and epic. Staiger moves from here to an excavation of the meaning of the temporalities for genre study and thus to a radically new understanding of the basic concepts of poetics. As I have noted earlier, critics failed to perceive the nature both of his intent and his achievement. They looked on his renovations as relatively minor additions to conventional genre criticism, on his excavations as tinkerings with its extant structure, and on his new foundation-laying as an imposition of alien (philosophical) thought on the genres' immutable essences.

It is true that in seeing in Heidegger's temporal ecstasies an opportunity to understand the genres in a way that they have not previously been understood Staiger adds to the always growing fund of information "about" them, and that he can thus be correctly located among genre critics. But in saying this it is necessary to remember that a genre criticism that has embraced Staiger will be one whose dimensions and whose understanding of itself have profoundly changed. It will be a genre criticism with a completely new foundation, and one that bears marks of the changes consequent upon this throughout the range of its thought. Thus it is a radical misunderstanding of Staiger's work and of what becomes of genre criticism in encompassing it if he is placed there without prior explanations of the special nature of his understanding and of his place vis-à-vis the tradition, of the special form that our own understanding of his modus operandi must take if we are to apprehend him satisfactorily, and of what becomes of genre criticism in the process. For Staiger does with the practice of genre criticism what Heidegger does with that of philosophy: He turns it inside out.

Rather than look upon a given genre as a first principle, as it were, and derive an understanding of a given poem deductively from its points of correspondence with or divergence from this principle—the genre's historically testified form—Staiger derives the fact of genre itself inductively from the way of being that is embodied in given works. This way of being he understands as necessarily temporally constituted—as a version of time in the process of temporalizing itself. But the import of our awareness of even this assertion may be finally enhanced by looking again for a moment at the practice of genre criticism before Staiger, who was not the first to link the genres with temporal modes, but whose doing so occupies a different conceptual space from that of former attempts.

Certainly since Kant it has seemed clear that the temporal and the spatial are the two primary coordinates, or matrices, of thought within which knowing and reason become possible for human beings. Thus it is not surprising that one of humans' primary ways of knowing, literature, should have been aligned with the temporal modes. This was recognized even before the phenomenologists appropriated the temporal as one of the several modes in whose terms they could describe experience. But since, according to Kant, time was a concept *a priori*, this left the genres also rooted in the *a priori*. And they had never been effectively freed from it. Thus genre forms seen as literary versions of temporal modes remained inhabitants of a metaphysical world. Even in the work of so recent a group as the Chicago Critics the genre forms appear clearly as essences. They are the universals of which R. S. Crane speaks when he argues:

> It is impossible that there should be, for example, a history of tragedy as such, or of lyric poetry, or of the epic. These terms are universals; they represent natures which do not change, however differently at different times they may be defined by critics or embodied by artists in particular works; as essences they lend themselves only to general and scientific, *not to histori-cal*, statement. (Italics added.)[23]

23. R. S. Crane, "History vs. Criticism in the University Study of Literature," in *The Idea of the Humanities and Other Essays Critical and Historical* (Chicago: University of Chicago Press, 1967), 8.

Staiger's work in the *Poetics* represents a profound reversal of this tradition. In Heidegger's temporal ecstasies Staiger sees an opportunity to open the genres to the possibility *of* historical statement by revealing them to be, in themselves, profoundly historical. The form Staiger's understanding takes is important—he sees the genres as versions of foundational human experiences and so links them to concrete historical existence. Thus, what Staiger confronts in his insights is the imperative of a thoroughgoing reconstitution of genre theory that would begin with an understanding of its basic concepts. His *Poetics* should be read as his response to this imperative.

Unlike Crane, Staiger sees the genres not as essences but as versions of ongoing processes of foundational human experience and thus as versions of concrete historical existence. Their radically historical character is suspended for the conventional understanding by their being recorded permanently in linguistic form. But in the detailed descriptions that make up the praxis of the *Poetics* Staiger demonstrates the validity of his view: He grounds the genres in poets' actual ways of being, in given temporalizations of experience, rather than in catalogs of aesthetic objects organized by kinds and described in their terms. This perspective permits him to achieve two important and immediate goals: first, to detach the genres finally from the world of the *a priori* (where they had continued to hover), and, second, to demonstrate that at their foundational level the genres are *not* susceptible to arbitrary multiplication. Staiger achieves this by grounding the genres in the primordial temporal modes.

Staiger thus successfully removes the genres themselves from the world of metaphysical essences, and he removes what have traditionally been considered the basic genre structures from the realm of primary consideration altogether. The structures he points to as primary, or basic, are ways of being that translate into literary qualities. His trio of primary generic qualities is based on primary experiential possibilities that cannot be expanded. These in turn ground the primary genre kinds. The multiplicitousness of subgenres can be dealt with at another level of theory.

Stated most simply, the link Staiger proposes between foundational human experience and the primary genres, the set of alignments for which his *Poetics* serves as the phenomenological description and the justification, is this: Lyric corresponds to pastness, epic to presentness, drama to futurity. It has been argued on the contrary, however, with varying degrees of persuasiveness, and from a conventional point of view, that Staiger's application of Heidegger's temporal categories to the genres is profoundly arbitrary, unsuitable (Salm). The point has been made that a more suitable arrangement is the more traditional association of epic with pastness, of lyric with presentness, and of drama with futurity.

But while such arguments are not always unconvincing, they are so only from a conventional point of view. It is essential to recall in this connection that Heidegger reminds his readers again and again that the modes as he understands and describes them are not apprehendable as conventional time designations. Moreover, if one takes as valid, and as given, the structure of the ecstasies as Heidegger apprehends and describes them, Staiger's alignments are not merely valid, they are inevitable. This is not to say that what dissenting observers argue is without merit. It is, rather, to observe that, when seen from a Heideggerian point of view, Staiger's alignments are easily recognizable as proportionately more suitable than those of other critics. For the present, however, it will suffice to say that with the term "proportionately" we are pointing indirectly to the fact that Staiger himself, when describing equivalences between the trio of primordial temporal modes and the primary genres, observes that no genre is pure. It could be maintained, however, that in his desire to illustrate the correspondences he fails to emphasize this point sufficiently. It is an important one and corresponds to Heidegger's insistence that every way of being in the world is inevitably suffused by all the modes, since the modes are profoundly interdependent, but that as a rule one predominates. The dominant function of one subordinates the others but seldom completely annihilates their functions. Thus every temporality is characterized by the interdependence of all three primordial temporalities, or temporal possibilities.

If one accepts Heidegger's temporal explanations as provisionally valid, as a set of first principles constituting a satisfactory position from which to begin to understand Staiger's genre descriptions, one is equipped with a means of sympathetically reexamining the *Poetics*. Accepting Heidegger's temporalities as the place for criticism of the *Poetics* to begin makes possible a reconsideration and understanding of it through assumptions that match Staiger's—that is, through assumptions not alien to his at the outset. Gelley recognizes the need for such a reconsideration and understanding:

> In my opinion the *Grundbegriffe der Poetik* is, correspondingly, not to be viewed as a comprehensive system of the genre forms as so many of its critics have done to the exclusion of all other considerations. The *Poetik* interprets the traditional genre categories—lyric, epic, and dramatic—as modes of temporalization

and specifically connects them to the three *Ekstasen*. Admittedly, there is an implicit claim of universality here, and it has been cogently argued that Staiger's field of reference is too restricted to allow his theory general validity—see, for example, E. M. Wilkinson in *MLR* 44 (1949), 433–37. But the objection can be met, I think, if one understands Staiger's identification of lyric with past as referring not to *the* past as such, but to a mode of temporalization which, adequately described, would be seen to be a form of past. And so for the other two modes as well. What is important in Staiger's book is not that he has classified the literary types by means of temporal categories, but that he has begun to overcome the arbitrary, indeed chaotic terminology based on historical and normative criteria, and to replace it with one based upon fundamental attitudes of human existence as they are temporally manifested.(211)

According to Heidegger, each way of Being available to humans realizes itself as one of the primary temporal modes. Before he goes on to describe the modes as discrete phenomena, however (and also repeatedly during the course of these descriptions), Heidegger emphasizes the profound extent to which each can be understood in terms of the others and in fact *must* be so understood if it is to be comprehended fully and accurately. He emphasizes the extent to which each is in fact incomplete without the contributory dimensions, and the content, of the other two. Thus, while he views the modes as distinguishable from one another, he sees each at the same time as also a function of the other two and constituted by them.

In order to describe the temporal modes, and to prepare his readers to understand their constituent relation to human ways of being, Heidegger identifies a number of such ways and interprets them phenomenologically. In doing so, he describes them by the temporalities that make them up. The basic, or primordial, ways of being that he identifies are mood, or state of mind; the moment of vision, or of bringing things into awareness; and resoluteness, or care—the moment of bringing things into awareness for a specific purpose.

Heidegger sees the way of being describable as being-in-a-mood, or as state-of-mind, as constellated primarily by its relation to pastness, or having-been. He sees it characterized by a preponderance of the necessity for having-been in its constitution. Mood, or state-of-mind, is always a function of having-been. It is an attitude toward or a way of disclosing or viewing something, and it has its roots in having-been. The moment-of-vision, or of bringing things into awareness (and to this extent into being), is characterized, rather, by a preponderance of the necessity for presentness in its constitution; and resoluteness, or care, by a preponderance of the necessity for futurity in its constitution.

It is thus that Staiger connects the genre "lyric"—consisting, characteristically, he feels, of works that are preponderantly linguistic disclosures of mood—with having-been. In the same way, he connects the genre "epic" (with its disclosure of the moment-of-vision, or bringing the phenomenal world into unconcealment, a disclosure that is primarily present-oriented), with the present. And it is thus that he associates drama, with its emphasis on unconcealment-with-a-purpose-having-its-goal-in-the-future, with futurity. In his view, then, lyric becomes understandable as a being-toward-the-past, epic as a being-toward-the-present, and drama as a being-toward-the-future.

XI

At the outset of his project in the *Poetics* Staiger's aim was dual, but it was to be accomplished with a single structure. Rather than argue against traditional genre theory, he would demonstrate its shortcomings by displacing it with a critical practice adequate to its subject, as traditional practice was not. He would show the traditional theory's irrelevance—its superficiality, inadequacy to its subject, and consequent lack of explanatory power—by establishing in its place a relevant practice. By focusing not on poetic form but on the nature of the experiences of consciousness that assume this form, the new practice could explain and thus understand the concept of genre and its constituent basic concepts as they had not been understood before.

But by the time Staiger has completed his task and looks back on it from a temporal perspective of several years, he can see the significance of his achievement and its potential critical role differently. He can see his work in the *Poetics* less as an invalidation of traditional theory than as a possible source of explanation for it, and his accomplishment less as an implicit rejection of tradition than as a possible means of understanding it. He would still deny traditional theory a role as a *basis* for criticism. The *Poetics* itself seeks out this basis in Heidegger, and further defines and explores it for the ends of literary understanding. But Staiger can see in the *Poetics* a possible foundation, and hence a source of meaning and of validation, for the traditional system, which heretofore had lacked all three. This insight is suggested only with the preface to the second edition, however, and is no more than suggested. It exists in his text for a moment only, then disappears. Moreover, it is not to be developed in later works. If this moment of insight itself exists more than fleetingly, Staiger does not view the need to effect a rapprochement between his just-developed practice and a still very largely alien prior theory as a need that he himself must meet. We mention it here as a guide to reading, however—as an indication of the potential of Staiger's practice for carving out a theoretical space in which the extremes of both absolutist and relativist criticism could be accommodated, and within which the two criticisms could be reconciled. This is the promise that Staiger's thought holds out for literary theory.

The *Poetics* can claim two primary achievements. First, it establishes criticism proper on a new theoretical footing, a philosophical rather than a literary one (though as we have seen, via Heidegger, this distinction might now be viewed as unnecessary). Second, it presents the foundational elaboration of the new theory's consequences for an understanding of literary art—for an understanding of poetic language in general and of the nature of genre distinctions in particular. In short, Staiger constructs a new theory of genre and of poetic language on the basis of speculative thought.

With this statement I am making no claim of novelty for a speculative basis for literary theorizing in general. Nineteenth- and twentieth-century *Geistesgeschichte* in Europe and the history of ideas in North America amply refute such a claim, as does the pre-Staigerian use of Husserl's thought as a means to literary understanding. And both *Geistesgeschichte* and Husserl represent important moments of Staiger's intellectual lineage. Moreover, that speculative philosophy should form a basis for literary theorizing is surprising least of all today, when the boundary between philosophy and literary theory is scarcely any longer distinguishable. What is surprising is that speculative philosophy should so patently characterize the work of a theorist automatically considered New Critical, when its speculative basis is anathema to New Criticism. It represents a sidestepping of Husserl's insistence on freedom from theoretical encumbrances, which was taken as a rallying point by Formalism and by New Criticism, though never thoroughly adhered to. Staiger's participation in the phenomenological program (the renunciation of theory as an approach to literary phenomena) and his simultaneous grounding of his apparently unmediated practice in speculative philosophical thinking not earlier used as a basis for systematizing literature make his theory unmistakably paradoxical. And this paradox may be the source of some of the difficulty that readers have clearly had with it. That it is Heidegger's philosophy that forms its point of departure makes Staiger's theory of particular consequence.

At the time Staiger's work appeared and enjoyed its first critical success, its link to Heidegger received mechanical acknowledgement as a determining aspect of its meaning, but was perceived neither as a chief source of its appeal nor as an especially illuminating means of understanding it. If we remember that Heidegger is part of a tradition still considered subversive and heretical in the very recent past, we can perhaps understand why. If they reflect Staiger's earlier audiences' general orientation to Heidegger, Hilary Lawson's recent descriptions of typical negative responses to the philosopher's work provide an explanation. Lawson speaks of Heidegger as being one of several figures taken to exemplify "the worst aspects of continental philosophy" and reports views of these thinkers as enemies "of reason and even of humanity."[24] One in fact still often enough encounters such words as "dense," "impenetrable," "obfuscating," and "pernicious"— and others in their general range of meaning—as descriptions of Heidegger's work emanating from scholars more comfortable with the thought paradigms of the Anglo-American analytical tradition.

In the absence of a conviction of Heidegger's indispensability to an understanding of Western thought and to its development, and in the absence of a consequent willingness on the part of scholars to recognize his importance as the core of Staiger's inspiration and as the root of his theory, there developed no impetus for an exhaustive investigation of Heidegger's thought for an understanding of Staiger's, and hence no real understanding of Staiger. Gelley's article is the exception here. With increasing contemporary interest in the potential of Continental philosophical (and in particular of Heideggerian) thought for informing and validating—even for rejuvenating—literary theory, however, Staiger's work and its Heideggerian provenance become increasingly relevant to contemporary concerns.

24. Hilary Lawson, *Reflexivity: The Post-Modern Predicament* (La Salle, Ill.: Open Court, 1985), 11 and back cover.

Basic Concepts of Poetics

Introduction

In speaking of *Basic Concepts of Poetics* we mean the concepts of epic,
lyric, dramatic, and possibly also tragic and comic—but taken in a
different sense from the one that has been in use up until now;
therefore, we must explain what we mean at the very beginning.
The title *Poetics* no longer signifies a practical guide to enable the
inexperienced to write poems, epic poems, and dramas corresponding
exactly to the rules. But the more recent writings that go by the name
of Poetics still resemble the older works in one regard: They see the
essence of the lyric, the epic, and the dramatic fully exemplified in
specific models of poems, epic poems, and dramas. This way of looking at things has been handed down to us from antiquity. Then, every
poetic genre was represented in a limited number of models; for
instance, a poetic creation corresponding in basic structure, length,
and meter to what the nine classic poets—Alcman, Stesichorus, Alcaeus, Sappho, Ibycus, Anacreon, Simonides, Bacchylides, and
Pindar—had produced was called lyric. Thus, the Romans could consider Horace a lyric poet but not Catullus, because he chose different
meters. Since ancient times, however, the models have increased
immeasurably. If poetics were to continue to do justice to every single
example, it would encounter almost insoluble difficulties, the solution
of which would yield little of value. In regard to the lyric genre, for
instance, such a poetics would have to compare ballads, *lieder*, hymns,
odes, sonnets, epigrams; it would have to follow each of these types
through more than a thousand years and find something common to
them all out of which to forge the concept of the lyric. But whatever
would be common to all types could only be so general as to be

meaningless. Furthermore, it would lose all significance as soon as a new lyric poet appeared with a hitherto-unknown model. For these reasons, people have often disputed the feasibility of a poetics. They flatter themselves into thinking that they are following historical development "without prejudice" and reject every kind of systematizing as inappropriate dogma.

This attitude is understandable as long as poetics claims as its goal to file every poem, epic poem, and drama ever written into slots set aside for this purpose. Since no two poems are alike, principally as many slots are needed as there are poems—and when this is the case order is abolished.

But even though it is hardly possible to determine the essence of the lyric poem, the epic poem, and the drama, a definition of the lyric, the epic, and the dramatic is conceivable. For instance, we use the expression "lyric drama." Here, "drama" refers to a poetic creation that has been conceived for the stage; "lyric" refers to the key it is written in and is considered to be of greater importance in determining the essence of this poetic creation than the "externality of the dramatic form." What determines the genre here?

If I characterize a drama as lyric or—as Schiller does with *Hermann und Dorothea*[1]—an epic poem as dramatic, I must already know what lyric or dramatic signifies. I cannot know this simply by recalling all lyric poems and dramas in existence; such profusion is merely confusing. Rather, I have an idea of lyric, epic, and dramatic. At one time or another, an example made this idea clear to me. The example was probably a specific literary work, but not necessarily. I might have experienced the "ideal meaning" of "lyric"—to use Husserl's words[2]— in looking at a landscape; I might have experienced what is "epic" at the sight of a stream of refugees; a heated verbal exchange might perhaps make clear to me the meaning of dramatic. Such terms remain constant. It is absurd, as Husserl has shown, to say that they could vary. The content of the individual poetic works, works that I assess according to the idea (of lyric, epic, and dramatic), can vary; the individual work might be more or less lyric, epic, or dramatic. Furthermore, those "acts which bestow meaning" can suffer from lack of

---

1. Friedrich Schiller to Johann Wolfgang von Goethe, 26 December 1797, *Briefwechsel zwischen Schiller und Goethe in den Jahren 1794–1805* (Stuttgart: J. G. Cotta, 1828–29); in English: *Correspondence between Schiller and Goethe from 1794 to 1805*, trans. L. Dora Schmitz (London, 1877–89).

2. Edmund Husserl, *Logische Untersuchungen*, 4th ed. (Halle, 1928), 2:91ff.; in English: *Logical Investigations*, trans. J. N. Findlay (London: Routledge and Kegan Paul, 1970), 1, 322ff.

certainty. Once I have an idea of "lyric," however, it is as unshakable as the idea of the triangle or as the idea of "red"; it is objective, far removed from my caprice.

But even though the idea may be constant, it is perhaps incorrect. If a person is colorblind, he cannot have a correct idea of "red." True! But this question deals only with terminological usefulness. My idea of "red" must correspond to what is commonly called "red." Otherwise I would be using the wrong word. Thus, the idea of "lyric" must correspond to what people call lyric without having a clear concept of it. It is not simply the mean of all the elements that according to external characteristics are considered lyric works. We do not think of an epigram when we hear the terms "lyric mood" or "lyric tone"; we think of a poem. And no one is reminded of Klopstock's *Messias* upon hearing the terms "epic tranquility" and "epic plenitude." Homer would most probably occur to us first, and not even the entire Homer but preeminently epic passages, followed by other more dramatic or lyric ones. Examples such as these must be used in working out the genre concepts.

To a certain extent, there is a connection between the lyric and lyric poetry, the epic and epic poetry, the dramatic and the drama. The prime examples of the lyric are most likely to be found in lyric poetry, and of the epic in epic poetry. But we cannot safely assume that we will encounter a work somewhere that would be purely lyric, epic, or dramatic. On the contrary, our investigation will lead us to the conclusion that every genuine poetic work partakes of all the genre concepts to varying degrees and in varying ways, and that this varying participation is at the basis of the multiplicity of literary types that have evolved historically.

We could ask whether the triad lyric-epic-dramatic can be taken absolutely for granted. Irene Behrens has shown that this triad did not occur in Germany until the end of the eighteenth century.[3] But there too, the terms do not signify our ideas, but rather specific poetic models. So for the moment, we shall refrain from taking up this question. Instead, we shall make use of the commonly accepted terms as a working hypothesis. Whether all types of possible poetic creation can be judged from that vantage point remains to be seen.

As a matter of principle our examples should be taken from the whole of world literature. But it can hardly be avoided that the selections reveal the personal circumstances of the observer. The German

---

3. Irene Behrens, *Die Lehre von der Einteilung der Dichtkunst* (Theory of Classification in Poesy), Special Issue, *Zeitschrift für romanische Philologie*, 1940.

and the Greek poets are given preference here, simply because I am most familiar with them. But my circumstances would also be revealed if I were better read in Slavic, Scandinavian, or even non-European literature. It would still be a case of someone whose mother tongue is German trying to describe this body of literature. Such limitations exist no matter what. Of course, the harm is not as great here as if we were dealing with a poetics in the traditional sense. And yet it could be that everything is seen from a point of view that is of interest only to those in the area of German. This is not for me to decide, however.

I ask only that the reader reserve judgment on the various sections of this presentation until the end. Because of the nature of the problem it is even truer than usual that the individual elements can only be assessed correctly within the context of the whole. Specifically, many initially vague terms such as "inwardliness," "spirit," and "soul" only gradually gain in clarity. But since this process only serves to make the use of such terms more precise, no serious problems should arise.

And so the purpose of this book lies in an attempt to clarify terminology so that, in the future, everyone will know what he means when he says "lyric," "epic," and "dramatic." Therefore, this book should be regarded as an introduction to literary scholarship and as a tool for the interpreter of literature, enabling him or her to come to an understanding of general concepts quickly, thus making room for analyses of individual works of individual writers. But beyond this, we should like to consider this book of value in and of itself, namely, insofar as the question of the nature of the genre concepts leads on its own to the question of the nature of humanity. Thus literary scholarship contributes to philosophical anthropology in the form of a fundamental poetics. In this respect it ties in with my book *Time as Poetic Imagination*, published in 1939, which attempts to work out possible forms of human existence using poems of Brentano, Goethe, and Gottfried Keller. Whoever takes the trouble to compare this book with my earlier one will of course notice that some of the terminology has changed. In particular, I would no longer characterize a lyric existence as "time rushing on." What is even more important, the distinction between individual reality and purely ideal nature has only been carried through with the necessary terminological exactitude in *Basic Concepts of Poetics*.

Lyric Style: Remembrance*

I

Goethe's "Wanderers Nachtlied" (Wanderer's Night Song) is considered one of the purest examples of the lyric style. Critics have often shown how, in the poem's first two lines,

Über allen Gipfeln   Over all mountain tops
Ist Ruh . . .   Reigns peace . . .

the long "u" and the pause following it make the silent twilight audible, how the word rhyming with "Ruh" in the lines

In allen Wipfeln   In all the tree tops
Spürest du . . .   You feel . . .

is not as profoundly calming because the sentence does not end here, thus the voice remains raised, and this corresponds to the last faint rustling in the trees; finally, the critics point out how the pause after

Warte nur, balde . . .   Wait, soon . . .

gives the impression of waiting, waiting until in the final line,

*An asterisk indicates a translator's note.
Staiger uses the word *Erinnerung* (here translated as "remembrance") both in the sense of remembering and of interiorizing. By interiorization he means that the lyric poet and his object become one. The object world is assimilated by the poet, and this assimilation, in turn, is externalized in the form of *Stimmung* [mood] in the poem.

> Ruhest du auch . . .   You shall rest too . . .

in the last two drawn-out words, everything becomes calm, even that most restless of all beings, man.

One could make similar observations about Verlaine's stanza:

Et je m'en vais	And I depart
Au vent mauvais,	Into the bad wind
Qui m'emporte	Which carries me away
Deçà, delà,	Here, there
Pareil à la	Like
Feuille morte.	The dead leaf.

The second line sounds almost like the first except that the nasal—so it seems—has been displaced in carefree play. The words "vais–mauvais" and "delà–à la" can hardly be felt to rhyme. The tongue forms the same vowel as if it were babbling senselessly. The fleeting rhyme word "la" removes all sense of heaviness from the language. Thus, one could say, something hopelessly frivolous becomes audible; the mere sounds inspire us with the mood that arises in us at the sight of autumn leaves drifting in the wind.

If we can trust our feelings for classical verse, we are tempted to hear at the end of the well-known Sapphic stanza

> Stars around the beautiful moon

and in the Adonic line

> On the sea and the land

the pure and widespread peace that the full moon brings to land and sea.

Stylistic analysis takes great pleasure in such observations. There is nothing wrong with this, but the layperson, the unpretentious amateur of poetry, is unpleasantly affected by it. He or she feels that an attempt is being made to foist an intention upon the poet. Yet only that which is spontaneous is enjoyable and any trace of intention is irritating.

The so-called expert has good reason not to disregard the opinion of the amateur, for his own judgment remains true only as long as he remains an amateur. But it is perhaps possible to settle the dispute.

The expert would simply have to admit that we are not dealing with onomatopoeia in the examples discussed above.

Onomatopoetic lines are familiar to us in great number from the epic poems of Homer, as, for example, in Voss's translation of the often-cited, highly praised and controversial hexameter

Hurtig mit Donnergepolter entrollte der tückische Marmor.

Hurtling with rumbling of thunder the treacherous marble rolled down.

Or in the sentence "Dumpfhin kracht' er im Fall" [Dully he fell and crashed down], which renders the Greek δούπησέν τε πεσών perfectly in German; or the line that describes Calypso's wooing of Odysseus:

Αἰεὶ δὲ μαλακοῖσι καὶ αἱμυλίοισι λόγοισι

Always with gentle and flattering words. . . .

Here, phonetic elements of language are applied to an action. "To apply to" signifies that language and the action it describes are separate entities. Therefore, we say—and rightly so—that language "re"-produces the action. The concept of "imitatio" is appropriate here. Imitation by means of language is an accomplishment that can be analyzed to some extent: This unbroken series of dactyls reproduces the rumbling of falling marble; this wealth of vowels, the seductive talents of Calypso. Such analyses are not really irritating, because the reader simply assumes this is the author's intention or at least thinks it possible, and because the analysis seems merely to substantiate the poet's pleasure in having succeeded so well at his task.

The lyric style does not reproduce an action in words, however. In "Wanderers Nachtlied" (Wanderer's Night Song) we do not have the evening mood on the one hand and, on the other, language with its sounds ready to be applied to its objects. The evening creates itself as language; it does so without the help of the poet. There is, as yet, no subject-object dichotomy. Language merges with the evening mood, the evening with language. Therefore, the analysis of individual phonetic relations is bound to irritate the reader. An interpretation separates elements that, originally, were mysteriously united, and it can never quite unveil the mystery. For the union is more intimate than the most penetrating perception ever realizes, just as a face is more revealing than any physiognomic analysis and a soul is deeper than any attempt at psychological explanation.

The value of lyric verse as such lies in this union between the meaning and the music of words. It is spontaneous music, whereas onomatopoeia—mutatis mutandis and without value judgment— might best be compared to program music. Nothing is more delicate than the spontaneous expression of mood. Therefore, every word, every syllable in a lyric poem is completely indispensable and irreplaceable. Let the reader who can bear to do so replace "spürest" with "merkest" in "Wanderers Nachtlied"; let him erase the "e" in "Vögelein" and ask himself whether the line is not seriously impaired by this change. Of course, not all poems are as vulnerable as this particular one. But the more lyrical a poem is, the more untouchable it is. We hardly dare to read it out loud for fear of contradicting the tone of the poet by lengthening or shortening syllables, by stressing them too much or too little. Epic hexameters are much more robust. One can, at least within certain limits, learn to recite them. Lyric verses, however, if they are to be recited, only sound right to the extent that they arise anew from a deep immersion in a tranquillity far removed from the world—this is true even for lines of light verse. They need the magic of inspiration, and anything that could arouse the suspicion of an intention is irritating here too.

This is what makes translation into foreign languages difficult or even impossible. When dealing with onomatopoeia an inventive translator might perhaps find a solution. It is highly unlikely, however, that words having the same meaning in different languages also have the same lyric unity of sound and meaning. Ernst Jünger cites an example in *Lob der Vokale* (In Praise of Vowels).[4] It is the Latin stanza:

Nulla unda	No wave
Tam profunda	As deep
Quam vis amoris	As the power of love
Furibunda.	Furibund.

The force of love is being compared here to that of water, and the rhyme words "unda, profunda, furibunda" conjure up the wellsprings of feeling from which the unfathomable, unknown even to ourselves, can rise. This is the German translation:

4. Ernst Jünger, *Blätter und Steine* (Leaves and Stones) (Hamburg, 1934).

Keine Quelle	No source
So tief und schnelle	As deep and rushing
Als der Liebe	As the sweeping
Reißende Welle.	Of love.

The "e" corresponds to the dark "u," the double "l" corresponds to the "nd." Again we think we hear water; however, this time not from the innermost depths, but as a rushing stream. And this is a different kind of love, not a restrained demonic force, but an overpowering passion. The meanings of the new or altered words correspond to this different kind of love. "Schnelle" is not to be found in the Latin text, nor is "reißende." The harmony between sound and meaning is just as pure as in the original. Yet the entire poem is completely altered.

But if the translation of lyric verse is almost impossible, it is also much easier to do without than is the translation of epic and dramatic verse. For each reader of a poem in the original believes he or she senses something in a lyric poem, even if its language is foreign. He or she hears the poem's sounds and rhythms and, before arriving at a discursive understanding of it, is affected by the mood of the poet. We are suggesting here the possibility of conveying a meaning without the use of concepts. A remnant of paradise seems to be preserved in the lyric.

This remnant is music, a language without words, but one that can, nonetheless, be sounded by means of words. The poet himself admits this with the *lied*, which he intends to be sung. For it is precisely in song that the melodic curve, the rhythm, is worked out. The listener does not pay much attention to the content of the sentences, and sometimes even the singer himself does not quite know what is being said in the text. Love, death, water—any vague, enchanting thing satisfies him. In the meantime he sings on without thinking, yet he is still completely absorbed in his task. He would be hurt if he were to be told he had not understood the *lied*. He is, of course, not doing justice to the whole work of art, for the meanings of words and sentences are after all integral parts of the *lied*. Not just the music of the words alone, and not just their meanings, but both together make up the miracle of lyric poetry. Yet we cannot blame anyone for being carried away by the immediate effect of the music. Even the poet is quite ready to accord a certain precedence to the musical element. For the sake of tone or rhyme he will himself occasionally depart from the rules and customary usages of language that is basically oriented toward meaning. He will syncopate a final "e," change a word sequence, omit indispensable grammatical elements:

Viel Wandrer lustig schwenken
Die Hüt' im Morgenstrahl . . .

Weg, du Traum! so gold du bist;
Hier auch Lieb und Leben ist . . .

Was soll all der Schmerz und Lust?

Many wanderers gaily
Wave their hats in the morning light . . .
(Eichendorff, "Wanderer's Song of the Prague Students")

Begone, dream, no matter how golden;
Love and life can be found here, too . . .
(Goethe, "On the Lake")

Why all this pain and desire?
(Goethe, "Wanderer's Night Song")

In epic verse such things would be noticed; in lyric verse we can accept them without being offended because the musical spheres of influence that place the words in a certain order apparently are more powerful than the need for grammatically correct and conventional forms.

Furthermore, there are poems whose motif or content is ever so slight, indeed insignificant, and yet they blossom for centuries in the hearts of a people without wilting. But Goethe denied this. In his conversations with Eckermann we find a discussion of Serbian *lieder*.[5] Eckermann is pleased with the motifs Goethe has summarized as follows: "Girl does not want the man she does not love," "love's joys gossiped about," "the beautiful serving girl's lover is not among the guests." Eckermann comments that the motifs are so vivid in themselves that they leave him little desire to read the poem. Whereupon Goethe answers:

> You are quite right, it is true. This demonstrates the great importance of motifs, which no one is willing to understand. Our women have not the faintest notion of it. This poem is beautiful, they say, and think only of the emotional qualities, of the words, of the verses. But it does not occur to anyone that the true power and impact of the poem lies in the situation, in

5. Goethe to Johann Peter Eckermann, 18 January 1825; in English: *Conversations with Goethe*, trans. Gisela C. O'Brien (New York, 1964).

the motifs. And for this reason thousands of poems are written whose motif is nonexistent and which give the illustion of some sort of existence through mere feelings and pleasant sounding words.

Goethe expressed this same appreciation of the motif in the fine arts, to the dismay of the romantic painters. He even went so far as to say that only a translation of a poem into prose would show how much real life a poem possessed. If need be, we could accept this when talking about the drama or about epic works. For example, the voyages of Odysseus fascinate the reader even in Schwab's *Tales of Classical Antiquity*. A vigorous retelling of Schiller's *Wallenstein* is conceivable. But poems retold in prose lose their most essential quality; on the other hand, a totally insignificant motif can become a work of art of the first order when put into lyric language. With many of Eichendorff's poems it would be difficult to pick out a motif. And does not one of the most famous of Goethe's poems, "An den Mond" (To the Moon), contradict his harsh judgment? For more than a hundred years experts have not been able to agree on the situation upon which the poem is supposedly based. Is it addressed to a woman or a man, and if a man is meant, is it a role poem?* Or is it a duet? And if it is a duet, how should the stanzas be divided up among the two partners? All these possibilities have been weighed and all discarded. But the critics have agreed on one thing: This incomprehensible poem belongs among the most beautiful in world literature.

Goethe formulated his requisite for a good poem late in life, when his aesthetics was based on concepts he had derived from nature and the fine arts. These same concepts became the basis of German literary history, particularly the problematic concept of form, which, however we look at it, still presupposes something to be formed and a force that forms or a sort of mold in which forms are made. It is precisely this duality between a form on the one hand and a thing to be formed on the other that does not manifest itself in lyric poetry. The concept of "forming" can, however, be applied to the epic, where the most different elements, pain and joy, the clamor of weapons and the return of the hero, are poured into the one "form," the hexameter, which remains constant through all change. In lyric poetry, however, the

---

*The word Staiger uses here is *Rollengedicht*, for which English offers no satisfactory term. In a *Rollengedicht*, thoughts and feelings are expressed not by a lyric "I" but by a speaker; see, for example, Brentano's *Der Spinnerin Lied* (Song of the Spinning Girl) and Rilke's *Lied des Bettlers* (The Beggar's Song).

meter, rhyme, and rhythm are generated as integral parts of the sentences. One element cannot be separated from another: One does not just comprise content and another does not just comprise form.

From this it seems to follow that in lyric poetry there have to be as many metric structures as there are moods to be expressed. A trace of this is evident in the history of lyric poetry. Because of the variety of its meters ("varietate carminum"), lyric poetry creates difficulties for the older poetics, which tries to determine genre according to metric characteristics. The older poetics finally is forced to concede that it is precisely this "varietas" that is characteristic of the genre. Furthermore, the designations "Asclepiadean," "Alcaic," and "Sapphic" verse show that, at least originally, every master of Melos sang his own tune, an ideal that attained renewed importance in the Middle Ages. It seems, however, that the ultimate has not been reached until not only every poet, but every poem, has its own tune, its own stanza, and its own meter. This is true of the short poems Goethe wrote in the early Weimar years, in "Rastlose Liebe" (Restless Love), in "Herbstgefühl" (Autumn Feeling), and even more perfectly in "Wanderers Nachtlied" (Wanderer's Night Song) and "Über allen Gipfeln ist Ruh" (Over All Mountain Tops Reigns Peace). Because it reveals the finest metric flexibility in every line, this wonderful poem cannot be fitted into any fixed metric pattern and is thus protected from any sort of imitation. The short poems of Mörike should be listed here too: "Er ist's" (He Is the One), "In der Frühe" (In the Early Morning), "Septembermorgen" (September Morning), "Um Mitternacht" (At Midnight), and "Auf den Tod eines Vogels" (On the Death of a Bird).

However, it would be wrong to attribute too great an importance to the uniqueness of the metric structure and to consider the countless poems written in regular iambic and trochaic verse less lyric from the outset. For even within the same metric structure rhythmical changes are possible that completely satisfy every individual mood. Mörike's "Verborgenheit" (Seclusion), for instance, is written in the usual trochaic four-line stanza:

Laß o Welt, o laß mich sein!	Let, o world, o let me be!
Locket nicht mit Liebesgaben,	Lure me not with gifts of love,
Laßt dies Herz alleine haben	Let this heart receive alone
Seine Wonne, seine Pein!	All its joy and all its pain!

Yet the tone corresponds completely to the content. A gentle gesture of refusal, a retreating movement, are audible in the slight emphasis that rests on the first syllable and in the subsequent timid pause marked by a comma:

Laß, o Welt, o laß mich sein!   Let, o world, o let me be!

It is as though the poet wanted to anticipate the enticements of the world. The "l" that opens the line three times contributes to this feeling, too, but here again, only subtle indications are possible; then the tone becomes calmer; the gently refusing gesture was enough; the world is willing to leave this heart to itself.

The third stanza sounds altogether different:

Oft bin ich mir kaum bewußt,   Often I am hardly aware of
Und die helle Freude zücket   myself,
Durch die Schwere, so mich   And bright joy flashes
    drücket,   Through the inner darkness
Wonniglich in meiner Brust.   which so oppresses me,
                                              Rapturously in my bosom.

The metric structure remains the same. But now the melody rises. At any rate, the initial syllables "oft" and "durch" do not carry the same weight as "laß," "locket," and "läßt." However, the ends of the lines gain in emphasis. "Bewußt," "zücket," and drücket" are more emphatic than "sein," "haben," and the two final syllables of "Liebesgaben." Because the tone heightens toward the end, this stanza is gently ascending, whereas the first stanza, with its descending tone, seems to recede. Hugo Wolf recognized this and provided the third stanza with a special melody. His composition reveals the meaning of the verse in such a way that it does not even offend the most sensitive amateur.

II

Such poems as "Wanderers Nachtlied" (Wanderer's Night Song), "Er ist's" (He Is the One), "In der Frühe" (In the Early Morning) offer the clearest idea of what Friedrich Theodor Vischer calls "the instantaneous illumination of the world in the microcosm of the lyric subject."[6]

6. Friedrich Theodor Vischer, *Ästhetik; oder Wissenschaft des Schönen* (Aesthetics; or the Science of the Beautiful), 2d ed. (Munich, 1923), 6:208.

They are poems consisting only of a few lines. All true lyric poetry should be limited in length. This follows from what has already been said and will be borne out again by what is to come. The lyric poet does not *do* anything. He gives himself up—and this is to be taken literally—to inspiration. Mood, and together with it language, are given to him. He is not capable of divorcing himself from one or the other. His writing occurs spontaneously: "Out of the abundance of the heart the mouth overflows." To be sure, even such a poet as Mörike reworked his poems many times. But the poet's reworking is not to be equated with a dramatist's revising of his plot outline, or with an epic poet's insertion of new episodes or attempts at clearer formulation of what he has already written. The lyric poet attunes himself again and again to the given mood; he brings it forth anew just as he will re-create it in the reader. In the end he regains the magic of the moment of inspiration lost along the way, or at least he conveys the impression of spontaneity, as have many poets of declining eras who were heir to a great literary heritage. Conrad Ferdinand Meyer very frequently proceeded in this way, from the first draft to the final version. But Meyer can hardly be considered a prototype of the lyric poet. Clemens Brentano composed quite differently, bent over his lute and improvising to the astonishment of his friends. We can tell when we hear his *lieder* that they have arisen in him of their own accord:

> Echo off the walls—
> Alas!—my heart asks fearfully:
> Is that her voice?
>
> O, the words of the wave!
> O, the wafting of the wind!
> O, blessed threshold,
> Where we are born!

The later stanzas of his longer poems rarely sustain the magic of the initial stanzas. The poet finds himself forced to make something of his inspiration, to enlarge upon it, to round it off, or possibly even to explain it. He detaches himself from the initial lyric inspiration in order to confront it and hence steps out of the realm of grace. Of course, the poet can help himself by falling back upon the poetic treasure he has amassed in his earlier *lieder*. Brentano did this extensively. But an imitator, even someone who imitates himself, cannot deceive sensitive ears.

A problem becomes evident here and will be looked at more fully later, when we intend to show that the concept "lyric" is a concept that can never be fully realized as poetry—not because of human weakness on the part of the poet but because of the very nature of the lyric. Therefore, the lyric needs to be complemented by an epic or a dramatic element. For an inspirational mood lasts only a moment; it is a single resounding chord that fades away or else is followed by a new chord. But when these moods follow one upon the other, when the poet drifts along on the waves of his innermost feelings and his verse follows the change limnographically, where is the unity that the work of art as such demands? There are poems of this type in free verse, in which every line gives the impression of spontaneity and in which the entire creation flows on, unchecked, without beginning and without end. The poet strives toward an ideal of uninterrupted lyric flow; but artistically this is no longer possible, and leads to complete dissolution of the lyric itself.

Does this mean, then, that lyric poetry must be restricted to a very limited sphere? At this point I would like to insert an example, Goethe's poem "Auf dem See" (On the Lake):

> And I draw fresh nourishment, new blood
> From a free world;
> How gracious and good is nature
> Which holds me at her bosom!
> The waves lift the boat upward
> In rhythm with the oars,
> And mountains, reaching, cloud-covered, to the sky
> Come toward us on our course.
>
> Why, o why, am I lowering my gaze?
> Golden dreams, are you returning?
> Begone, dream, no matter how golden,
> Love and Life can be found here too.
>
> On the waves, a thousand
> Suspended stars are twinkling,
> Soft mists drink
> The towering distance all 'round;
> Morning breezes wing around
> The shadowy cove,
> And in the lake
> Is reflected the ripening fruit.

The entire poem is divided into three parts: The first part, which begins with an unaccented syllable, sounds lively and fresh; the second part, with the longer lines, is a memory and has a retarding effect; in the third, the journey continues with the poet's rapture slightly subdued. Three times the "instantaneous illumination of the world" occurs in the poet, each time in a different way, so that we cannot really speak of three separate stanzas. The poet's inspirations are simply strung together, for they belong together temporally and thematically. But we do not really know whether we are dealing with a poem or a cycle. The distance between the sections is too small for a cycle and too large for a poem. The separate sections represent lyric moments of a journey. What unifies these moments is not expressed in mood and language—it is a coherence that exists only biographically and that, duly enlarged, unites all of Goethe's poems as "fragments of a confession."

Thus, the question still remains: How do *lieder* of considerable length, existing as a unified whole, come into being?

Only *repetition* saves lyric poetry from disintegration. Yet some sort of repetition is inherent in all poetry. The most common is the beat, which is the repetition of equal units of time. Hegel compares the beat to the rows of columns and windows in architecture, and he points out that the "I" does not consist of limitless continuation and unrestrained duration; it establishes a sense of self only through meditation and self-reflection:

> The satisfaction that the "I" derives from the beat in this recovery of itself is all the more complete since unity and uniformity are not characteristics of time or of musical notes as such. Rather this satisfaction is something which is inherent only in the "I" and which the "I" has placed in the stream of time for its own satisfaction.[7]

This holds true for blank verse as well as for hexameter or for the rhythm of a *lied*, to the extent that it can be established. When Hegel states in accordance with the premises of his metaphysics that uniformity is not a characteristic of time and of musical notes but rather of the "I," he means that identical beats never occur "in reality" except in a performance executed by a metronome; uniformity is instead perceived merely as a regulative idea that asserts itself in ever greater or smaller variations. Heusler, as well as Hegel, describes this regula-

7. Friedrich Hegel, *Sämtliche Werke*, Jubiläums-Ausgabe (Stuttgart, 1928), 14:161 (further reference to Hegel's *Sämtliche Werke* is to this edition); in English: *Aesthetics: Lectures on Fine Art*, trans. T. M. Knox (Oxford, 1975).

tive idea as the opposition of beat and rhythm.[8] Whether beat and rhythm in natural delivery approach each other or diverge widely essentially determines the style of a poet. Not infrequently in Schiller's ballads, the rhythm approaches the beat so closely that the lines sound disjointed. In Mörike's "Verborgenheit" (Seclusion) the uniformity of the beat in each stanza recedes behind the change in the rhythm and merely seems to be a watchful eye, which inconspicuously keeps the lines from disintegration. In "Wanderers Nachtlied" (Wanderer's Night Song) the beat is no longer recognizable at all; various adjustments are possible, depending on what the length of the syllables and of the pauses is estimated to be. Longer poems in such a vague cadence would dissolve into formlessness.

The more purely lyric a poem is, the more it inclines away from a neutral repetition of the beat. This does not mean that it inclines toward prose but rather a rhythm that changes in keeping with the mood. This is only the metrical expression for the fact that in lyric poetry an "I" and an object just barely oppose each other as separate entities. In Schiller's poetry, however, the distance between them is especially great. This corresponds to the marked antithesis in his aesthetics between a Person who remains constant in the midst of all change, and a changeable condition.

But if the beat is not essential, are other repetitions possible? Eichendorff's "Nachts" (In the Night) consists of two stanzas that are both the same metrically:

Ich wandre durch die stille Nacht,
Da schleicht der Mond so heimlich sacht
Oft aus der dunklen Wolkenhülle,
Und hin and her im Tal
Erwacht die Nachtigall,
Dann wieder alles grau und still.

O wunderbarer Nachtgesang:
Von fern im Land der Ströme Gang,
Leis Schauern in den dunklen Bäumen—
Wirrst die Gedanken mir,
Mein irres Singen hier
Ist wie ein Rufen nur aus Träumen.

---

8. Andreas Heusler, *Deutsche Versgeschichte* (History of German Verse) (Berlin and Leipzig, 1925), 1:17ff.

> I wander through the quiet night,
> And the moon steals silently, softly
> In and out of the dark cover of clouds,
> And here and there in the valley
> The nightingale awakes,
> Then all is gray and still again.
>
> O, wonderful eveningsong:
> From afar in the land the rivers course,
> Soft tremors in the dark trees—
> You are muddling my thoughts,
> My confused singing here
> Is like someone crying out in a dream.

Differences of meter appear here as infrequently as in the four stanzas of Mörike's "Verborgenheit" (Seclusion). Rhythmically, too, these stanzas hardly differ from one another. The rather heavily accented opening syllable in the first stanza is repeated in the same place in the second stanza:

> *Oft* aus der dunklen Wolkenhülle
> In and out of the dark cover of clouds
>
> *Leis* Schauern in den dunklen Bäumen—
> Soft tremors in the dark trees—

The same thing occurs in the final lines, where in both cases the accent on the opening syllable is almost imperceptible, but nonetheless still audible:

> *Dann* wieder alles grau und stille . . .
> Then all is gray and still again . . .
>
> *Ist* wie ein Rufen nur aus Träumen
> Is like someone crying out in a dream.

The accentuations are distributed in a noticeably similar manner. Only in the fourth line is the rhythm perceptibly changed:

> Und hin und her im Tal . . .
> Here and there in the valley . . .
>
> Wirrst die Gedanken mir . . .
> You are muddling my thoughts. . . .

It is clear that further, barely tangible differences exist. But they do not prevail against the rhythmic similarity of the two stanzas. That is to say: The musical pattern of the first stanza is repeated in the second. The same chord resounds once more, emits a second, very similar tone. The vibrations of this tone seem to blur even the differences in the content of the two stanzas, like a chord held by a pedal over which a melody is continued.

Mörike's "Um Mitternacht" (At Midnight) takes us a step further:

> Gently, night came onto the land,
> Leans dreaming against the mountain wall,
> Her eye now sees the golden scales
> Of time quietly resting in perfect balance;
> And the wellsprings rush on more boldly,
> They sing into the ear of their mother, the night,
>   Of the day,
> Of the day that was today.
>
> The anciently ancient lullaby,
> She does not heed it, she is weary of it;
> To her the blue of the sky sounds sweeter,
> The perfectly balanced yoke of the fleeting hours.
> Yet the wellsprings continue to talk
> The waters sing on even in sleep
>   Of the day,
> Of the day that was today.

The evenly balanced yoke of time is mentioned in the same line of each stanza, the wellsprings are mentioned in the same pair of lines, and the two stanzas even end in the same words. The rhythmic repetition gradually eliminates the differences in content; it is as though this repetition had won the struggle against a gradually diminishing resistance on the part of speech seeking to perpetuate itself.

Such repetition is only possible in lyric poetry. It could be argued that in Homer's epic poetry, lines are also repeated literally. However, this objection is not valid, even though we frequently read:

> When the rosy-fingered dawn awoke . . .

> They reached out their hands for the good food that had
>   been prepared for them. . . .

But here it is merely a question of the poet's choosing the same words he has already previously used to depict another meal and another morning. By contrast, lyric repetition, in using the same words, does not express anything new; the same unique mood is evoked again.

A veiled repetition of the sort that occurs in Eichendorff's "Nachts" (In the Night) is quite rare and can prolong the lyric mood for two or three stanzas at most. Whatever goes beyond that becomes tiresome. Thus, the first repetition in Brentano's "Spinnerin" (A Girl Spinning) pleases us; the second time it sounds monotonous. By contrast, literal repetition is called refrain and is common in both the oldest and the most recent poetry of many countries. In Mörike's "Um Mitternacht" (At Midnight), the use of the refrain is unique; for most refrains are connected to the main text in a different way. In this poem the tone is lyric from beginning to end. The refrain is hardly distinguishable in its essence from the first lines of the stanza. Most of the time, however, particularly in folk songs and in folk-song-like poetry, the refrain is quite noticeable because of its musical diction. Not infrequently, in fact, the refrain seems to concentrate in itself all the poem's lyric character, whereas the rest of the lines tend more toward the epic or the dramatic.

Brentano supplies countless examples. Again and again in his longer poems, a balladlike event or even an experience is told in rather casual verse and is brought to a close almost chapter by chapter with an enchanting refrain:

> O, how her beautiful little crown sparkled
> Before the sun would go down.
>
> O star and flower, spirit and robe,
> Love, pain, and time and eternity.

And in the context of stanzas:

> I was dreaming out into the dark valley
> On narrow mountain ledges,
> And have called my sweetheart countless times
> Now here, now there.
>
> Truelove, Truelove is lost!
> My dear shepherd, now tell me
> Have you seen Truelove?
> She wanted to go to the lambs here
> And then to the well.—
> Truelove, Truelove is lost!

The main body of the text of such *lieder* is usually delivered in a somewhat recitative manner, and, whenever possible, by a single singer, so that the "story" can be understood. The listeners join in the refrain. The singing swells. The musical element outweighs the meaning of the words.

The refrain also occurs at the beginning and in the middle of the stanzas:

> To Seville, to Seville . . .
>
> Alone, I want to die . . .
>
> Now I am to go far away. . . .

Here again, Brentano is imitating the folk songs from *Des Knaben Wunderhorn* (The Child's Horn of Plenty). These examples probably show most clearly what the refrain accomplishes. A chord resounds spontaneously within the poet, and the poet strikes it once again, this time knowingly and with purpose, and he listens to its tone for the second, third, fourth, and fifth time. What has emanated from the poet in the form of language again produces the same mood and makes possible a return to the moment of lyric inspiration. In between, he can tell a story or reflect upon the mood of the poem; the larger whole maintains its unity through the lyric element. The refrain at the end of each stanza is basically no different from the stanza itself; the lyric element is only artificially postponed. And it is right that the refrain should appear in the title, as it does in "Treulieb, Treulieb ist verloren" (Truelove, Truelove Is Lost). For in truth the poem actually does begin here: The refrain is the musical wellspring of the whole.

As examples of different types of repetitions, poetic forms must be cited that, like the rondel, show a circular movement, or that return to earlier lines in some sort of interweaving pattern.

> The gold of the days has faded away,
> The brown and blue colors of evening:
> The gentle fluting of the shepherd died away,
> The blue and brown colors of evening:
> The gold of the days has faded away.
> (Georg Trakl, "Rondel")

In a larger framework, Strindberg's play *Nach Damaskus* (To Damascus) is constructed in this way. Starting in the middle, the poet repeats the stage settings in reverse order and finally arrives back at the first one. Thus, the play truly acquires a lyric nuance. The spectator is not swept away (p. 174) [force is not exerted on him as it is in the later example—Trans.]; as in *Traumspiel* (Dream Play), he or she is gently led into the mood of the play.

Lyric repetition pervades even the smallest segments of a poem. Brentano again provides an especially revealing example:

> The world repulsed me,
> Mountains were piled upon me,
> The sky was too low for me,
> I longed for you, for you!
> O dear girl, how bad you are!
>
> I roamed through the streets
> For two long years;
> At the corners I had to watch
> And wait just for you, for you!
> O dear girl, how bad you are!

The recurring use of "for you" provides the transition from the more recitative lines to the refrain. A musical composition suggests itself here. The melody for the first three lines would be very unpronounced. Toward the end of the fourth line, the music would intensify, becoming a painfully heartfelt song that, set free by the refrain, could then flow on. In this stanza, the lyric element becomes concentrated toward the end. It always becomes concentrated where single words or groups of words are repeated:

> After its springtime the heart seeks
> Continuously, continuously . . .
>   (C. F. Meyer)
>
> Deep flow, deep deep drunken flow . . .
>   (A. v. Droste)
>
> O love, o love! so beautifully golden . . .
>   (Goethe)
>
> Must I really, must I really leave this town . . .
>   (Folk song)
>
> She had black, black, black eyes. . . .
>   (Folk song)

Such repetitions are only possible in lyric expression. Put another way: Wherever we find such repetitions we experience the passage as lyric.[9] The effect of these repetitions is the same as that of the refrain. The "instantaneous illumination of the world" recurs; the poet listens once again to the chord he has struck.

This finally brings us to rhyme. Needless to say, we cannot do complete justice to it here, for its significance in the history of poetry is constantly changing. And we must realize that the multiplicity of its meanings calls for the utmost discretion.

Rhyme first appears in Christian poetry. It seems destined to re-place the metric complexity of ancient lyric poetry, which is gradually disappearing. It is as though the musicality of lyric were being drawn from a new source. Poems that combine meter and rhyme, for exam-ple, rhymed Sapphic odes, do not impress us too favorably; it is as though they contained too much of a good thing. Nonetheless, when it marks the end of the line, rhyme can possess predominantly metric qualities. This is precisely what Humboldt praises about Schiller's verse.[10] But here, we are only concerned with rhymes that produce magical effects; in other words, we are not so much concerned with rhymes that subdivide the stanza as with rhymes that draw the line magnetically on and that are capable of obscuring differences in the content. The rhymes and assonances in Brentano's *Romanzen vom Rosenkranz* (Romances of the Rosary) give us one of the very best examples:

Allem Tagewerk sei Frieden!
Keine Axt erschall im Wald!
Alle Farbe ist geschieden,
Und es raget die Gestalt.

May peace reside in all daily
  work!
Let no axe resound in the
  forest!
All colors are separate,
And form stands out.

Tauberauschte Blumen
  schließen
Ihrer Kelche süßen Kranz,

Flowers intoxicated by the dew
Close the sweet circle of their
  calix,

---

9. But compare here the altogether different repetitions in the pathetic style, as in the examples on page 141–42.

10. Wilhelm von Humboldt to Schiller, 18 August 1795. In *Briefwechsel zwischen Schiller und Wilhelm von Humboldt. Mit einer Vorerinnerung über Schiller und den Gang seiner Geistesentwicklung* von W. von Humboldt (Stuttgart: J. G. Cotta, 1830); in English: *Correspondence between Schiller and Wilhelm von Humboldt. Preceded by a Reminiscence about Schiller and the Course of His Spiritual Development* by Wilhelm von Humboldt.

Und die schlummertrunknen Wiesen	And the meadows drunk with sleep
Wiegen sich in Traumes Glanz.	Rock in the glow of the dream.
Wo die wilden Quellen zielen	Where the wild springs shoot Down from the rocks' edge,
Nieder von dem Felsenrand,	The deer wander freely and
Ziehn die Hirsche frei und spielen	Joyfully play in the gleaming sand . . .
Freudig in dem blanken Sand . . .	("Kosme's Penance")

And so it continues for sixty-three stanzas, always with the same hypnotic alternation of "i" and "a." The same sounds always elicit the same mood. And the reader who after only one reading was able to say exactly what the poet is talking about would have to be very insensitive musically. Evening—peace—sleep: That is all that remains, whereas the rest flows on in a tide that cannot be stemmed.

III

In the lyric, unity of mood is especially necessary since the coherence we would normally expect of an utterance is here sometimes only vaguely evident and often not at all. In its lyric expression, language seems to renounce much of what it has gained in the way of logical clarity: a gradual development from parataxis to hypotaxis, from adverbs to conjunctions, from temporal to causal conjunctions.

Spitteler's "Bescheidenes Wünschlein" (A Modest Little Wish) begins:

> At that time, at the very beginning,
>   If I had had to say
> What, in case I could wish for something,
>   I would want to wish for. . . .

This is charming but only because, in friendly irony, it pokes fun at the true nature of lyric. Spitteler makes a virtue of necessity and emphasizes his lack of lyric talent with overly logical constructions. But when a writer of *lieder* expresses himself in all seriousness in such a clearly logical way, his poem lacks musicality, for thinking and singing do not go together. A poem of Hebbel entitled "Lied" begins with the stanzas:

Komm, wir wollen Erdbeern
    pflücken,
Ist es doch nicht weit zum
    Wald,
Wollen junge Rosen brechen,
Sie verwelken ja so bald.
	Come, let us pick
	    strawberries,
	It is really not far to the
	    forest,
	Let us break off young roses
	After all, they wilt so fast.

Droben jene Wetterwolke,
Die dich ängstigt, fürcht ich
    nicht;
Nein, sie ist mir sehr
    willkommen,
Denn die Mittagssonne sticht.
	Up above that storm cloud,
	Which frightens you—I do
	    not fear it;
	No, I welcome it,
	Because the noon sun is
	    burning.

The poem's chilly effect on the reader can be blamed on the seemingly harmless little words "doch" [after all], "ja" [yes], "nein" [no], and "denn" [for]. If these words are dropped then these didactic lines come closer to the *lied*:

Wir wollen Erdbeern pflücken, Es ist nicht weit zum Wald, Und junge Rosen brechen, Rosen verwelken so bald. . . .	Let us pick strawberries, It is not far to the forest Let us break off young roses, Roses wilt so fast. . . .

Lieder are not equally vulnerable to all conjunctions. The causal and intentional conjunctions seem to have the most unpleasant effect. An occasional "wenn" [if] or "aber" [but] hardly seems to affect the mood. The most natural construction, however, is simple parataxis, as for example in Eichendorff's "Rückkehr" (Return):

> With my guitar
> Which sounded so beautiful
> I return through many countries
> To this town.

> I roam through the streets,
> So dark is the night
> And everything so deserted,
> I had pictured it differently.

> At the fountain I stand for a long time,
> It rushes on as before,
> Many a person comes and goes,
> No one knows me any more.
>
> I heard then fiddling, fluting,
> Windows shone from afar,
> And there many strangers, happy people
> Whirled and danced.
>
> And my heart and my soul were on fire,
> I felt driven out into the wide world,
> The musicians played
> And I fell down in the field.

The objection that such a paratactical construction is uniquely romantic in style is only justified to the extent that German romanticism reaches a pinnacle of world-literary excellence in the *lied* and hence in the purest form of lyric poetry. We find the same structure in Goethe's "An den Mond" (To the Moon) and "Über allen Gipfeln ist Ruh" (Over All Mountain Tops Reigns Peace), and in poems by Verlaine. We even find it further back, in lyric highpoints of the baroque, a century that is otherwise so passionately interested in logical junctures; an example would be Hofmannswaldau's poem "Wo sind die Stunden der süssen Zeit" (Where Are the Hours of Sweet Time). Admittedly, however, the lyric language here is not created by spontaneous writing, but by the most conscious artistry. This is especially evident in the last stanza:

> I swam in joy
> The hand of love
> Spun a dress of silk for me,
> The page has turned,
> I walk in sorrow,
> I weep now since love and sunshine
> Are always full of fear and clouds.

A single dependent clause concludes the poem. But it is at this very point that the lyric effect grows perceptibly weaker and the singing changes into recitation. The conjunction "da" [here; since—TRANS.] clearly belongs to the unlyrical conjunctions. Folk songs must be mentioned here and, from ancient Greece, the odes of Sappho, that primeval lyric sound that comes to us as an intimate secret from out of the distance of two and a half thousand years:

> The moon and the Pleiades
> Have set. It is midnight
> And the time goes by.
> But I sleep alone.

But lyric language is not yet adequately defined by the word "para-tactic." For epic language is also paratactic; hence, one could just as well say: The more paratactic, the more epic (see p. 118). In the epic, the various segments of the sentences are independent; in the lyric, they are not. In more recent poetry this is immediately evident in the punctuation: Here, entire sentences are often only separated by commas. It would not only be dull and pedantic, but also stylistically inconsistent, to attempt to proceed according to the dictionary with Eichendorff's "Rückkehr" (Return) or with Goethe's "An den Mond" (To the Moon). The lyric flow would be halted. The difference becomes even clearer if we compare Eichendorff's prose, for example, with the prose of Kleist or Lessing. In the latter two, we have a wealth of punctuation; in the former, a reluctance to insert signs of distinct division—a reluctance reminiscent of the letter-writing style of women. These are the same women Goethe criticizes in such an unfriendly way in his conversations with Eckermann, because of their penchant for purely musical poems. Perhaps we see a feminine charac-teristic of lyric poetry revealing itself here, or a lyric element in wom-an's nature.

Furthermore, the various segments are not complete in themselves: Often the complete sentence gives way to a less closely knit syntactical sequence or even to single words:

> And here and there in the valley
> The nightingale awakes,
> Then again all is gray and still. . . .
> (Eichendorff, "In the Night")

The last line is as far from being a sentence as is the beginning of the second stanza:

> O wonderful evening song:
> From afar in the land the rivers course,
> Soft tremors in the dark trees. . . .

Fragments of sentences appear here that cannot stand alone. They are like mere waves in the lyric stream: Before the white cap can form on the crest, the wave has already dissolved again. The never-ending flow prevents the completion of a single part. It is the same in the first stanza of Annette von Droste's *"Im Grase"* (In the Grass):

> Sweet peace, sweet intoxication in the grass
> Surrounded all around by the aroma of the herb,
> Deep flow, deep deep drunken flow
> When the cloud dissolves in the azure sky,
> When upon the tired swimming head
> Sweet laughter is fluttering down,
> Dear voice murmuring and trickling,
> Like lindenblossoms, onto the grave.

or in a Goethe poem:

> Twilight descended from above,
> Already everything close is distant;
> But the first to be raised up,
> The evening star with its gracious light!
> ("Chinese-German Poems of the Day and Year," VIII)

True, sometimes a grammatical connection between the parts can be found, but it is not sought, at least not by the unreflecting reader. Eichendorff's "Wanderlied" (Wanderer's Song) is an example:

> Through fields and beech groves,
> Now singing, now gayfully silent,
> Above all, may he who chooses traveling
> Always be merry!

Grammatically, this could be reworded in the following way: Whoever likes wandering should be sometimes singing, sometimes joyfully quiet, through fields and beech woods, above all merry. We need not waste a word about the senselessness of such a rendition of the grammatical meaning.

Not infrequently, only single disjointed words remain. In the second stanza of Annette von Droste's "Im Grase" (In the Grass) the following appears without any connection to what precedes or follows: "Tote Lieb', tote Lust, tote Zeit" [Dead love, dead desire, dead time]. And Brentano's famous refrain

> O star and flower, spirit and robe,
> Love, pain, and time and eternity . . .
> ("What Is Ripe in These Lines")

seems to be altogether like the water of life that the poet lets run through his hands: Nothing complete, nothing clearly outlined remains; only these fleeting words, words full of promise, recur again and again as the fruit of lyric existence.

Wherever in a narration the thread of a sentence is lost we feel the passage has a lyric quality to it, as for example these lines in Eichendorff's *Julian*, a short verse narration:

> Upon which, renewed deep silence
> And the knight walked in great haste. . . .

Or in *Spiritus Familiaris des Rosstäuschers* (*Spiritus Familiaris* of the Horse Dealer) of Annette von Droste:

> Deep, deep night, only the stealthy gnawing of a mouse rattles
>   In the cupboard!

Only in the style of pathos are such incomplete sentences and even single words equally possible. But their significance is entirely different. Incompleteness in pathos signifies a demand (see p. 144). The lyric poet does not demand anything; on the contrary, he gives in; he lets himself be carried wherever the fleeting mood takes him.

Strictly speaking, one would misunderstand these syntactical findings if one were to interpret them as ellipses. The concept "ellipsis" signifies that something is missing from a grammatical construction, something that belongs to it but is not indispensable for comprehending it. If the missing element is inserted, then the grammatical structure of the sentence coincides exactly with the sentence's meaning. In our examples, however, it would be impossible to insert anything without falsifying the lyric meaning.

> From afar in the land the river's course:
> (Eichendorff, "In the Night")

If the word "rauscht" [rushes] is inserted here, the sentence acquires a clarity that is far from what the poet intended. And if the main clause in the first stanza of "Im Grase" (In the Grass) were to be appended to the conditional clause by adding: "Sweet stillness is in the grass;

the tide is deep when the cloud dissolves in the azure sky," then it is clear that precisely this "is" clashes with the lyric tone. Even where the poet uses "is," she can hardly be taken to mean existing in the sense of enduring existence. Werther's words—without the pessimistic undertone, of course—hold true for the lyric poet: "Can you say: That is! When all is transitory . . . ?"

In other words: For the lyric poet, there is no substance, there are only chance occurrences; nothing tangible, no contours. She may have fiery eyes and a bosom that stirs him, but no breasts in the sense of a three-dimensional form and no pronounced physiognomy. A landscape has colors and lights and smells, but no base, no earth as its foundation. Hence, when we speak of images in lyric poetry we must never think of painting, but, at most, of images in a dream that arise and disappear again, unconcerned with their relation to space and time. And where the images have more substance, as in many poems by Gottfried Keller, we feel far removed from the innermost circle of the lyric. In Goethe's poem "An den Mond" (To the Moon), things near and far in time and space flow together, just as in Mörike's "Im Frühling" (In the Spring) and in Droste's "Durchwachte Nacht" (Night Vigil). We call such phenomena jumps of the imagination, just as we are accustomed to speaking of jumps in grammatical construction. But they are jumps only for the perceiving and reflecting mind. The soul does not jump; it glides. In the soul, even the remotest elements are as close together as they appear to be. And the soul does not need connecting links, since all elements are already joined in it by mood.

IV

Logical connections are not necessary within a poem, and the poem as a whole does not need an explanation. In epic poetry, when, where, and who have to be more or less clearly established before the tale can begin. And more than anyone else the dramatist presupposes a scene of action; whatever is needed for an understanding of the whole he adds later.

Of course, a poem can also begin with a sort of exposition. Mörike, for example, gives us the occasion for a certain feeling:

> Here I lie on the spring-like hill. . . .
> ("In the Spring")

However, this is not necessary. Eichendorff's "Gärtner" (The Gardener) starts right in with the full confession of love:

> Wherever I go and look. . . .

Taking a hint from the title, the reader can supplement the lines with a situation in which these words are possible, if he feels the need to do so and if he is not familiar with the scene in *Leben eines Taugenichts* (The Life of a Good-for-Nothing) from which these verses in his collection of poems were taken. A poem by C. F. Meyer begins:

> Do not leave, you whom God created for me!
> Let your horses' hooves drown out
> The sound of the call to depart!
> ("Let Your Horses Pass the Ground")

Who wants to start out on a voyage? Who is trying to hold back the person who is leaving? We come to know the answers only vaguely; hence many possible situations can be supplied. In connection with these lines by Marianne von Willemer,

> What does this stirring mean?
> Does the east wind bring me a joyful message?

Goethe's biography informs us that he has left Frankfurt, and now the wind blows toward her like a messenger sent by him. Such information can heighten the reader's pleasure in the poem. Yet, it is not indispensable and most readers do not demand it. It is even less likely that it would occur to anyone to ask what direction is meant in Mignon's lines.

> Alone and cut off
> From all joy
> I look toward the firmament
> In that direction.
> (Goethe, "Only Those Who Know Longing")

Mignon's songs are not at all dependent on the context of *Wilhelm Meisters Lehrjahre* (Wilhelm Meister's Apprentice Years). How many people love them and sing them without knowing the novel!

Against all reasonable usage, a poem can even begin with "und," "denn," "aber" [and, for, but] and similar conjunctions:

> And fresh nourishment, new blood . . .
>
> For what man in his earthly
>   limitations . . .
>
> As if he were listening. Quiet.
>   A remoteness. . . .

In such instances it becomes especially clear just what the significance of the missing explanation really is. At some point in the course of an ordinary day, life is transformed into music. This is the "occasion" that brought Goethe to call every genuinely lyric poem an occasional poem. The occasion as such appears in the context of a life history. It can be explained biographically, psychologically, sociologically, historically, or biologically. Late in his life, in *Dichtung und Wahrheit* (Truth and Fiction), Goethe himself explained the occasion for many poems from the context of his life, and Goethe scholarship has carried on this work with great care. Yet the poems can forego an explanation. They have to forego it because at the time of inspiration, the poet himself is not aware of its source; and they can do without it because they are immediately understandable. But this immediate understandability does not depend on the reader's being able to apply the words to a similar occasion from his own life. Whenever this happens, the reader cannot experience the poem in its entire purity. He overvalues whatever element in it permits a reference to his own life, ignoring other elements. Often, no personal reference is possible, and, if it does exist, it is not until afterward that the reader can account for his finding joy or comfort in certain verses because of his familiarity with a similar experience. In a true reading experience he is carried along by the poem without comprehending it, without any reason whatever for doing so. Only the reader who does not fully participate needs reasons. Only the reader who cannot participate spontaneously in the mood demands that the mood be both possible and comprehensible.

But whether a reader is carried along by the poem or whether he doubts the truth of a mood is of no concern to the lyric poet. For he is alone, knows of no public, and writes for himself. But such a claim needs to be explained. Lyric poetry is also published. The harvest of years is collected and presented to a public. All this is certainly true. But in a volume of poetry "these passionate stammerings"—to use Goethe's words—"seem so strange in writing." And Goethe was not alone in thinking that the collecting of the separate pages is absurd. When a volume of poetry is presented to the public, what is the public to do with it? Lyric poems can be recited, but only with as much success as an effective stage play can be read. A recitation cannot do them justice. A reader presenting purely lyric poetry to a full auditorium almost always makes a painful impression. A recitation is much more effective in a small group, carried out in the presence of people who, we trust, are in sympathy with us. But lyric creation can really flourish only if it is read in quiet and in solitude. And even this is a pleasure that will not be bestowed on the reader every day. We leaf through a collection of poems. Nothing appeals to us. The verses sound empty, and we are amazed that the poet should be so conceited as to write such poems, to assemble them in book form, and to expect his or her contemporaries or future generations to read them. But suddenly, in a special moment, a stanza moves us, an entire poem. Later, there are more, and we realize, almost with dismay, that a great poet is speaking. This is the effect of an art that neither captivates the reader as does epic, nor excites him and creates tension as does drama. The lyric infuses itself into the reader. If this infusing is to succeed, the reader has to be open. He is open when his soul is keyed to the soul of the poet. Thus, lyric poetry reveals itself as the art of solitude; the art that can be experienced in all its purity only in solitude by people who are attuned to it.

The love poem in which a poet addresses the beloved and the poet are "one heart and one soul." A lament over unrequited love can also contain the intimate "you," but the "I" knows that it will never merge with this "you."

The poet can, of course, prepare the listener for the mood. And from the poet's point of view, this is the reason for the composition of a *lied*. Schubert, Schumann, Brahms, Hugo Wolf, and Schoeck are masters of the art of creating—in a few introductory beats—a magic formula that rejects everything extraneous to the text and rids the heart of its apathy. With their music, they have opened the way to priceless treasures of lyric poetry for the German-speaking peoples. Hugo Wolf in particular has done this; he is always concerned with the truest interpretation and hardly ever drowns the word of the poet in the music.

But in the concert hall, too, the listener is alone with himself and the *lied*. For the *lied* does not bring individuals together as does a symphony by Haydn, where each person feels a polite affection for his neighbor, or as does a Beethoven finale, which, one feels, is capable of bringing everyone to his feet in a single decisive movement. Applause, which is appropriate after such music, offends us after lyric songs. For first we are alone and then suddenly we are expected to be with others again.

Goethe and Schiller, in their efforts to discover the genre principles governing epic and dramatic poetry, proceeded from the relationship of the rhapsodist and mime to the public.[11] A similar relationship could be established for the lyric, which they do not discuss.

The poet who is not addressing himself to anyone and is only speaking to a few kindred spirits does not need powers of persuasion. Hence the concept of the lyric excludes all rhetorical effect. The writer who wants to be heard only by people in tune with himself does not need to explain. Explanations in lyric poetry are indelicate, as indelicate as a lover's explaining to his beloved the reasons for his love. Moreover, the poet feels as little compelled to elucidate obscure words as he feels a need to make explanations. A reader in tune with the mood of the poem possesses a key that can open more than ordered ideas and logical thinking can. The reader almost feels he has composed the song himself. He repeats it quickly to himself, knows it by heart without consciously memorizing it, and voices the lines as though they had originated in his own heart.

But it is precisely lyric poetry's direct accessibility that makes the mediate, discursive understanding of it difficult. That is to say: It is easy to grasp a poem, or better still, it is neither easy nor is it difficult—understanding comes of its own accord or not at all. But it is almost impossible to talk about lyric poetry, to evaluate it, and to justify our evaluation. For it is likely that our evaluation will hardly ever concern itself with the lyric worth of a poem, but will concentrate instead on the sort of thing that is in every poem—on the significance of a motif for example, or on a daring comparison. The difference between lyric and dramatic poetry becomes very clear here. It is not easy to grasp a drama by Ibsen, Hebbel, or Kleist, to comprehend it in every detail. But when we do understand it, explaining our understanding of it is no longer difficult, because the drama itself is motivated to the last detail. It belongs to the same sphere as the language that explains and comes to conclusions. This is why aesthetics shows a preference for the drama, whereas the lyric often leads an apocryphal existence or is treated self-consciously. Thus, the great absence of unity in the evaluation of poems. Today, the masters of classicism and romanticism have proved themselves beyond any doubt. But there is always controversy raging over new poets who have not yet done so, and it can take the form of some very peculiar arguments, made all the stranger by the fact that no one is willing to accept reasons in an

11. Goethe and Schiller, correspondence of 23 and 26 December 1797; in English: See footnote 1 above, page 40.

evaluation of lyric. The inexperienced reader is always going to overestimate poems. He notes that this is the way he feels, too. Therefore, he thinks the poem is good. But genuine lyric poetry is unique and inimitable. An *inviduum ineffabile*, it opens up totally new moods, moods never before felt. The reader must be able to grasp the poem, and the poem, in turn, must delight him with the insight that his soul is richer than he himself imagined up until now. Thus, lyric poetry must satisfy conflicting demands. Consequently, experienced readers find almost everything they are shown bad. If they hit upon a good poem they are likely to consider it a miracle—and quite rightly so, because every genuinely lyric line is an inexplicable miracle that endures for centuries. It does not create any bonds; it lacks all rationally demonstrable truth, all persuasive power and conclusive evidence. There is nothing more private, more unique on earth than the lyric verse. Yet it unites those who hear it more intimately than any other type of poetic creation. To the extent that all genuine poetry reaches down into the wellsprings of the lyric and glistens from the wetness of this source, all poetic creation has its beginnings in the unfathomable, in a "sunder warumbe" [without asking why] of a special sort. At this level an explanation of the beauty and the rightness of the poetic creation is no longer possible. Furthermore, it is no longer necessary.

V

If a single concept of the lyric underlies all the stylistic phenomena we have described up to now, then we must be able to prove that this one concept exists and we must be able to define it. A unity between the musicality of the words and their meaning; the immediate effect of the lyric without any explicit comprehension on the part of the reader (see section I); the danger of the dissolution of the poetic creation stayed by the refrain and by other types of repetition (see section II); the renunciation of grammatical, logical, and concrete connections (see section III); the poetry of solitude, heard only by a few who are attuned to the poet (see section IV): All this signifies that no distance exists in lyric poetry.

This statement must be examined more closely and amplified with new evidence.

We can understand most readily that the reader does not put any inner distance between him- or herself and the poem. It is not possible to analyze* the lyric essence of a poem in order to understand it. Either it appeals to us or it leaves us cold. We are moved by it to the extent that we find ourselves in the same mood. Then the verses resound in us as though they came from our own heart. Admiration seems the more appropriate response in the presence of epic or dramatic poetry. But participation in lyric poetry deserves the more intimate designation of love.

In lyric poetry the musicality of the language attains the greatest significance. Music addresses itself to the ear. In the act of hearing we do not place ourselves opposite what we hear—as in seeing we place ourselves opposite what we see. The phenomenology of the senses is, as a matter of fact, very underdeveloped as yet; and it is precisely in these areas that we find ourselves confused by ambiguities. At any rate, this much can be said: If we want to look at a painting, we have to step back a little if we are to be in a position to get a full view of it and see all the parts distributed in space as a unified whole. Here, distance is essential. When listening to music, we find proximity and distance important only insofar as the instruments sound best from a certain ways away. The proper distance from an instrument can be compared to the most favorable lighting of a painting. However, distance does not place us opposite music as it places us opposite a painting, which is "set before us" and which we can still visualize when it is no longer in front of us. Moreover, what Paul Valéry has to say about music holds true: Music dissolves space. We are in the music, and it is in us. The true listener is "esclave de la présence générale de la musique" [slave of the omnipresence of music], sequestered with it like a Pythia in the smoke-filled chamber.[12] Perhaps this comparison seems a little too weighty when applied to the intimate, lyric sphere. And we would have to add that not all music can be considered lyric. A Bach fugue is not lyric. We cannot discuss here whether an inner distance exists between the listener and the fugue, or enlarge on the special significance this might have. However, the music that Schiller condemns so sharply in his essay on the sublime is lyric:

> The music of the more modern composers also seems to have a singular preference for the sensual. Thus it caters to the taste

---

*Staiger uses the German word "sich auseinandersetzen," which means to comprehend something by analyzing its various components. By hyphenating this word and putting it in quotation marks, "auseinander-zu-setzen," he emphasizes the literal meaning of the word, which is "to take something apart."

12. Paul Valéry, *Eupalinos* (Paris, 1924), 126; in English: *Eupalinos; or, The Architect*, trans. William McCausland Stewart (London, 1932), 36.

of the day, which only seeks titillation; people do not want to be touched, deeply moved, elevated. Therefore, the public prefers all that is *cloyingly sweet*, and no matter how great the noise is in the concert hall, people are suddenly all ears as soon as a cloyingly sweet passage is played. Then, an almost animal-like expression of sensuality usually appears on everyone's face, their glazed eyes swim in tears, their mouth is open and full of lust, a voluptuous shiver takes hold of their entire body, breathing is rapid and shallow, in short, all the symptoms of intoxication appear: clear proof that all the senses are revelling in voluptuousness. But the mind or the principle of freedom in man is the victim of the violence of the sensual impression.[13]

The music of language, which Herder describes in a manner quite similar to Schiller's, but in highly enthusiastic words, is also lyric:

These tones, these gestures, that simple flow of the melody, this sudden turn, this fading voice—I can't list them all. These things have a much greater effect on children and on simple people who live solely through their senses, on women, on sensitive people, people who are sick, lonely, sad—they have a much better effect than the truth itself would have if its soft, delicate voice were to sound from heaven. In our childhood, when we heard certain words, a certain tone, a surprising turn of events in some gruesome romance, etc. for the first time, they invaded our souls, I could not say with how great a number of connotations of terror, of solemnity, of fright, of fear, of joy. A certain word rings out, and like a host of spirits they arise all at once in their dark majesty from the grave of the soul. They obscure the pure, clear meaning of the word which could only be grasped without them. The word is gone, and the emotive tone rings out. Obscure feelings overcome us: even the person who normally takes things lightly is frightened and trembles—not because of thoughts, but because of syllables, tones from childhood; and it was the magic power of the speaker, of the poet which turned us into children again. No premeditation, no thinking, only the law of nature caused this: "the emotive

---

13. *Schiller's Werke*, vollständige historisch-kritische Ausgabe (Leipzig, 1910), 17:402 (subsequent reference to Schiller's *Werke* is to this edition); in English: *Naive and Sentimental Poetry, and On the Sublime: Two Essays,* trans. Julius A. Elias (New York, 1966).

tone shall put the person who is in sympathy with it in tune with it."[14]

Distance does not exist between the poetic creation and the listener, nor does it exist between the poet and what he speaks about. The lyric poet usually says "I." But he says it differently than does the author of an autobiography. One can only speak of one's own life when an entire era lies in the past. Then, one looks at the "I" in perspective and gives it form. But the lyric poet does not "give form" to himself any more than he "comprehends" himself. The words "give form" and "comprehend" presuppose an opposite. "To form" might seem appropriate for autobiographical writing, while the word "to comprehend" might perhaps seem appropriate for a diary, in which a person takes stock of a period just passed. But this material only *seems* to be more recent than that found in an autobiography, it only seems so according to time as measured by the clock. The person writing a diary makes himself the object of a reflection. He reflects, he "bends" back over that which has just passed. In order to be able to "bend" back, he must have turned away first. Indeed, the word "reflection" holds true in its literal meaning. The writer of a diary unburdens his mind from each day's cares by gaining perspective on and thinking over what has happened. If he does not succeed in doing this, he speaks spontaneously, and, therefore, his diary will be lyric in tone.

This leads us to consider the grammatical tense of the lyric. In the lyric, the present tense predominates, so much so in fact that it would be a waste of time to list examples. We can learn more by observing that the preterit has a different meaning when it occurs in the lyric than it does in the epic. Let us read Eichendorff's *Rückkehr* (Return) (pages 63–64) once again. The poet vacillates between the present and the preterit in a strange way, as though it did not matter which tense he used. It is only in the last line, "And I fell down in the field," that the preterit can scarcely be replaced by a present, for this line tells of an event that lies in the past and it is clearly being seen as removed in time. But this line no longer has a musical ring to it. Eichendorff has awakened from the magic spell, and he is saying this line to himself as though he were in a daze; his song is over. However, the

14. Johann Gottfried Herder, *Sämtliche Werke*, ed. B. Suphan (Berlin, 1891), 5:16f. (subsequent reference to Herder's *Sämtliche Werke* is to this edition); in English: *On the Origin of Language: Jean-Jacques Rousseau, "Essay on the Origin of Languages"; Johann Gottfried Herder, "Essay on the Origin of Language,"* trans. John H. Moran and Alexander Gode (New York, 1967).

other preterit forms that could be replaced by the present do not represent any temporal distance. The past they signify is not remote and over with. Not formed and not comprehended, the past is still in motion and it moves the poet and us with the same magic that Goethe's *lied* "An den Mond" (To the Moon) radiates, and that Keller praises, more dispassionately, in "Jugendgedenken" (Memories of Youth):

> I want to see myself mirrored in those days,
> Which have disappeared like the wind in the crown
> Where the silvery chord being struck,
> Gave the first clear yet trembling tone,
>> Which resounded my whole life long,
>> And today again,
> Even though the chord was broken long ago.

The past as the object of a narrative is stored in that part of the mind from which memories can be recalled at will.* The past as a theme of the lyric is stored, as something very precious, in that part of the mind from which memories arise spontaneously. Thus, Goethe, in his later years, remarked, "I will not let any memory take possession of me."[15] By that, he means he will not grant the past any power over the present. And yet, the lyric moments of Goethe's later years all derive from remembrance, "Dem aufgehenden Vollmond" (To the Rising Full Moon) for instance, where the encounter with Marianne von Willemer, which lies ten years in the past, fills his soul once more, or the *Divan* poem:

> And the air is perfumed as it was long ago
> When we still suffered from love. . . .
>> ("In the Present Past")

---

*We have found it necessary to circumscribe *Gedächtnis* and *Erinnerung*. Both words are usually translated with "memory." However, *Erinnerung* means not only the ability of the mind to remember, but also that which it remembers. The word *Gedächtnis* means only the ability of the mind to remember. Since English has no word to denote the distinction between memory as a capacity of the mind and memory as an object of this capacity, we have attempted to circumscribe the two terms. One usually thinks of the *Gedächtnis* as containing the sort of material that can be recalled at will, whereas the *Erinnerung* can also contain memories that cannot be recalled at will, but which arise of themselves, spontaneously. The best example of this type of memory is Proust's experience with the petite madeleine. We will call this type of memory "remembrance."

15. Goethe to F. O. Müller, 4 November 1823.

Smells belong more to the sphere of remembrance than do visual impressions. It sometimes happens that we cannot recall a fragrance at will, but the remembrance of it can suddenly arise on its own. When this occurs, we suddenly reexperience a long-forgotten event; our heart beats faster, and finally, a remembrance emerges as a definite recollection and we can say where this fragrance intoxicated us in the past. That smells belong so much to remembrance, and so little to voluntary recollection, doubtless has to do with the fact that we cannot give them form; in fact, often we cannot even give them a name. Unformed and unnamed, they do not become objectified. And we are only free of that which a perception or a concept has objectified. Only in relation to an object can we "take a stand."[16]

The person who is immersed in the lyric mood does not take a stand. He glides along in the flow of life. For him, what is momentary takes on a definitive power—now this tone, now another, predominates. Each line so captivates him that he is at a loss to say how subsequent lines relate to preceding ones. Hence, his gliding is interrupted whenever a connection is expressly stated, contours are outlined, or segments are related to each other by such logical conjunctions as "because," or "therefore." We feel the spell has been broken; that is to say, we feel unmoved, feel we have been brought back to shore when we would have preferred to let ourselves be carried farther by the current as we had been invited to do:

> Let the Greek press
> His clay into forms,
> And the son of his own hands
> Heighten his delight;
>
> But for us it is pure joy,
> To reach into the Euphrates
> And to drift back and forth
> In this watery element. . . .
> (Goethe, *Divan*, "Song and Shape")

Thus did Goethe contrast *"Lied und Gebilde"* (Song and Shape). Of course, when the third stanza speaks of water gathered in the pure hand of the artist, classical aesthetics appears to be asserting itself against lyric poetry. Or perhaps the line simply signifies the miracle of the fluid aspect of lyric poetry taking shape as language, an enigma

16. Compare Schiller, *Werke*, 18:51.

we will try to solve later. At this point, we need only realize that the inappropriateness of the term "form," the paratactical sequence without sharp distinction between parts, the need to achieve an otherwise unattainable unity by using the refrain and other types of repetitions—that all these can be explained by the lack of distance that characterizes all lyric phenomena.

It is always the same distance that is missing in lyric poetry. We could have been calling it the subject-object distance for a long time now, if the terms "subject" and "object" were not just as confusing and ambiguous as the term "form." "The lyric is not objective": This has been the standard formula, dating back to idealist aesthetics. This same formula, stated positively, would have to read: "The lyric is subjective." This results in a three-way division of poetic creativity according to the following model: lyric poetry—subjective, epic poetry—objective, the drama—a synthesis of the two. Here the thinking of idealism is substantiated by means of such opposites as ego–non-ego, spirit–nature, or the Hegelian dialectic. Idealism as a system or as a metaphysics no longer determines humanistic thought. But the terms "subjective poetry" and "objective poetry" have remained and been given new interpretations. Thus, the objectivity of the epic poem has been interpreted as meaning that it represents reality as it exists, independent of the person of the poet. "Objective" then means the same as "factual" and, further, as "universally valid." Lyric poetry, on the other hand, is understood to show the reflection of things and events in the individual consciousness. But even here, the terminology is already becoming confused. If "independent of the person" is supposed to mean "in itself," then this definition is quite clearly wrong, for no object can be perceived "in itself." Precisely because it is an object, and stands opposite someone who perceives it, it can only be viewed from a certain vantage point, from a perspective which is that of the poet, his time, or his people (cf. pages 97–98). Therefore, "objective" cannot be equated with "independent of the poet."

But the contradiction can also be explained in another way. The epic poet is said to depict the external world, the lyric poet his own inner world. Lyric poetry is understood as poetry of the inner world. What does this mean? In the epic there is an opposite, as we shall see: On the one side we have the narrator, unmoved by his tale; on the other, the turbulent action. What does "of the inner world" mean? The same as "introverted" perhaps? This would falsify the nature of the lyric. The psychological contrast between "introverted" and "extroverted" has nothing to do with the contrast between "lyric" and "epic." For example, as manifestly epic a poet as Spitteler is

introverted. In the case of Brentano, everything points to the extroverted type.

The expressions "inner" and "outer" derive from the idea that
man is a sort of peep show: The soul resides in the body and lets
the external world in through the senses, more specifically, lets
images in through the eyes. No matter how much everyone strives
to combat this idea these days, it is deeply rooted in our minds
and probably can never be completely eliminated. The sight of a
person walking toward us, his body clearly outlined and his soul
shining from his eyes, always calls this idea back to mind. Of
course, it is not completely nonsensical. The fact that we are
separated from an external world by our bodies is a perception that
belongs to a certain level of experience—the epic one (cf. page 107).
In the epic, the body is given a very substantial form. Therefore, in
the epic mode of existence, things appear to us as belonging to the
external world. In the lyric mode of existence, this is not so. Here,
there are no objects as yet. And because there are no things, no objects
yet, there is also no subject. And now we recognize the error that is
causing the confusion in terminology. If lyric poetry is not objective,
it cannot be called subjective either. And if it does not depict an
external world, it does not depict an inner world either. For "inner"
and "outer," "subjective" and "objective" are absolutely not divorced
from one another in lyric poetry.

It is worth noting that in Vischer's aesthetics, there is a flash of
insight into this, but it is obscured again by his concept of subjectivity.
He introduces lyric poetry with the words:

> The simple synthesis of the subject with the object in which the
> former subordinates itself to the latter (in the epic poem) cannot
> satisfy the essence of art; it requires a higher level where the
> world essentially infuses itself into the object *and is permeated
> by it.*[17]

This addendum is significant, but it is subsequently almost forgotten. The "infusion of the world into the subject" defines the essence
of lyric poetry almost definitively. Vischer describes feeling as it is
expressed in music similarly:

> Feeling lacks the clarifying alternation of subject and object; it
> corresponds to consciousness as sleep to waking, the subject
> sinks into itself and loses the contrast to the outer world.[18]

17. Vischer, *Ästhetik*, 6:197.
18. Ibid., 5:10.

It is true that an opposite no longer exists. But not, as Vischer says, because the subject sinks into itself. It would be just as correct and as false to say that it sinks into the outer world. For in the lyric, "I" am not a "moi" that consciously maintains its identity, but a "je" that does not maintain itself, but dissolves in every moment of existence.

We have now come to the place where we must explain the fundamental term "Stimmung."* "Stimmung" does not refer to the presence of an inner state. "Stimmung" understood as inner state implies that it has already been grasped rationally and has been contrived as the object of observation. Originally, however, a "Stimmung" is definitely not anything that exists "in" us. On the contrary, when "Stimmung" affects us, it is we who are "outside" in a very special sense; we do not stand opposite objects, but rather we are in them, and they are in us. The "Stimmung" opens up existence to us more directly than any perception or any comprehension. We are in a certain mood, that is to say, we are filled with the joy of spring or lost in fear of the dark, intoxicated with love, or anxious, but always "taken up" by what stands opposite us—in space or time—as a corporeal being. Therefore, it makes sense that the German language should speak of the "Stimmung" of the evenings as well as of the "Stimmung" of the soul.[19] Both are indistinguishably one. Amiel's statement is absolutely true: "Un paysage quelconque est un état de l'âme" [Any landscape is a state of the soul]. But this holds true not only for landscapes. Rather, everything that is exists in the "Stimmung" not as an object, but as a condition. Conditionality is the mode of existence of man and nature in lyric poetry.

What the "Stimmung" reveals to us is not "present" [gegenwärtig]:** neither the jest and the kiss of long ago, nor the luminous mist that is filling bushes and valleys at the very time that the poet is speaking.

---

*The German word Stimmung implies both an inner state (mood) and an outer condition (atmosphere). Since, in this passage, Staiger's use of the term Stimmung encompasses both mood and atmosphere, either English word would be too restrictive in meaning. Therefore, we found it necessary to retain the German word Stimmung in this passage.

19. Compare in this connection O. F. Bollnow, Das Wesen der Stimmungen (The Nature of Moods) (Frankfurt am Main, 1941), 17–36.

**The German word gegenwärtig is an adjective deriving from the noun Gegenwart, and it means present either in time or in space or in both simultaneously. Gegenwart is translated into English as "present tense" or "presence." Vergegenwärtigen is usually translated as "to bring to mind," "to visualize"—that is, we call something from the past back into the present and before our mind's eye. All these words share the prefix gegen, which implies oppositeness. This prefix is also found in the word gegenüber, "opposite."

For the word present [*gegenwärtig*] is to be taken literally. It is meant to indicate an opposite [*Gegenüber*]. Thus, we may say that the narrator recalls the past into the present and before his mind's eye [*vergegenwärtigen*]. But the lyric poet does not do this with the past any more than with the present. Rather, both are equally close to him, closer, in fact, than any present time or present thing [*Gegenwart*]. He merges with them; that is to say, he "interiorizes" [*erinnert*].* We shall use the word "interiorization" [*Erinnerung*] for the absence of distance between subject and object, for the lyric interpenetration (*Ineinander*). The present, the past, even the future can be interiorized and remembered in lyric poetry. Goethe's "Mailied" (May Song) remembers and interiorizes what, seen at first glance, is the present; Mörike's "Im Frühling" (In the Spring), at the end, "remembers" "bygone and nameless days"; some of Klopstock's odes "remember" the future beloved or the grave.

But it is not as though the "lyric inner world" were renewed. "Interiorization" does not mean "the complete dissolution of the world in the subject," but a perpetual interpenetration of the two, so that we could just as well say: The poet "interiorizes" nature, as: Nature "interiorizes" the poet. The latter would, perhaps, correspond even more to the experience of many lyric poets than the former, and would stress even more the significance of the "Stimmung" (mood)—its blessings or its curse.

But doesn't the lyric approach the mystical in this explanation? In Hofmannsthal's "Gespräch über Gedichte" (Conversation about Poems), there are sentences that are close in meaning to what we have been saying here, and just as close to the mysticism Hofmannsthal writes about in "Traum von großer Magie" (A Dream of Great Magic) and *Ad me ipsum*:[20]

> Aren't the feelings, the half feelings, all the most secret and the deepest states of our inner self strangely woven into a landscape, a season, a certain quality of the air, a gentle breeze? A certain movement of yours when you jump down from a high wagon; a sultry starless summer night; the smell of damp stone tiles in an entrance hall; the feeling of ice-cold water

---

*When the noun *Erinnerung* occurs, we sometimes translate it as "interiorization" and sometimes as "remembrance"; but the reader must always bear in mind that *Erinnerung* encompasses both. When Staiger uses the word *erinnern*, particularly when he uses it as a transitive verb (this is not standard usage in German), we sometimes found it necessary to make the double meaning clear. Therefore, we translate *erinnern* as "to remember" and "to interiorize."

20. E. W. Brecht, ed., *Jahrbuch des Freien Deutschen Hochstifts*, 1930.

running from a fountain over your hands: your whole inner life is bound up with a few thousand such earthly things, all your ecstasies, your longing, your intoxication. More than bound, rooted to it with the roots of their existence so that were you to cut them with a knife from this ground, they would wither and shrivel to nothing in your hands. If we want to find ourselves, we cannot descend into ourselves: we are to be found outside ourselves, outside. Our soul arcs over the endless downward flow of existence like the ethereal rainbow. We are not in possession of ourselves: it blows our way from outside, it escapes us for a long time, then it returns in a gentle breath of wind. —Our "self"! The word is such a metaphor. Vague feelings return which have nested here once before. And is it really they again? Isn't it rather their offspring, driven back here by some mysterious homing instinct? No matter, something returns and something in us encounters something else. We are nothing more than dove-cote.[21]

Later, Hofmannsthal adds that "we and the world are not two separate things." But what does "world" mean? Here, it apparently signifies "total being." The mystic feels himself to be one with this totality that is eternal and divine. He closes his eyes—μύει—to the multiplicity of things, he creates unity out of profusion, and dissolves time in eternity, the "sunder warumbe" [without asking why] of God.

However, the "sunder warumbe" of the person attuned to the lyric mood is narrowly limited. He or she feels one with this landscape, with this smile, with this tone, that is to say, not with the eternal, but with the most ephemeral. The cloud dissolves, the smile dies.

> Whatever we see is constantly changing,
> Day sinks into dusk. . . .

And, in the same way, man's inner being changes. The lyric poet is moved, whereas the mystic preserves unassailable peace in God. It is possible, of course, for the lyric mood to become purified to the point of mystical peace, in the sense that, as always in life, one thing blends unnoticeably into another. But literary criticism, which is obligated and duty bound to differentiate between terms, must determine clearly what "lyric" and what "mystical" mean in order to make orientation possible in this fluid and fluctuating existence.

21. Hugo von Hofmannsthal, *Gesammelte Werke* (Berlin, 1934), 2, 2:236.

VI

What we have been discussing here in abstract language, the poets have known instinctively for a long time. We simply must get used to taking seriously what we read in poems. We must accept a lyric statement as a document of humankind, in the same way as we accept dramatic pronouncement. Once again, we can refer to Vischer, who, among the teachers of aesthetics, is the most sensitive expert on the nature of lyric. He points out that the lyric poet, in order to express a dark inner state, borrows his images from the sphere of the human body:

> My peace of mind is gone
> My heart is heavy . . .
> My poor head
> Is crazed,
> My poor mind
> Is in pieces . . .
> My head is reeling,
> The pit of my stomach is on fire. . . .
>   (Goethe, *Faust*, I)

However, Sappho's poem still surpasses all newer examples:

> . . . even if I only look
> Fleetingly toward you, sound
> Dies in my throat,
> My tongue is numbed, a delicate
> Fire runs through my skin, suddenly;
> With my eyes I see nothing, a roaring
> Fills my ears,
> And beads of sweat run down, and my whole
> Body is seized with trembling, and I am paler
> Than the grass, and I seem already near
> Death, Agallis. . . .

Vischer calls this type of imagery "a sort of dark symbolism in which the physical state reflects the state of the soul."[22] As in the description of feeling and of subjectivity in lyric poetry, he recognizes

22. Vischer, *Ästhetik*, 6:204.

the phenomenon perfectly, but falsifies it with his conceptualizations. Here it is precisely of reflection that we cannot speak, and we cannot speak of "obscure symbolism" either. Only someone who artificially separates body and soul can speak in such terms. But anyone who says "I am in pain" and anyone who cries tears of joy and sadness knows nothing of this artificial separation.

Since the German language provides us with the two terms *Körper* and *Leib*, however, it ought to be easy to make a distinction.* A physical pain, from a wound or a toothache for instance, of course remains outside the realm of the soul. It can disturb us, even depress us, and in this way, perhaps, if it lasts a long time, can gain influence over the soul. But the soul itself does not dissolve in the face of such physical pain. Hamlet's "heart-ache," however, or Sappho's shiver of sensuousness is something entirely different. Such "sensations" or "feelings" represent the corporeal reality of the mood as it manifests itself in the body-soul. This reality, scientific considerations aside, confirms Schleiermacher's statement: "To be a soul means to have a body." The lyric poet does not borrow images from the realm of the body in order to express something else, namely the state of the soul; rather, the soul itself is body, and it changes with the feelings that befall, not the body, but the body-soul. But even with this, the mood is not interiorized. The body alone is clearly delineated; it appears as a form into which one can penetrate from the outside. The body-soul, on the other hand, designates everything that dissolves the distance between us and the external world. It is precisely when Sappho breaks out into beads of sweat and when she begins to shiver that she is not "in herself," but "outside herself," beside herself. From the burning pain in the pit of her stomach, Mignon senses how far she is from her beloved homeland. As body-soul we do not feel ourselves to be individuals or persons or beings determined by our life's history. We feel the landscape, the evening, the beloved—or more precisely: we sense *ourselves* in the evening and in the beloved. We merge with that which we feel.

Nonetheless, even the lyric poet, caught up in the generally accepted terminology stemming from epic writing, often speaks of inner and outer worlds. And he especially designates as "inner" the past and the future, namely that which is interiorized [*jenes Erinnerte*] and which is not before his eyes at the time he is speaking. Inexpressible, bygone days of love wander "through the labyrinth of the breast"

---

*In accordance with Staiger's definition on page 184, we shall translate *Körper* with "body" and *Leib* with "body-soul."

(Goethe). "In the heart, thoughts" (Eichendorff) are also remembrances of things past. But even this more localized "inside," which regards the breast, the heart, as a sort of hollow form, still only means the same as "not present." There is no clear distinction between this and those interiorizations [Erinnerungen] of life as it actually manifests itself in space. The interpenetration of the inner and outer worlds in such interiorizations is expressed more or less purely in the simple language of the poet:

> O love, o love,
> So beautifully golden,
> Like morning clouds
> Upon those mountain peaks. . . .

In these lines from Goethe's "Mailied" (May Song) the "like" retains a slight trace of oppositeness. But if we try to interpret it in all seriousness as the Homeric "exactly like," which introduces a simile, we can easily see that this will not work. The comparative particle is not more than a figure of speech. Perhaps, in an almost imperceptible way, it foreshadows the later Goethe, who does indeed see *himself* opposite nature, but yet recognizes that he and nature are basically identical. Hence, he remains open to the lyric as well as to the epic. The simplest explanation, however, is that love can be felt in the golden, beautiful morning clouds. Mörike expresses himself in the same way in "An einem Wintermorgen vor Sonnenaufgang" (On a Winter Morning before Sunrise):

> O downy-soft time of the dark early morning!
> What new world are you stirring in me?
> Why is it that all at once I glow in you
> With the gentle voluptuousness of my life?

"You . . . in me," "I . . . in you": The poet still knows that from another point of view I and you are differentiated, and yet at the same time he knows that that viewpoint is not applicable here. This is evident throughout the poem. The "you in me" dominates the line in which Mörike compares images and thoughts within his bosom to little fish; the "I in you" dominates the one in which he speaks of the flight of the soul to the heights of the sky. The same thing occurs in the poem "Im Frühling" (In the Spring), where the cloud becomes "my wing" and where the breath of the spring landscape merges with the breath of the soul to one delightful rising and falling.

In "Wanderer in der Sägemühle" (Wanderer in the Sawmill) Kerner dreams of what is actually before his eyes, "remembers" the landscape and the mill. Such remembrance is possible because in the little stream that fills and lowers the paddle chamber, he feels the melancholy of his own life that is drawing to a close; in the beautiful tone of the sawblade, which painfully cuts through the pine wood, he feels the painful origin of his creative activity; and in the preparation of the coffin, of death, he feels the final meaning of his life.

In this respect, Eichendorff is probably the most daring:

> When man's clamoring desires are still:
> The earth rustles as in a dream
> In a wondrous way with all the trees,
> What the heart barely knows,
> Old times, gentle sorrows,
> And soft tremors
> Flicker like summer lightning through my breast.
> ("Evening")

The earth rustles—the accusative is astonishing—old times. It rustles what the heart barely knows. The soul dissolves completely in the landscape, the landscape in the soul.

From all sides, the most inexhaustible topic of lyric poetry, love, beckons. Most of the great lyric poets were great lovers—to name but the most important ones: Sappho, Petrarch, Goethe, Keats. Often at a young age already an epic poet is an old man. Some of the great dramatists, for instance Kleist or Hebbel, shock us with harsh and cruel traits, which they display, especially, in their relationships with women. By contrast, the lyric poet is "soft." "Soft" means that the contours of the self, of the poet's own existence, are not fixed:

> Her gaze like the presence of the sun,
> Her breath like spring breezes,
> Melts what has kept itself in frozen rigidity for so long,
> The sense of self, deep in wintry vaults;
> No self-interest, no self-will lasts,
> With her arrival they shuddered and turned away.
> (Goethe, "Trilogy of Passion—Elegy")

The sense of self dissolves. Thus, we admire the "molten" aspect of lyric language. "Molten" means that something solid becomes fluid. We are dissolved by love and the *lied*. This is why music, as Shake-

speare says in *As You Like It,* is "the food of love"; and according to
Tieck, "love thinks in tones." Here, language reveals the whole wealth
of the lyric interpenetration. The time-tested saying reads: "You are
mine, I am thine." It expresses devotion, a "giving of self." The lover
immerses himself—a wondrous word—in the face of the beloved. The
lovers are one in the spring and in the night, which embraces them
both, hides the intrusive body from view, and heightens the sensuousness of the body-soul, which becomes one in the embrace.

All the elements of the lyric: musicality, fluidity, interpenetration,
are brought together in Brentano's version of the myth of the Lorelei
and have been passed along to the later romantics. Her name alone,
consisting of vowels and liquids, resounding and fluid tones, is music,
and as such it is inspired by the name of the rock at Bacharach. Her
name is as fluid as her eyes, and her eyes are as fluid as her singing.
A demon of the fluid element, she lives in the river, in the rustling of
the forest, in everything that glides, waves in the wind, and floats.
Everyone who hears her or sees her glistening at the bottom of the
Rhine succumbs to her. In her presence one has no more freedom, no
self-will—just as the poet under the spell of the lyric is certainly the
most unfree of persons, giving himself, beside himself, carried away
by waves of emotion.

There are, of course, other kinds of love than this is lyric love of
the man who gives himself and yet who preserves some sense of self
and thus grants love duration for the first time.[23] But the love of
intoxicated youth, which is oblivious to the world, which flows forth
and rids itself of all individuality, also belongs to the sphere of lyric
existence. Gottfried Keller tells about this at the end of his novella
Romeo und Julia auf dem Dorfe (Romeo and Julia in the Village), where
the lovers leave the disjointed world and entrust themselves to the
gliding river, perishing in each other's arms. Death and such love
belong together as the dissolution of the self.

VII

Here again, we are made aware of the brevity of lyric poetry. We have
spoken before of the highly transitory character of mood (see section
II), and we now better understand this transitory character as depending on the nature of the interpenetration between the poet and

23. See in this connection Ludwig Binswanger, *Grundformen und Erkenntnis mensch-
lichen Daseins* (Basic Forms and Understanding of Human Existence) (Zurich, 1963).

the world, which is delicate and always in danger. It abolishes all resistance and it sets up an opposite. A resistance is something that is out of tune—the poet, calm in the peace of evening, encounters resistance when he is suddenly startled by a rabbit or when a drop falls on his hand. The epic poet would consider such distraction at most as a loss of time. But the lyric poet finds that it destroys his unique mood forever—a tragicomic frailty that humorists have always noticed and laughed at, for instance in Wilhelm Busch's *Balduin Bäh-lamm*, whose title character is absorbed in the sky and suddenly feels an earwig crawling around in his ear. Yet, the pesky insect and the other comic incidents Busch invents would not even be needed to foil the character's poem. Even the sky, the moon, a tree, can suddenly become objectified—the poet only has to look at them more closely. Then the landscape is no longer "right": It is out of harmony with the soul. The moon is not "right" as an astronomical body or as a crater field but as a silver gondola; the hill is "right" as a blurred streak, the forest as a rustling sound or as a shimmering of lights and shadows, the lake as radiance. The most fleeting things are lyric—if solidity and objectivity manifest themselves, then the most fleeting form of poetic creation, the *lied*, is ended.

But should this coming to an end be put into words, or does the poet just suddenly break off? We have seen how he or she begins, often with an unmotivated "and" or "also." Perhaps if we ask about a possible way to end, we will gain even deeper insight into the nature of the lyric. Let us read Eichendorff's "Auf einer Burg" (In a Fortress):

> He fell asleep while lying in wait,
> The old knight up there;
> Overhead a shower of rain descends,
> And the forest rustles through the bars.
> His beard and hair have taken root,
> His heart and collar have turned to stone,
> He has been sitting for many hundreds of years
> Up there in his quiet cell.
> Outside it is quiet and peaceful,
> All have gone into the valley,
> Birds of the forest sing all alone,
> In the empty archways of the windows.
> A wedding party passes by down there
> On the Rhine in the sunshine,
> Musicians gaily play
> And the beautiful bride is weeping.

This is an excerpt from the mood of a landscape, arbitrarily selected. It is true that in the last line the emotional tone becomes somewhat more concrete. This might perhaps be enough to awaken the poet and make him think of the girl's story. Yet the poem could also go on in the same way for a long time. It does not really come to an end.

Annette von Droste's "Im Grase" (In the Grass) is different. After the first two stanzas, which are among the most wonderful in the lyric poetry of world literature, and in which the poetess, her head tired and swimming in the summer-tired and swimming air, feels her whole being sink down in the dizzying sway of fragrances and voices—after these stanzas she goes on:

> Hours, more fleeting than the kiss
> Of a ray of light on the sorrowing lake. . . .

She is speaking here now about her feelings and reflecting on her situation. With this, she leaves the spirit of the *lied*. The second half of the poem is matter-of-fact, and in order to veil this matter-of-factness it is bolstered somewhat with rhetoric.

What is disturbing here, because it occurs too soon and is continued for too long, can, under some circumstances, end a poem meaningfully in a few lines or even in a single line. Again, "Wanderers Nachtlied" (Wanderer's Night Song) can serve as an example:

> Wait, soon
> You shall rest too.

Here, the poet himself is aware of the deep, inner meaning of the evening landscape. But at the moment of comprehension, lyric creation ceases, the mood becomes objectified. At the end of his poem, Eichendorff, too, often indicates what direction remembrance is taking, for example in "Zwielicht" (Twilight), where the seemingly disparate dream images are united in the end, after a pause for thought indicated by the dash. This suddenly results in:

> Beware, remain watchful and alert!

This was implicit in every line. It emerges explicitly and the *lied* is ended. The same thing is true in "Frühlingsnacht" (Spring Evening):

Over the garden, through the air
I heard the birds on the wing,
That means the fragrance of spring,
Below, things have already begun to bloom.

I would like to shout for joy, to weep,
For I feel it cannot be!
Old wonders shine in again
With the glow of the moon.

And the moon, the stars say it,
And in dreams the grove rustles it,
And the nightingales sing it out:
She is yours, she is yours!

Only when a *lied* is carried out with a conscious use of artistic means can one say that the poet is summarizing the mood because he wants to end the poem. When inspiration, when lyric spontaneity predominates, the reverse is usually true: Because the poet can now reflect on the mood and give it a name, the *lied* is over.

Those poems in which language fails go in the opposite direction. Again and again, Rilke experimented manneristically with this possibility—for instance in "Abend in Skåne" (Evening in Skone), in the version in *Buch der Bilder* (Book of Images), where, at the end, it says about the evening sky:

Wondrous structure,
In itself fluid and yet self-contained,
Forming configurations, giant wings, faults,
And mountain peaks before the first stars
And suddenly, there: an opening into such distances
As perhaps only birds know. . . .

The dots mean that something is still pending; something still has to be said, namely in the line that is to rhyme with "know," but this last line is inexpressible. This is a gesture of powerlessness, a renunciation in the face of something altogether too intimate; in Rilke it sometimes strikes us as affected, but it is without a doubt deeply grounded in the essence of lyric. Rilke, who has probably done more than any other modern poet to enlarge the range of what can be expressed in poetic language, derives great satisfaction from proving those right who say that verse which is never written, which is inexpressible, is the most beautiful. This question usually separates the artist from the dilettante, the masters of language from those who feel effusively but cannot express their feelings. It seems impossible for them to reach an understanding on this point. The artist takes the position that all poetic creation is a work of art in words, that whatever is left unsaid is not poetry. In taking this position he makes us aware of the contradiction inherent in the term "the silent word," "the unspoken line," and—as a poet—he is doubtless right. However, the sensitive dilettante is right, too, when he says that pure feeling cannot be put into words. He can refer to Schiller's words:

Spricht die Seele, so spricht, ach, schon die *Seele* nicht mehr.
As soon as the soul *speaks*, alas, the *soul* speaks no more.
                                        ("Votive Tablets," #41, "Speech")

Thus it becomes evident that the quarrel is over the differentiation that has already been brought up in the preface to the present attempt to lay the foundations of a poetics (page 41) and that the reader is asked to keep in mind at all times: The artist is speaking of the lyric *poem*, the dilettante of the phenomenon of the lyric. Hence we cannot but become aware of a contradiction between the lyric and language in all its characteristics. In language used as an instrument of cognition we take apart and analyze existence in all its elements; then we establish certain relationships between them. Language itself takes apart, only to unite again, in the structure of the sentence, precisely what it has taken apart. In contrast, we characterized the lyric mood as interpenetration that needs no interrelationships because everything has already been unified in the mood. Every single word establishes (see page 104) and orders the transitory phenomena of existence to a lasting whole. The person who is in the lyric mood simply glides along; as soon as he begins to discriminate things, he is sobered. Thus, he actually finds himself coerced by some of the functions of language, by its intentionality, which, as such, constitutes an opposite, and by its "logic," if λόγος from λέγω is taken to mean "a gathering together of many things." Thus, if the poet wants to express himself lyrically, he has to succeed, if possible, in obscuring these very characteristics of language. We have seen this happen in the dissolution of the syntactical structure (see section III), in the reduction of sentences to single, disconnected words (see section III), in the reluctance to use the auxiliary "is," which has the power to establish things all too definitely (see section III), and most particularly in the musicality of language, which seems to dissolve the intentionality and objectivity of language.[24] Of course, this never succeeds completely except in those few syllables that no longer mean anything but are only pure tone, for instance "eia popeia, $\alpha\ddot{\imath}\lambda\iota\nu o\nu$, om." But such syllables could never constitute a poem, any more than a series of chords can result in a symphony or a series of color tones in a painting. Thus, since even the purest type of lyric, the *lied*, is poetry, not even a *lied* can realize completely the idea of the lyric. For it consists not just of syllables; rather it is made up of words, which are always also concepts; it is made up of sentences, which always also signify objective relationships, even though such relationships are not intended by the lyric poet. And it has a beginning and leads somewhere, even though movement toward a goal does not lie in the nature of the lyric, its movement being constant gliding. In those poems that end in a clarification of feeling, the hidden concomitants of language, particularly its conceptual elements, reappear: The *lyric* poem never comes to an end. On the other hand, in those poems in which language finally fails, the wellspring of feeling overflows, making any rational analysis impossible: The lyric *poem* comes to an end. The *creating of lyric poetry* is a rendering of the soul in words—something that in absolute terms is impossible. In the lyric, language does not want to be taken literally; it shies away from its own all-too-concrete reality and wants to free itself from all logical and grammatical coercion. We shall see that the essential characteristics of language that are blurred here are clearly evident in epic and dramatic poetry. This means that every poetic creation takes part—to a larger or smaller degree—in all three genre concepts. For no poetic creation, as a work of art in words, can rid itself completely of language with all its characteristics.

VIII

We have yet to speak of the limits of lyric poetry and to determine what it *cannot* give to the poet and to the reader. Frequently, we found ourselves forced to speak of the wondrous nature of lyric language. It cannot be grasped rationally and it is not an accomplishment on the part of the artist since it cannot be forced into existence. What Duhamel says about lyric creation is true: "Miracle n'est pas oeuvre" [A miracle

---

24. See in this connection also, and in particular, Herder's words quoted on pages 75–76 above.

is not an artistic accomplishment].[25] The lyric poet does not "achieve" anything (see section I). The epic poet must be industrious, the dramatic poet even dogged in his efforts, but the lyric poet can be as languid as Mörike or as irresolute as Brentano. Elements that make up the epic must be gathered together; those that make up the dramatic have to be coerced into being. But the lyric is given through inspiration. The only thing the lyric poet can do is wait for inspiration. But he who always waits for grace must depend on grace alone and expect no help from his own strength, his will, or his patience. Even the timorous reworking of lyric poems is not exempt from this. To be sure, it is possible to produce a *lied* through the skillful use of artistic means, but when this does occur, new shades of meaning can only emerge from renewed inspiration.

"A miracle is not an artistic accomplishment" also means: "Poems are kisses which we bestow upon the world; but children are not conceived from kisses alone." This is said playfully and yet it is as rich in meaning as much that Goethe has passed on to us in questions of aesthetics. First of all, he means—to stay with the imagery—that the lyric is not conceived, not carried to maturity, and not born. Conception, maturation, and birth—these would only apply to the type of poetic creation that awakens the seed of life in the "substance" and then gradually takes shape. But Goethe also means that nothing in the lyric rests on firm foundations. We have seen that the lyric mood itself is without rational foundation and that it needs no such grounding (see section IV). But it is precisely for this reason that the lyric mood does not lay any foundation in the reader and does not found any tradition. The style of every *lied* is unique and definitely should not be imitated. The mood is thoroughly individual and can only unite those who are in the same mood, but it cannot create any common ground on which a heterogeneous group of people could be brought together. It is not possible, either, on the basis of a *lied*, to gain an experience that could be substantiated elsewhere. We cannot gain greater maturity with purely lyric poetry, because it is completely fortuitous. Chance assumes no responsibility. Furthermore, responsibility can only take place when a second party is involved.

Thus, the lyric poet does not build anything, but of course he or she does not destroy anything either. A tragedy can destroy one's faith by revealing discrepancies in the view of life of an entire generation (cf. pages 167–68). But the lyric poet is not aware of discrepancies because

25. Georges Duhamel, entry in the guestbook of the Bern, Switzerland, Free German Students' Association.

he is carried along by the flow of existence, because at every moment he forgets the previous moment and, therefore, does not establish any relationships. In a poem of Brentano we read:

> Night is full of lies and deception,
> We can never see enough
> In her black eyes;
> Love is hot and night is cool,
> O! I look far too often
> Into her black eyes!
>
> The sun did not want to set,
> Stopped in curiosity at the edge of the hill;
> Night arrived;
> Quiet night, in your womb
> Lies man's greatest fate
> Enveloped maternally.
> ("From the Echo of the Walls")

Night is full of lies and deception; night is the maternal womb. I never see enough, I look far too often into her eyes. These things follow each other without connection. It does not disturb the poet, because he does not think and does not assume anything.

For this reason, a single *lied* proves nothing. An epic poem, a dramatic work proves, to begin with, that its creator is a person of creative talents. But someone without talent can occasionally succeed, as a matter of sheer chance, in creating a *lied*. In German poetry, there are many chance creations of this sort, for instance, the few *lieder* of Luise Hensel or of Marianne von Willemer, or the poem "Zu spät" (Too Late) by Friedrich Theodor Vischer. But epic poetry and dramatic works prove much more. An epic poem proves a unity of existence and, further, an ethnic unity (see page 131). A dramatic work can prove that a certain historical period has become untenable (cf. pages 164–65). Thus, epic poems and dramatic works have a historical function. A *lied* produces no consequences. It is created, it leaves some cold and a few others love it. But we do not let our lives be affected by a *lied*, as might be the case when we select as a model a hero from an epic poem or a dramatic work. The *lied* proffers no model of how or how not to live. We cannot turn to it for advice when we have to make some decision, whereas a maxim from some dramatic work might give us strength in a difficult hour. The *lied* is noncommittal. It solves no problems. We cannot fall back on it. Who would think of calling up, as a witness, in some important matter, a fragrance, a certain vague something hovering in the atmosphere? A *lied* can comfort us but not help us. It is more a lover than a friend on whom we can lean when we have to steel ourselves for action; it is more a lover than a wife who is a man's constant companion. All this emerges from the fact that lyric poetry does not overcome anything, that it possesses nothing substantial against which it could test such a thing as strength; in short, it is full of soul, but without spirit.

Or is this because the *lied* is always brief? The few lines of a poem do not "represent anything." How could they make history or be dependable in any way? We cannot object to this explanation. However, we now know that brevity is an essential characteristic of the lyric. Every *lied* is brief, because it can only last as long as Being is in harmony with the poet. In other words, this means that the lyric poet has no destiny. At the point where destiny, where the resistance of an alien existence could set in, his creating always ceases. He does not think about what this ceasing means: that that life which was music is now alien and distant again. He probably senses this and feels regret. But as long as he senses it, he cannot express himself as a poet. He has no choice but to await a renewal of grace, when he and the world will once more be in harmony. Then, he can sing a few more verses, only to fall silent again. An unheard-of fate: The poet must pay for the renewal of grace with a pitiful helplessness in everything that requires an independent accomplishment; he must pay for the joy of one moment of inspiration with painful days, devoid of inspiration, for which there is no remedy.

Epic Style: Presentation

I

Usually the distinction between epic poetry and the drama forms the core of a poetics. The poet asks himself whether the material at hand is better suited for the stage or for a narrative, and he looks for a criterion. With such a goal in mind, Goethe and Schiller also examined the possibilities of epic and dramatic creation. Much less frequently, epic poetry is distinguished from lyric poetry. Everyone recognizes the difference between them and it is impossible to be in doubt as to which genre to choose. But when the question of the basis for the poetic genre concepts is posed without any practical goal in mind, as is the case here, then even what seems perfectly clear deserves our undivided attention. To begin with, a distinction should be made between the "varietas carminum" [variety of meter] in lyric poetry and the regularity of the meter in epic poetry.

A single meter, the hexameter, dominates the *Iliad* and *Odyssey* from their first to last line—dominates, in fact, the whole of Greek epic poetry. We are not yet ready to ask what the superior qualities were that assured this meter the favor of poets for centuries. For the present, we shall merely observe that regularity is an essential characteristic of epic poetry. Klopstock's *Messias* is, for example, less epic than lyric when, as it sometimes does, it modulates into free verse. The same holds true for Leuthold's *Penthesilea*, where the narrative is told in long, drawn-out stanzas with very different meters.

The regularity of epic verse expresses the equanimity of the poet who does not fall prey to any mood, and whose feelings do not vary. Homer emerges from the flow of existence and stands firm and unmoved in the face of things. He sees them from a single point of view, from a particular perspective. This perspective is established in the rhythm of his verse and it secures his identity for him, a constant element in the flood of appearances.

An archetype of such a confrontation is that scene in the *Iliad* where Zeus harnesses his horses, drives to the top of Mount Ida, and looks down from there to the fortress of Troy in order to decide the outcome of the war. Another such scene is the *Teichoskopie*, the view from the walls, in the third song, where Priam has Helen tell him the names of the Greek heroes. Similarly, from a secure vantage point, Homer looks at life. He does not participate in it himself. He is not submerged in the action; it does not carry him away as it does the lyric poet. How little he himself is moved is shown in his digressions, to which we eventually grow accustomed but that astonish anyone who reads them for the first time. For example, in the fourth song, Agamemnon is urging his army to battle; he finds Diomedes idle and accosts him harshly:

> Woe is me, son of Tydeus, the fiery tamer of horses,
> How you do fear! full of fright you look 'round at the paths
>   of encounter!

Homer is far from sharing the king's emotions here; on the contrary, he confers his own contemplativeness onto Agamemnon, who, unmoved by the urgency of the situation, begins to tell a story of the bravery of Tydeus:

> Never once, truly, did Tydeus despair so completely,
> Far ahead of his own companions he battled the enemy.
> Thus they all say who have seen him in battle, for never have I
> Encountered or seen him, but, so they say, he outdid all others.
> Once, long ago, and far from the war, he came to Mycenae,
> A guest, with Polynices, the god-like, gathering people,
> For in battle they besieged the sacred bastions of Thebes;
> And then, with fervor, they pleaded for brave companions in
>   battle.
> The others were ready to give and to grant what they asked
>   with such fervor;
> But Zeus averted all this with signs of impending disaster. . . .
>   (IV, 37ff.)

And so on for twenty verses. After calmly delivering them, Agamemnon again works himself into a rage:

Such was Tydeus once, the Aitolian! his son here
Is a poorer hero in battle, but he is a far better speaker.
Diomedes has long known what his father Tydeus
    accomplished at Thebes.

Thus, a brief reminder of his courageous father would have better echoed Agamemnon's impatience. But could Homer ever resist a temptation to tell stories? A similar thing occurs in the sixth song when Hector is taking leave of Andromache (407–34). The beginning of Andromache's speech corresponds exactly to her feelings of anxiety. She pictures the death of her husband. She imagines her loneliness afterward, for her parents are both dead. Achilles killed her father— here, Homer seems to pause suddenly: What was Achilles' involvement again? Homer has complete freedom to take off in whatever direction he wants, whenever he wants. Thus he has the grief-stricken woman describe in detail how this came about, how Achilles freed her for a great ransom, how he left the dead man's weapons with him and made a burial mound upon which the nymphs planted elm trees. And only after she has also told of the fate of her seven brothers does she continue, again in great agitation:

Hector, listen, father and mother you are to me now
And my one and only brother, and also you are my
    flourishing husband.

Andromache digresses because Homer is not overcome by the pain of the situation, or at least he is not completely swept away by it.

The distance he puts between himself and his narration may occasionally diminish at some points in his tale, but it never disappears completely. Homer and Troy, Homer and the wanderings of Odysseus remain forever separated, opposite each other. This does not mean, however, that the poet disappears behind his material. On the contrary, in his role as narrator, he places himself very much in the foreground; he addresses the Muses. He not infrequently interrupts the narration in order to address a remark, a plea, to the gods. He is also present as the "I" who addresses that heartfelt "you" to the favorites Eumaeus and Patroclus. Of course, he does not expect to be noticed as anything other than the narrator, the man who sees and shows things in a certain way, who stands there with his staff in hand—to use Vischer's words[26]—pointing to the images as they arise.

26. Vischer, *Ästhetik*, 6:129.

Because he places himself opposite these images, everything that happens is objectified.* The object itself may change, but the narrator himself maintains his equanimity, and this becomes audible in the regularity of his verses.

Everything that happens is also objectified because it belongs to the past. That is to say, the epic poet does not immerse himself reminiscingly in the past, as does the lyric poet; rather, he reflects. And in reflecting he maintains temporal as well as spatial distance. What is far away is recalled into the present: It stands before our eyes, and for that very reason it stands opposite us as a different, wonderful, and greater world. The *Song of the Nibelungs* begins, "In ancient tales we are told many wondrous things."

Homer, too, tells of ancient tales. He does not describe his own time; rather, he is quite obviously seeking to create a patina of the archaic. Thus in the *Iliad*, for example, there is no cavalry and no trumpet signal, though both certainly existed in Homer's time. This temporal distance is maintained even more emphatically by the repeated assurance that long ago, when the Trojan war took place, people were stronger. The formula "the way mortals are" again and again compares contemporary existence unfavorably to the great past. But even this great past has to suffer the same sort of criticism. For among the heroes, Nestor steps forward, and declares with the conceit of age:

> For long ago I used to be with stronger men
> Than you are; and still those stronger men did not disdain me!
> Never again have I seen such men and never shall I.
>
> (I, 260–63)

Homer's contemporaries are weaklings compared with Hector and Achilles, but even these heroes are weaklings compared with those of a still earlier age. Thus, the greatest vitality lies in the depths of the past and no opportunity is missed to plumb these depths. When two men ready themselves for combat with each other they ask for name and origin, and the man questioned relates the history of his clan back to the oldest forefathers, even to the god who founded the family. When Agamemnon takes hold of the scepter, we hear its whole history, who made it, who carried it, how it went from Zeus to Hermes, from Hermes to Pelops, and finally came into Agamemnon's hands.

---

* The German word for object, *Gegenstand*, which is used in the text, literally means "something that stands opposite something else." Cf. translator's note, page 81.

Odysseus' marriage bed has its history too. And sometimes a pitcher or some other utensil is deemed worthy of a legend about its origin.

What this means is most clearly illuminated in the famous dialogue between Glaucus and Diomedes in the sixth song of the *Iliad*. Diomedes asks the usual question,

> But who are you, o noble one, of the mortal inhabitants of
> the earth?

But Glaucus gives an answer that is totally out of place:

> Tydeus' courageous son, why ask about my kinship?
> As leaves in the forest, so are the succeeding generations of
> men;
> Some the wind strews down onto the earth, and others
> Are brought forth in the burgeoning forest, produced in the
> warmth of spring.
> And so it goes with human generations: one grows and one
> diminishes.
>
> (VI, 145–50)

Finally and unwillingly he gets around to telling about his ancestors. Whether Homer does this here in order to show the attitude of the Lycians, a matriarchal people, is a question that cannot be answered at this point. We see only that Glaucus does not recognize the value of epic reflection. For it is precisely the merit of epic reflection that it stems the pressing flow of people and things. The epic poet asks: "From where?" This question points to the dimension of being about which the lyric existence, itself swept along in the flow of time, knows nothing. Thus I can only ask "From where?" if a fixed "here" exists; likewise, the position of "here" can only be determined by knowing "from where." The answer to the question anchors in a solid base all that is in question. This base is in the past, which, being something complete, stands still and can no longer change. Whoever asks the question "from where" must take up a position in relation to this past. Thus opposite sides are created: The position of the person asking the question as well as the position of the object of the question is fixed.*

And that is the whole point. The question of the nature of the past, which Glaucus does not want to answer, is a most important part of

---

* The German word for "to fix" or "to ascertain" is *feststellen*. This literally means "to fix things and events firmly."

the activity of the epic narrator: He fixes. This the lyric poet can and will not do, for he himself is not fixed; he is part of the flow of life. Therefore, he is never able to say "this is" (cf. page 68):

> He looks at walls and palaces
> Always with different eyes.

The sun rising in the morning is his hope and his courage. The sun setting in the evening is a magnificent and shattering experience. He is of course vaguely aware that it is the same sun that rises and sets, because he makes use of language and says "sun." But it is of no consequence. This sameness recedes behind the changing of the impressive spectacle.

In the epic, however, it is precisely that sameness that is emphasized. Because the epic poet himself occupies a firm vantage point he is able to see that something returns and is the same. How happy this discovery makes him is revealed by the stereotyped formula in the Homeric epics: "Hector readied for battle, fleet-footed Achilles, owl-eyed Athena, Zeus, the ruler of thundering clouds." Hector, Achilles, Athena, Zeus are fixed once and for all. They have identified themselves thus and they are called again and again. And it is always the same Eos who appears, rosy-fingered, in the morning, the same sleep that relaxes the entire body. Further, when the Trojans and later the Greeks are feasting, when Athena or Iris sweeps down from Olympus, the same situation in a different setting is told in the same words:

> And they reached out their hands for the good food that
>   had been prepared for them.
> ....
> And she swept far down from the top of the high Mount
>   Olympus.

Of course the fact that the narration is improvised can explain this practice. The rhapsodist needs a large store of ready-made verses, which he occasionally inserts, so that in the meantime he can reflect on what is to follow. But this historical explanation does not exclude the aesthetic interpretation. The happiness that the return of the familiar brings, the triumph of knowing that now life no longer flows on without stopping but is something lasting, and that objects have a firm, stable existence and can be identified—all this is so powerful that even today every unspoiled reader experiences in it an inspired feeling for the early days of mankind. Having become a proven means of highly developed art, the stereotyped phrases of Homer seem to conclude the process that Herder undertook to interpret in his essay on the origins of language.

According to Herder, language has its basis in consciousness or reflection:

> Man shows reflection when the force of his soul acts so freely that from out of the whole ocean of feelings rushing through all his senses he is able, so to speak, to isolate one wave, to hold it up, to direct attention toward it and at the same time to be conscious of his own awareness. Man shows reflection when, from the entire dreamlike flow of images which glide past him, he can collect himself in a waking moment, can voluntarily direct all his attention to one single image, look at it quite calmly and brightly and pick out characteristics which distinguish this object from all others. Thus he demonstrates reflection when he can not only recognize all characteristics vividly or clearly, but also when he can pick out one or several truly distinguishing features. The first step in this act of recognition yields a clear concept; it is a man's first act of judgement— and—how did recognition occur? With the help of a feature which he had to isolate and which, being a feature of consciousness, stood out most clearly in his mind. Good, let us address him with Εὔρηκα! *This first feature of consciousness was a word from his soul! With it, human language was invented!*
>
> Let that lamb, as an image, pass before his eyes: it appears to him in a different way from the way it appears to other animals. As soon as he feels the need to get to know the sheep, no instinct will deter him, no feeling will bring him too close to the animal or keep him away; it stands there just as it impresses itself upon his senses. White, soft, wooly—man's mind, training itself to reflect, seeks a distinguishing feature. *The sheep bleats!* He has found a distinguishing feature: his mind is at work. This bleating which has made the strongest impression on him, which has isolated itself from all other characteristics of sight or touch, which stood out and penetrated his senses most deeply, remains in his mind. The sheep returns. White, soft, wooly—man looks, touches, reflects, looks for a feature— it bleats, and now he recognizes it again. "Ha! You are the one who bleats!" is what he feels deep inside; he has recognized

the sheep in a human way since he recognized and named the animal clearly, i.e. with the help of one feature. . . .[27]

In a word that is not just pure expression, such as the "cry of feeling"* (cf. pages 75–76), in a word that means something, an object is always established; hence it and objects of its kind can be recognized again at any time. In his stereotyped formulas, Homer seems to enjoy this same sort of recognition—an elementary achievement of language. These phrases determine an object or an event as being constituted or as proceeding in a given manner. They "present"** it—let us use this word in order to encompass in our terminology the relation of subject to object, the act of presenting things from a fixed vantage point. Presentation in this sense is the essence of epic poetry.

II

Epic language presents. It points to something. It designates. The contrast between it and the language of lyric has already been mentioned in our discussion of the difference between onomatopoeia and music (page 46). In lyric-musical language a mood is evoked. Epic onomatopoeia tries to elucidate something by linguistic means. Epic poetry is entirely a matter of elucidating, of showing, of making things visible. Spitteler calls it the "royal prerogative" of the epic poet "to transform everything into a living event"[28] and thus present everything before our eyes. Even states of the soul, he explains, are transformed by the poet into concrete phenomena. Spitteler himself has done this quite frequently. We are acquainted, in his *Prometheus und Epimetheus*, with the animals of Prometheus, the lion and the little dogs of the heart, which he strangles. Or in *Olympischer Frühling* (Olympian Spring) we are familiar with the will of Zeus, which, being a projectile, is hurled toward its goal and shatters the glass-fragile will of others. Even in prose, Spitteler refuses to dispense with this epic prerogative. In *Imago* we find the following description of his own soul:

---

27. Herder, *Sämtliche Werke*, 5:34ff.

* Herder's "Ton der Empfindung," the "emotive tone" of pages 75–76—Trans.

** Staiger uses the verb *vorstellen* here, which literally means "to place something before one's eyes."

28. See in this connection Carl Spitteler, *Lachende Wahrheiten* (Zurich, 1945), 232ff.; in English: *Laughing Truths*, trans. James F. Muirhead (London, 1927).

But in order to be completely certain, he even undertook a tour through the Noah's ark of his soul, from the top floor to the cellar of his unconscious, giving out admonitions and wisdom on all sides. In dealing with the noble animals, he appealed to their pride by telling them about future fame and triumphs, contrasting this to the pitiful role they would play as the unhappy lover of a president's wife, a Mrs. Wyss. The small animals he baited with sweets, reminding them of past pleasures of love and making them believe far greater pleasures were in store for them if they would only be patient a little while longer; and at the very end, he had the lions roar down the stairs, "Are you convinced now?"

"We are convinced."

"Good, then act accordingly and keep each other in check."[29]

The grim humor of this passage reconciles us to its strange mixture of very modern psychology and old-fashioned presentation. Otherwise, the passage would strike us as rather peculiar. For as Spitteler himself admits, he is in fact forced to *transform* states of the soul into concrete phenomena. Homer does no such thing. He does not know states of the soul to be anything other than visible occurrences. For him, feelings inhabit the breast as the winds inhabit the cave of Aeolus. The ninth song of the *Iliad* begins:

So the Trojans kept watch there before Ilias. The Achaeans, however,
Were seized with gruesome fear, stark-staring terror's companion;
And unbearable grief took hold of them, even the very courageous.
As two ocean winds stir up the waves teeming with fishes,
North and howling west winds both are blowing from Thrace,
Arriving, racing and raging; and right away now darkening waves
Tower above, and often to shore they fling the grass of sea:
And thus by disquiet was the heart of the noble Achaeans torn asunder.

Literally translated, the eighth line goes as follows:

29. Carl Spitteler, *Gesammelte Werke* (Zurich, 1945), 4:366f.

And thus in the breasts of the Greeks the θυμός was torn
asunder.

Θυμός, the seat of the emotions, is as real to them as our heart is to
us. And pain and anxiety, which tear it apart, are just as concrete.
They pierce through the seat of the emotions. The figurativeness of
language, which we are often reluctant to avail ourselves of today,
has kept its literal meaning here. It says exactly what it means. Of
Menelaus it is said in the seventeenth song:

When he thought about all this in the seat of emotions, the
diaphragm. . . .

(106)

The diaphragm is the seat of the emotions, but since these are themselves seen as things, it can often scarcely be differentiated from them.
Thoughts are stirred, shoved back and forth like objects. Thus, Homer
imagines even thinking to be action in space, usually by having the
thinker conduct a dialogue with himself. In the same song we read:

Deeply he sighed and then spoke to his noble emotions. . . .

And what Menelaus says here to his emotions is shortly afterward
designated as words of his beloved emotions addressed to himself.
Thus it is that we often read in the *Iliad* about "words," where, according to our use of language, only "thoughts" could be meant:

Hera, do not at all hope that you will know all of my words.
(*Iliad*, I, 545)

However, the words that the suitors had secretly harbored
within them
Did not long remain unknown to Penelope.
(*Odyssey*, IV, 675–76)

But very well, let us go and silently let us accomplish
That word, which we all have resolved within our
diaphragm.
(*Odyssey*, IV, 776–77)

It is clear that such a literal translation is impossible. But it is worth
showing, in connection with the Greek text, that thought itself here

is a corporeal being that is stored somewhere in the body and then sometimes makes an appearance through the well-known "enclosure of the teeth."

However, a poet who looks at everything and presents everything in objective form will not remain for long in such immaterial regions, which are, after all, rather difficult to depict objectively. He prefers to direct his eye outward—for there is an outer world here, just as there is an inner world now—and he looks at the immeasurable wealth of life that presents itself to his eyes: weapons, warriors, the tumult of battle, wondrous countries and people, the sea and sand, animals and plants, household goods and artistic creations. Just naming these things and being able to say: This is how it looks! fills him with joy. Ore gleams, the sea is the color of wine, the grapes are dark, the swan is long-necked, the cattle have long straight horns and the ships high prows, the dogs are nimble, the girls have beautiful curls, Hector is surrounded by helmets, Chryseis has beautiful cheeks, Thetis is silver-footed, Athena owl-eyed, Hera white-armed. The wealth of words is immeasurable and this wealth alone represents a significant poetic achievement of the most ancient epic poetry. Here we find expressed what is most characteristic of gods and of men and of all things. By this means the eyes of the listener are opened and he looks at life in its well-differentiated fullness. The imagery of the Homeric vision becomes exemplary for the Greek world.

The creative power of Homer's vision asserts itself in the plastic arts. Finsler[30] is convinced that the poet is describing works of art that did not yet exist in his time, such as Achilles' shield, the gold and silver dogs that guard the house of Alkinoos, or the sceptre of Agamemnon and the mixing pitcher of Menelaus. Mere mortals did not create these artifacts; Hephaestus, the divine artist, did; and this artist, envisioned by Homer, is zealously imitated by the later artists of Greece. In the creation of the images of the gods, too, these artists remain under Homer's spell. Zeus with his great wavy mane, Athena in her father's armor, Apollo with his long hair, his lyre, and his silver bow, Hermes with his sandals, which carry him over land and sea: For centuries, Greek art was concerned with these Homeric themes and gradually learned to create what the poet had seen with his inner eye. Thus in truth, as Herodotus said, Homer created the gods for the Greeks. But this creation of the gods is only a part of his overall accomplishment: He revealed far and wide the brilliant visibleness of life.

30. Georg Finsler, *Homer*, 2 vols. (Leipzig, 1913, 1918).

In order to see, one needs light. In the light that epic speech spreads, the actual revealing word, Olympus and the human realm stand clearly outlined. To live in light is the greatest joy of Homeric man. Zeus is the god of the greatest brilliance, literally and metaphorically speaking. The brightness of mountain heights surrounds him, brightness in the sense that no secret any longer surrounds his appearance. One could deplore in this a loss of magic power. But the epic poet gladly sacrifices this and lifts the veil of the sacred again and again for the sake of making it visible. Thus the sun becomes the light of the renowned Homeric rationalism. The brilliance of Homer is enlightenment, and as such is sober but strong, healthy, enduring, and clearly defined. Of course all this is acquired at the price of an insuperable aversion to night and death. If a hero falls in battle, we read the stereotyped formula:

> Screaming he fell to his knees and the shadow of death
>   was upon him.

Or:

> . . . straight away came
> Nightlike death together with almighty destiny and
>   dimmed his eyes.

Lyric existence does not know such a dread of the dark and death, when the eyes close. On the contrary; it sinks into the night as into the inner depths of the self and feels surrounded and secure. Of course it would be misleading to say that night belongs characteristically to the realm of the lyric and day to that of the epic. For lyric, light is also possible, but it is more a glistening and gliding light; it does not establish an opposite, hence making itself interchangeable with the dark, which likewise makes no distinctions. On the other hand, darkness robs epic man of his essential nature. In the dark he no longer sees anything, and, since his existence is grounded in the visual, he "is" no longer. The gods abandon the dying man. He sinks into μὴ ὄν, into nothingness, for which the shades of Hades are the somewhat self-conscious simile of a poet who must still somehow make the invisible visible. The voyage to Hades is the most awesome venture of the godlike sufferer Odysseus. The line that the hero crosses here marks a more radical boundary of the world than do the columns of Hercules past which the ship of Dante's Ulysses must sail.

Another realm is excluded here, too, which for lyric man is closely related to night and to death, namely, love. Of course Homer is acquainted with faithfulness in marriage and has erected a monument to it in Andromache and Penelope. He also knows the lust for possession of a woman. The Trojan war breaks out over Helen, and Achilles' anger is ignited because of Briseis. But one finds in his work no trace of love's bliss and love's longing. Briseis is like a goblet of wine; the thirsty man drinks and turns again to the business of war. Achilles would have been no less angry had Agamemnon taken a weapon or a jewel from him. He has lost a lovely plaything, and therefore he has lost face. This, in turn, is how Agamemnon sees it, when in the ninth song he declares himself prepared to make the following atonement:

> Ten talents' worth of gold; in addition tripod petals
> Numbering seven, not yet fire-blackened, and twenty
>   shimmering cauldrons;
> And twelve mighty horses, drowned with prizes in races.
>   . . .
> And seven women I will give him, good and skilled
> In their work; they are Lesbians whom I chose when he
>   conquered flowering Lesbos.
> In charms, they surpassed the daughters of every mortal on
>   earth.
> Now these I will give him; and with them shall go the one I
>   abducted
> The daughter of Briseus; and then I will swear with most
>   sacred oath
> That I never dishonored her bed and I never approached
>   her
> As in all mankind the man is wont to approach the woman.
>   (IX, 122–34)

Love is not an epic theme, inasmuch as it has a fluid quality (cf. pages 87–88) and dissolves the contours of a differentiated existence. Eros, "unconquered in battle, who lurks at night on the cheeks of the virgin," is unknown here. Even Aphrodite lacks that all-consuming grace and demonic power of which Sappho and Phaedra in Euripides' *Hippolytus* speak. Homer's Aphrodite is an amusing goddess, lovely, but often enough close to being ridiculous. However, in the Nausicaa scenes in the *Odyssey* a soft lyric breath is discernible; as a matter of fact this later epic poem occasionally approaches the lyric, for example in the delicate landscape depictions, in their blend of colors.

The nature of Dionysus can be assessed in a similar way. The *Iliad* is, to be sure, acquainted with this god. Diomedes tells the story of Lycurgus, whose act of violence so terrified Dionysus that he hid in the sea. But the epic poem knows nothing of the orgiastic power of this god. And he does not appear on Olympus. He would be an enemy of the clear differentiation of all forms and of the fixed oppositeness of things in their relation to each other.

Thus, since night, death, Eros, and the intoxicated god are excluded here or are at least pushed aside, light triumphs over all and with light the corporeal, delineated world of objects. In the words of Goethe's *Faust:*

> The proud light which once contests
> The ancient rank and space of mother night,
> It emanates from bodies, and it makes bodies beautiful. . . .

III

Hence the epic demonstrates its relatedness to the visual arts, as did the lyric its relatedness to music. But in the same way that the fixed concrete meaning can never be eliminated from lyric expression, epic language can never escape the consecutiveness of time. For the epic is not a plastic art, nor is the lyric music; both are poetic creation. However, the poet may attempt to fulfill the dictum "ut pictura poesis" in such a way that he or she tries to depict in words things that occur side by side in space. In Haller's *Die Alpen* (The Alps) we find the lines:

> Here a bold pair struggles, uniting solemnity with play,
> Winding body around body and twining hip around hip,
> There a heavy stone hurtles towards its destined target,
> Given life by a strong hand through the divided air.
> Another is led by the desire to undertake something more noble
> Toward a lively crowd of noble shepherdesses.
> There a speeding bullet hits the distant mark,
> It flashes and rends the air and the target simultaneously;
> Here a round ball rolls along its given track
> Towards the chosen goal in long bounds.
> There a colorful circle dances, hands intertwined,
> In the trampled grass to a village shawm. . . .

Haller adds that this entire description has been painted according to real life. But we do not find it very lifelike, precisely because the continuous change of perspective, the "here" and "there," distracts our attention, and because the reader cannot keep in mind all the parts of the picture that accumulate as the lines progress. Here we touch upon the question that Lessing poses in his *Laokoon* and that he attempts to answer in the sixteenth paragraph with the well-known assertions:

> Objects that exist next to each other or whose parts exist next to each other are called bodies. Consequently, bodies with their visible qualities are the basic objects of painting.
> Objects that follow each other or whose parts follow each other consecutively are called acts. Consequently, acts are the basic objects of poetic creation.
> All bodies, however, exist not only in space, they also exist in time. They endure and at any given moment of their duration they can appear differently and can stand in a different connection. Any one of these momentary appearances and connections is the result of a previous one and can be the cause of a subsequent one, thus constituting the core of an act. Consequently, painting can also imitate acts but only in an allusive way through bodies.
> On the other hand, acts cannot exist in isolation, for they are dependent on certain entities. Inasmuch as these entities are bodies or are regarded as bodies, poetic creation also describes bodies but only in an allusive manner through acts.

These sentences have been admired as often as they have been contested. To begin with, it should be made clear that Lessing plainly wanted only to establish the limits of *epic* writing. Lyric poetry does not describe at all and depicts no objects, neither bodies nor acts. Lessing really has no clear-cut concept of the lyric as yet. But in the following he indicates something about its nature:

> Not because Ovid shows us the beautiful body of his Lesbia part by part but rather because he does it with such voluptuous ecstasy that our own longing is readily aroused, can we feel we are savoring the same sight that he savored. (paragraph XXI)

The reader does not assemble the parts Ovid describes here into a three-dimensional whole; rather, he participates in the intensification of sensual pleasure that arouses the poet at the sight of Corinna's beauty.[31] We could say the same about Ariosto's description of Alcina, which Lessing criticizes unjustly. Here too, the depiction of each separate part is unimportant. The portrait of Alcina is as though dipped into a haze, and this haze enchants us, creates a mood, and carries us along from stanza to stanza.

Lessing's question, then, is justified only when that which stands opposite the poet is clearly delineated and when the poet wants in the literal sense of the phrase to depict the objective world—that is, that which is opposite him. But does the solution lie in assigning bodies to the artist on the one hand and acts to the poet on the other? What Lessing means by act is discussed in a fragment of the *Laokoon* from his posthumous papers:

> A series of movements which are all directed toward a final goal is called an act.[32]

However, this more aptly describes the movement of dramatic poetry. In the drama we are in suspense about the end from the very beginning (cf. page 148) and every part fits in with every other, as Lessing says at another point, "to achieve a final goal."[33] But where tension predominates, calm presentation is no longer possible. There, the object world becomes a mere means to an end; but the epic poet enjoys an object for its own sake. Differences between the genres is not the point of issue in Lessing's *Laokoon*. Every existing poetic work—as is noted again and again—participates in all three genre concepts in varying ways and to varying degrees. Still, it cannot be denied that Lessing judges poetry too much by dramatic standards. This is so even in his essay on the fable, where he forbids all descriptions that have nothing to do with the moral at the end and has little understanding for the charming epic elements in La Fontaine's work.

At most, however, this merely emends Lessing's thesis; it does not refute it. The sharp contrast between depiction and the continuing flow of speech is maintained. The only question is: Does the epic

---

31. Lessing incorrectly writes "Lesbia"; he is confusing Ovid's loved one with Catullus's.

32. Hugo Blümner, *Lessings Laokoon,* 2d ed. (Berlin, 1880), 444. [Staiger is quoting here from extensions of the *Laokoon* in Lessing's *Nachlass* [literary remains], rather than from the *Laokoon* proper; hence the inadequacy here of available translations of this much-translated work.]

33. Ibid., 603.

poet deal with this contrast in a way that conforms more to visual representation than to the purposeful movement of the dramatic?

In the sixth song of the *Iliad* Diomedes wants to know whether Glaucus, whom he has never seen, is a mortal or a god, and he addresses him as follows:

> Who among mortal men are you, o noble stranger?
> Never before have I seen you in glorious, honor-filled battle.
> Now though, you tower above all your other companions,
> Boldly courageous in front of my powerful lance you
>   appear.
> None but the sons of unhappy parents oppose my great
>   power!
> But insofar as you are a true god and descended from
>   heaven
> Never shall I desire to fight with the powers of heaven.
> Even the mighty Lycurgus who was a descendant of Dryas
> Died very young when he rose up against all the heavenly
>   powers:
> He who had earlier chased all the nurses of mad Dionysus,
> Driving them all up the sacred mountain Mysaion; together
> Now they all threw down the leaf-covered sticks, since the
>   killer Lycurgus
> Wildly was beating them, using a goad; and in fear
>   Dionysus
> Plunged in the waves of the ocean and Thetis embraced
>   him, he who
> Trembled and fearfully heard the menacing voice of
>   Lycurgus.
> This man, thereon, enraged the divinities, placidly reigning.
> Zeus, called the thunderer, blinded Lycurgus and not long
>   thereafter
> Did he survive, for hated was he by all the immortals.
> Therefore, not with blessed immortals do I wish to do
>   battle.
> However, if you are mortal and nourished by fruits of the
>   earth
> Come, then, approach me that speedily you shall encounter
>   death.
>
> (VI, 123–43)

The tale of Lycurgus can be dispensed with if the only question here is of finding out who Glaucus is. Then the tale is—to use Lessing's words—not a part vital in the formation of the final goal. We could provide many more examples. But we shall cite only one of the clearest, from the sixteenth song of the *Iliad*. The battle between the Trojans and the Greeks is approaching its climax. Already flames are leaping from the ship of Prothesilaus. Help is urgently needed. Achilles recognizes the great danger and calls to his friend:

> Rouse yourself, Patroclus, noblest of heroes and brave men
>   in battle!
> For on our vessels I see the raging of enemy fire.
> Soon they will capture our ships; then, escape will no
>   longer be possible.
> Thus you must put on your armor and I shall assemble the
>   people.
>
>   (126–29)

As we can see, there is great need for haste. But in stating this, Homer has satisfied his final goal. He then goes on to tell how Patroclus arms himself. He interjects a comment on Achilles' heavy spear. And he cannot resist giving a genealogy of the horses. The Myrmidon hordes gather their forces. Homer describes their throng, using a long-drawn-out simile. Then he tells the stories of several of the subordinate leaders of the Myrmidons. One of them is Menestheus, son of the heaven-born stream Sperchaeus and of Polydora; officially, however, Borus, son of Perieres, was recognized as his father. Eudorus is another leader. His story is told, too: who he is, who his parents were, and where and how he spent his youth. Then Achilles gives a speech. Afterward he gives an offering to the gods, and again Homer describes in detail how Achilles takes a goblet from the shrine, how shrine and goblet look, how he puts the goblet away again and finally emerges from the tent to watch the departure. Only then, after 120 verses, does the action reach its conclusion:

> Well armed they gathered around Patroclus, their brave leader;
> Then they set out and plunged with defiance into the Trojans.

Thus we see that in epic the final goal is not important. The dramatist utilizes people and things merely to illustrate great decisions, whereas for the epic writer great decisions are but a pretext for recounting as much of past events as possible. He does not proceed in order to reach a goal; rather, he sets himself a goal in order to proceed and, in doing so, to observe everything carefully. It is from this vantage point that Schiller made his distinction between epic and dramatic exposition, the latter of which literally takes place en passant. On 25 April 1797 he writes about this to Goethe:

> Since he [the epic writer] does not propel us to a conclusion the way [the dramatic writer] does, beginning and end move much closer to each other in their dignity and significance; and the exposition must hold our interest not because it leads to something but because it is something in and of itself.

For this very reason the epic writer seldom chooses the most direct route. He does not mind straying from the main plot or even going back and reexamining this or that. Even Herodotus, considered the "father of historiography," writes this way. His topic is the Persian wars. But the world-historic event merely constitutes the great work-frame for innumerable anecdotes, reports on countries and people, foreign customs and cultures, habits and conventions. An excursus is just as important as the outcome of the battle of Marathon. Whoever refuses to accept this will also fail to grasp the essence of the epic.[34]

But if the reader is not to await the outcome with impatience, the end of a poem must not be too weighty or exert too great an appeal. The *Iliad* concludes with Hector's burial. This conclusion certainly corresponds to the beginning, where the poet proclaims that he intends to sing of the anger of Achilles. When Hector's corpse goes up in flames, the last vestiges of anger have also been consumed. In between, however, Homer has told so much about the Trojan war that no unbiased reader would feel the last verse to be final. The *Iliad*, it seems to him, does not conclude: It just stops. It would be possible to continue in the manner of Goethe's *Achilleis*. But it would also have been possible to stop at the point of Hector's defeat. Wherever the situation and the story reach a point of dramatic excitement, the suspense is broken, as though the poet wished to tell the reader that the actual course of the action is more important than any end result. This means that the *Iliad*, taken as a whole or in its parts, is primarily epic in nature. The same applies to the *Odyssey*. In the return and victory of its hero over the suitors, it comes to its long-awaited conclusion, from which point a continuation is hardly possible. But precisely for this reason—because everything tends toward its natural conclusion—the poet does his best to avoid all build-up of suspense. As

---

34. See in this connection Ernst Howald, *Vom Geist antiker Geschichtsschreibung* (Munich, 1945).

early as the first song the gods decide to let Odysseus return. When even Zeus agrees to this, we know that nothing too serious remains to befall the long-suffering hero. This assurance is often repeated lest the listener forget it. Moreover, Odysseus himself recounts his most harrowing adventures—a living guarantee that the Sirens have not destroyed him, that the Cyclops has not eaten him, and that the sea has not swallowed him up. Thus reassured, the listener can observe with a steady eye what this many-faceted man has experienced—the marvels of foreign lands and oceans, of the entire, though mostly unexplored, world.

Goethe and Schiller expressed their views on the epos in this same vein. During the long controversy, Schiller on one occasion described the epic principle in the following words:

> The epic poet's purpose lies at every point along the way of his narrative. Thus, we do not rush impatiently toward a goal; rather, we tarry fondly at every step.[35]

With these remarks, Lessing is given due credit and at the same time stands corrected. As a poet heavily dependent on language, the epic writer progresses following temporal succession, in contrast to the artist, who stands still and captures the special relations of juxtaposition and perspective in space. The epic writer does, however, stop at every step in his progression, and he looks at a stable object from a stable vantage point. Now this, now that: Time passes as the poet perceives one image after another and reveals them to the listener. He will pause until the image he is presenting has made a clear impression, but not so long as to make it difficult for the listener hearing the succession of words to keep in mind the simultaneity they signify. Thus, we can explain everything Lessing says in praise of Homer without having to concur in the excesses to which he was driven by his polemical zeal.

IV

Schiller also expresses the same principle in these words:

> A main characteristic of the epic poem is the independence of its parts.[35*]

35. Schiller to Goethe, 21 April 1797; in English: See footnote 1 above, page 40.
* This and the previous note are numbered 35 in the original. Both quotations come from the same letter.—TRANS.

Each single line can be considered an independent part. A lyric line is not independent. I cannot do anything with a line like "the windows gleamed afar." I cannot even be sure of the line's rhythm until I know that Eichendorff wrote it, or until I am touched, as in the poem "Heimkehr" (Return Home) and carried by the lyrical flow of the whole. But the epic hexameter is an independent rhythmic entity that does not dissolve in the lyric flow. Rather, it stands and holds its own. It gains its support from the caesura. This becomes readily apparent when one compares hexameters without caesura to properly constructed hexameters:

Elim put sprouting twigs of the shadowing olive tree upon him.
(Klopstock)

And so the Trojans buried the warrior Hector's body . . .
(Homer)

Men of wisdom require far less the friendship of kings . . .
(Herder)

All situations are good which are natural and well-reasoned. . . .
(Goethe)

The caesura seems to act as a small peg to anchor the line so that it is not swept away by the onrushing stream of dactyls. Yet it is merely a gentle device, quite different from the much more rigorous caesura of the alexandrine, which divides the line so sharply into two parts that we are forced to see the division as marking a confrontation of the two halves and to construct a logical relation between them.

In the hexameter, then, a simple whole is clearly set apart. Homer, a late master of the hexameter, does make use of enjambment, thus occasionally endangering the independent whole of the single verse line. But the original function of the measure is still recognizable.

The rhythmic whole brings about the wholeness of the object world. Countless hexameters, though they are completely divorced from their surroundings, can bring us pleasure through the concreteness of their imagery. We are not speaking of stereotyped lines, but of lines like the following:

And a terrible sound escaped from the silver bow
(*Iliad*, I, 49)

> Pears upon pears all ripened, apples on apples reddened,
> Grapes upon grapes all darkened, and figs upon figs
>   grow wrinkled.
>
> (Odyssey, VII, 120–21)

Here are further examples from epics of the German classical period:

> At the gate she was met by the dog who was wagging his tail
>
> (Voss, Luise)

> Festive the sky and serene, and the earth was resplendent
>   with color.
>
> (Goethe, Reineke Fuchs [Reineke the Fox])

These examples also show that the length of the verse line corresponds to the usual length of a concise main clause. The independence of the parts is represented grammatically by a paratactic construction, one in which it would however be perfectly proper—in contrast to the lyric parataxis—to conclude each line with a period. This is not evident in Homer. But the Greek text manifests the independence of its parts in a different way, a way that can scarcely be imitated in German any longer, but that can be seen in other, younger languages, and that, as is the case with the epic in general, signifies an unrepeatable, early phase of human development. A glance into Kägi's Greek school grammar is enough to illustrate the point. When Homer does go off into a longer hypotactic construction, he often suddenly stops and breaks the tension by means of anacoluthon. One example of this, which Thassilo von Scheffer[36] manages to render into German, can be found in the sixth song of the *Iliad:*

> When, however, he reached the magnificent dwelling of Priam,
> Built all around with halls of smooth marble columns—
> Inside, however, were fifty chambers with walls of sleek stone,
> One room was built right next to the other and Priam's sons
> Lay there asleep by the side of their lawfully wedded
>   companions;
> But at the other end of the palace there were in the courtyard
> Twelve enclosed rooms for the daughters with walls of the
>   smoothest stone,
> One right after the other; the husbands of Priam's daughters
> Lay there asleep at the side of their chaste and worthy
>   companions—

36. Homer, *Iliad*, trans. Theodor von Scheffer (Berlin, 1920).

There, then, he was approached by his gentle and good-hearted
   mother,
Who was just going to Laodike, her most beautiful daughter.
                                                    (242–52)

In modern poetry such a construction could only be justified as a
conscious effort at being archaic. But for Homer it is quite natural,
apparently because he does not have nearly as strong a feeling for the
subordination of the dependent clause as we do. Thus, the relative
pronoun still has demonstrative meaning for him and introduces a
main clause. Hence, he does not say: "I have seen the house that is
located by the road," but rather: "I have seen the house; it is located
by the road." This phenomenon is repeated over and over again. We
are in the habit of saying that a preposition governs a case. With
Homer, however, the cases still retain some measure of independence.
The genitive of "house" can mean "out of the house"; the dative can
mean "in the house." Prepositions are still used adverbially: "in front
of" meaning "in front of it," and "in" meaning "in it." Therefore,
prepositions can be found in front of or behind the word to be governed. In such instances a case is not governed by a preposition; rather,
a postposition preposition has an explanatory function in relation to
a case.
    Further examples would continue to show the same thing: namely,
that the feeling for grammatical relationships is still only slightly developed, that even the smallest sentence segments, which later acquire
a purely functional significance, still stand pretty much on their own.
This is merely the grammatical reflection of the principle recognized
by Schiller.
    We must follow this further and shall now discuss similes. Very
frequently, they are only loosely connected grammatically to their
immediate context, since the poet likes to break away from the "as–
so" construction and not take it up again until later. Such is the case
in the following simile, where I have tried, using the Voss translation,
to approach the original text syntactically:

. . . and he fell in the dust like the poplar
Which in the water-soaked meadow in vast swampy lands stood
   tall,
Bare is its trunk, but leafy-green branches grow from its tip.
Now it is felled by the cartwright wielding his gleaming axe-blade
That he might bend it into the shape of a carriage's wheel rim;
Now though, wilting it lies at the edge of the onflowing stream:
Thus, Themius' son Simoisius . . .
                                                    (Iliad, IV, 482ff.)

From the sentence structure alone it is clear that the simile is an independent entity. If we investigate the simile's content we find that it only sustains its connection to the main line of action through the images of falling and lying. Interpreters of ancient times attempted at every opportunity to devise as many connections as possible. For example, the simile of Athena, who wards off the arrow the way that a mother chases a fly from her sleeping child, is arranged so that the mother signifies the goddess's concern for Menelaus; the sleep of the child, the unsuspecting man in peril, and so on. Although in this example the interpretations do not lead to complete nonsense, the reader does feel annoyed. The action of chasing away seems to him or her entirely adequate as a *tertium comparationis*. Anything further seems too construed, and, in its painstaking relating back and forth, is contrary to the epic process.

Almost every simile is connected by a single point with the action, and hence does not burden our memory. In the well-known series of similes in the second book of the *Iliad* the point of comparison is constituted by the swarming of the armies and of birds and flies in the summertime. But the swans' long necks and the milk can around which the flies are swarming do not follow through in detail with the simile; rather, they become independent images.

In this respect, the simile is somewhat akin to the episode, and episodes fill both the *Iliad* and the *Odyssey*. In the *Iliad* scenes of hand-to-hand combat abound; in the *Odyssey* it is a series of sea adventures. Their number could almost be increased or decreased at will. In the long history of Homeric scholarship this is exactly what has happened. First this, then that single-combat scene has been discarded as being a later addition. It has been claimed that the *Odyssey* was made equal in length to the *Iliad* through later interpolations. I cannot permit myself to become involved in these very difficult questions here. They require their own separate study. But it is perhaps permissible to address myself generally to these problems.

The excitement that Friedrich August Wolf's *Prolegomena ad Home-rum* afforded the friends of Homer has not yet subsided. For decades, philology looked down with a condescending smile upon those who refused to give up the idea of one author and one united work at any price. But at present even philologists seem inclined to point to the broad compositional interrelations in the *Iliad* and accordingly to speak at least of the predominance of a single powerful poetic genius.[37] Such

37. See Wolfgang Schadewaldt, *Iliasstudien* (Studies on the *Iliad*), Abhandlungen der sächsischen Akademie der Wissenschaften, philologische-historische Klasse, 1938; Renata von Scheliha, *Patroklos* (Basel, 1943).

investigations might strike us in some ways as forced, artificial, or too pedantic. But much about them is convincing and deserves to become a permanent part of the body of Homeric scholarship. Despite this, however, we will never be able, as Homer lovers would like, to see the *Iliad* as one *organic* whole. This, basically, is the core of the controversy. And in the name of Goethe the layman still protests against Wolf. Goethe was disconcerted by the results of Wolf's investigations because he could not conceive of a poetic creation as other than an organic whole. But if we take this concept seriously—as seriously as Goethe himself took it—then we must say: An organism is a construct in which every single part is simultaneously end and means,[38] that is to say, at once independent and functional, valuable in itself and at the same time related to the whole. Unmistakably, Goethe's *Hermann und Dorothea* is such an organism, but not the *Odyssey* and the *Iliad*. One cannot cut big pieces out of an organism without endangering the life of the whole. But the *Iliad* could be reduced to a half, to even a third of its length and no one who was not familiar with the remainder would miss it. This is only possible because even on a large scale the independence of the parts is maintained. It can be explained any number of ways, as the accumulation of individual songs handed down from generation to generation, or as the result of the special situation of the rhapsodist, who had to perform a piece of moderate length daily. Finsler is probably correct with his cautious explanation: "Even if a single poet had created the *Iliad*, the main thrust of poetic activity in the work would be on the single parts and not on the cohesion of the whole."[39]

The *main thrust* of poetic activity: This does not exclude the possibility that the poet—or *a* poet who appeared at some point and brought together epic material—let himself be guided by certain compositional considerations or that he was intent on creating and attempting to create a well-calculated effect of suspense up until the time of Hector's death.[40] From our standpoint this would mean that here the latecomer Homer is already overstepping the boundaries of the epic and preparing a poetic creation that will find its fulfillment in the drama. Yet Homer only paves the way. He never completely overcomes the self-sufficiency of each individual part. Even in the most "modern" songs of the *Iliad* there remain myriads of verses, scenes, deeds, and events

---

38. Immanual Kant, *Kritik der Urteilskraft*, Inselausgabe (Leipzig, 1924), 260ff.; in English: *The Critique of Judgement*, trans. James Creed Meredith (Oxford, 1952), 24.

39. Finsler, *Homer*, 1:315.

40. See in this connection Ernst Howald, *Der Dichter der "Ilias"* (The Poet of the *Iliad*) (Zurich, 1946).

that, as regards the whole, are expendable and in a strict compositional sense would have to be considered flaws. For this reason the person who focuses his attention primarily on the broad picture and begins to make connections between widely divergent scenes misses the heart of Homer's poetic activity entirely and makes it clear that epic poetry's naïve simplicity does not satisfy him.

The principle of composition most truly epic in character is that of simple addition. On a small as well as on a large scale epic brings independent elements together. The process of addition goes on continually. It would come to an end only if one were to succeed in pacing off the entire world and presenting absolutely everything, everywhere that is or has been. The boredom that threatens to ensue (which Herder, for instance, admitted experiencing with all epics) can definitely be alleviated by the epic poet through the use of special devices: He can surpass his work's earlier parts by its later ones, thus continually captivating his listeners' attention. The dramatist does not attempt to surpass earlier scenes by later ones. Nor does he captivate; rather, he creates tension. The impatience generated by the dramatic genre arises from the audience's knowledge that the earlier parts are lacking something, that they still need to be completed in order to make sense or to be understandable. This completion is the end upon which everything in the drama depends. The process of surpassing in the epic is very different. Here a single element is presented as an independent piece. So that interest does not flag, the next piece must be richer, more frightening, or more lovely—as is the case, to cite a brief example, in the sixteenth song of the *Iliad*, where Homer, in the rush of his narrative, pleads, sighing, to the Muses and heightens the struggle more and more until finally fire sweeps the ships:

> Thus, then, the two of them earnestly spoke, conversing
>   together.
> Aias no longer held firm for the volleys too closely beset
>   him.
> He was held back by Zeus' sacred will and the valiant
>   Trojans
> Hurling their spears; and around both his temples his
>   shimmering helmet
> Echoed the horrible din of the spearheads; for his embossed
> Armor was constantly hit; and his shoulder, the left one,
>   grew stiff
> Due to the weight of his shield which he kept in continuous
>   motion.

Still no one could beat him, though he was surrounded by
  death-bringing weapons.
Yet he was breathing quickly and hard, and the sweat was
  pouring
Down the whole length of his body and nowhere could he
  find respite
Since on all sides he encountered horror heaped upon
  horror.
Muses, o tell me now, you who inhabit Olympian heights,
How was fire first cast at the ships of the people of Danai.
Hector, hurling himself on the ash-wood spear of Aias,
Wielded his mighty sword, and close to the ring made of
  metal,
Severed the spear completely. Telemonian Aias
Twisted the shattered spearshaft around in his hand, but in
  vain
Since his spear was wrenched from him and fell with great
  din to the ground.
Aias realized, awestruck now in his most noble heart, that
Godly dominion was thwarting any endeavor at battle,
That to the Trojans high-thundering Zeus was bestowing all
  triumphs;
And he escaped the volley. Then flaming firebrands were
Hurled at the ships and suddenly all was a raging inferno.

                                                    (101–23)

This art can of course only fully develop on a large scale. The slaying
of the suitors in the *Odyssey* is a masterpiece. No one realizes how
dangerous such a topic is, how wearisome it could be, if one suitor
after the other were felled. But the poem increases the tension and
captures the listeners' interest by surpassing and contrasting. The
technique of contrasting, too, must be recognized as an excellent
artistic device of the epic. Like the device of surpassing what has gone
before, it is determined not by what is to come, but from behind, by
what has already been presented. Thus, in his capacity as an artist,
the epic poet prefers to look back. The goal toward which an action
as such must necessarily strive, however, has little effect on the way
he progresses, on his tempo, on his compositional arrangements. It is
simply a pretext for moving ahead, as when someone wants to enjoy
a walk in the open and thus takes the path to the hill or to the next
village.

V

In referring to the "parts," we were thinking of the beginning, the middle, and the end, of the songs, and of single verses of the epic poem. But their independence is only possible and meaningful when the segments that present life are also independent. It is precisely here that Homer's singular power can be found.

In his *Aesthetics* Hegel explains that Alexander's campaign could not really be considered an epic topic, because the army does not maintain any degree of independence from its leader; rather, it is blindly subservient to him, as to a despot. How totally different is Agamemnon's position in the *Iliad!* He is, to be sure, the commander in chief, but more in the sense of being primus inter pares. Heaven help him, should he take it upon himself to insist on his leadership. For then he would be told that he is not to command, that people have followed him of their own free will. They are under no obligation. Any one of them can leave as soon as he feels like it. The relationship of the God-father Zeus to the other gods is similar. In a powerful speech at the beginning of the eighth song he boasts of being able to wrench the sea, the earth, and all the gods who want to cling to them up into the skies: "I, the all-powerful, thus do surpass all gods and all mortals."

But, in these lines an older myth seems to have been preserved, traces of an awesome world about which Homer otherwise knows nothing. For the rest, the circumstances of Zeus's power are by no means so positive.To be sure, it is stated repeatedly that all decisions are in his hands. However, Hera, Ares, Athena, and Poseidon often hold opinions different from his; they complain when Zeus issues orders and they even have the audacity to get around his will with cunning and treachery. Then Zeus has to resort to cunning, too, or to thunderous threats, like Agamemnon in the war council. This spectacle is painful for Zeus. But it is precisely because he is not omnipotent that all the gods and heroes stand out so wonderfully. They are not just seen in relation to Zeus. Each has his or her own particular desires and concerns. Each is a freely developed individual.

In the same way, man retains his independence in relation to the gods. In antiquity it was already said of Homer that his heroes were puppets in the hands of the gods. But the attentive reader soon realizes that such criticism is not valid. To be sure, it is often stated that a god has inspired a man, has confused his thought, or guided him toward the good. But this does not exclude man's freedom of action. He can follow the will of the gods or rebel against it. He himself bears the responsibility for what he does and is completely aware of this fact. This is true even outside the human sphere. Even the animals are independent. The horses weep for Patroclus, and Zeus honors them with a reply. In a powerful climax to this event, Homer feels compelled to bestow the gift of speech on the horses, and even if this is an isolated case it still fits very naturally into his world. Each thing strives for its own individual existence. The lance trembles with the desire to hit the flank of the enemy. The arrows of Odysseus whirl their vengeance.

Where the particular stands out like this, the general remains dull. As Hegel expressed it: Epic poetry falls into that middle period "in which a people is awakening from torpor . . . but everything that later becomes fixed religious dogma or civil or moral law is still a living attitude inseparable from the individual as such."[41]

A comparison of these lines with recent conditions sheds the clearest light on Hegel's meaning. Modern man is a member of a church, of a nation. He works at a particular job and thus participates in economic life. He belongs to interest groups. More than he realizes, his life dissolves in functions—political, economic, moral, and social functions, in general domains he is forced to adjust to. The Homeric hero knows none of this. He lives and acts out of his own strength. His small country, by our standards an estate, can sustain him. His actions are not governed by any regulations because there are none. He finds his motivation in his "general attitude," which his particular nature and heritage have developed. Thus he creates a world for himself—no different essentially from each individual epic line. The event that brings the heroes to Troy is very significant. The son of the Trojan king has robbed Menelaus of his wife. The audacious crime is to be avenged and Helen brought home. But no one will believe that this is the reason why Achilles, and Ajax, join the fight. They go along because their sense of honor demands it and because they are lured by their lust for battle. Agamemnon and Menelaus are told often enough that their personal family concerns are basically of no interest to the others. We see that this relationship between men corresponds to the one between the individual episodes and the total design of the *Iliad* and the *Odyssey*. Just as the total design exists to provide space for the individual episodes, so the cause of the war is there so that the individual can show himself off. Nothing is more foreign to the Homeric hero than an ideological war. There is no relation of the

---

41. Hegel, *Sämtliche Werke*, 14:333; in English: *Aesthetics*, trans. T. M. Knox.

individual to a fixed obligation, there is no moral or political consideration. This does not mean that a Homeric hero cannot accomplish any good. But even then he is acting not out of any consideration for any eternal moral law but rather because he now wants to perform a good deed. It is not *the* good, it is *a* good, the kindness of Achilles, the bravery of Hector, not kindness and bravery in and of themselves, in which each individual should, in the Platonic sense, participate. The moral purpose remains united with the personal temperament of each individual.

In such a world the poet sees humankind differently than we do. We, the modern readers, approach each character with a preconceived notion. This consists in the fact that we judge each character in accordance with fixed ideas and values. We judge them according to one standard of measurement; only what falls into the sphere of this standard interests us, just as only what has a bearing on the misdeed of the accused interests a court of law. Nobody asks whether the thief is musical or whether he loves landscape. The epic writer has no such preconceived notions. Therefore humanity appears to him in the most abundant variety. Achilles, aroused by his fury, later playing the lute, the friend of Patroclus, the inhuman foe of Hector, acting with kindness in the final song: One trait after the other appears, as occasion demands, unhindered by the concept of the totality of the character, of the need to draw a balance. Later it is of course possible to bring together into a whole the many traits of Achilles. But to do so would be as difficult as tackling multifaceted life itself. Homer lends no assistance to such an endeavor; he shows what is visible at a given moment. The total picture does not concern him.

We suddenly gain insight into these things when we consider that the Homeric world does not know the written word. Homer seems to have been able to write but he views writing as something modern and hardly realizes its great significance. Because he describes ancient times, he avoids any mention of writing—a fact we obviously cannot rate highly enough. For the written word is, so to speak, the locus of enduring validity, of a validity divorced from the individual person. The tablets of the law in the Old Testament are set up and now stand, immovable, regardless of who comes and goes. There the written word preserves something universal that encompasses the entire people; it renders each individual member dependent. The autocracy of the individual, characteristic of the epic, is over. The same is true of any contract made in writing. The other party to the contract leaves us with something tangible: Through his signature he has given up his boundless freedom to change at any given moment. It is no longer completely possible for him to be one way now and another way later. In writing, an earlier element of his existence is related to a later one.

Of course even in the world of Homer there are some sanctions, for instance the oath. But the tremendous solemnity surrounding the oath proves how little it is trusted and how difficult it is to bind people to their promises and get them to be consistent in their behavior, to bring them to align the future days of their lives with this most significant hour.

The written word keeps us from forgetting in a way that goes beyond the epic way of remembering. When I take part in a consultation, I write down the main points so that finally, when I have to make a decision, I will be able to compare and check everything. As astounding as the memories of men who did not yet write may have been, only the written word allows us to bring together a multitude of things and to view what is widely ramified as a whole. It becomes an instrument of thought, of a synthetic act for which epic parataxis can only be considered the material. The total composition of the *Odyssey* and the *Iliad* does presuppose the written word. But because it does not yet permeate everything, because isolated elements again and again elude the prescribed framework, we recognize that the written word at this time is still at the beginning of its effectiveness and that the Homeric epics cannot deny their origins in oral tradition. The playful reference to Homer's little nap—*quandoque bonus dormitat Homerus*—can be appended here as ancient proof of the forgetfulness of one as yet unaccustomed to the written word.

Finally, it should be noted that it is not until the advent of the written word that an all-encompassing view of human existence becomes possible. Which of us has not read old diary notes with amazement? In this amazement we can still sense the new dimension of recognition that the written word allows man: This is the way I was before, this is the way I am now; how shall I be in ten years? Only the written word can give us such insight reliably. Where it is lacking we imperceptibly modify our earlier years and transform the past as we ourselves have been transformed. In such a case we make our past selves into what we now are; or else we no longer understand the past and we hear tell about ourselves as if about a stranger, strangely irritated that this stranger is supposed to be ourselves.

Homer knows nothing about development. In his work the later years of a person's life do not evolve from the earlier ones; they are simply added on. And because he neither thinks ahead nor looks back, the maturing process, or even just the process of aging, escapes him. In the *Iliad* this is not too noticeable because the action only covers fifty-one days. But Odysseus is always the man in his middle years, both when he comes to Troy, and during the campaign, which lasts ten years, and then during the home voyage, which again takes up a whole decade. The same is true for Penelope. After twenty years she still appears as the same mature, sought-after woman she was when Odysseus left her, and after his return she looks forward to long years of happy marriage.

Herein lies an essential difference between the epic and the novel, which, coming after its precursors of late antiquity, appears as a Christian convention and shows man developing within a given time frame in an essential way.

Thus, it is true in every respect: Epic man lives for each day. He enjoys the day with its light and does not look ahead anxiously— either to the end of his days or to a future closer at hand. Nonetheless, is there not still some measure of looking ahead here? Are there not oracles and seers, Calchas among the Greeks, Helenus among the Trojans, and Teiresias, whom Odysseus meets in the depths of Hades? Certainly! And they are consulted at length. But—this is the astonishing thing—despite great reverence for the gift of the seer, despite childlike curiosity about his pronouncements, these are still not taken seriously. In the Greek tragedies, entire destinies are determined by oracle, whether the hero, like Orestes, acts according to the divine decree or whether, like King Oedipus, he rebels against it, and tries to escape what has been decreed. His actions remain bound to the future, the predictions of which by the oracle generate the tension of the drama. It has long been prophesied to the Greeks in the *Iliad* that Troy will fall after ten years. But they act as if they know nothing of this. They undertake storming the walls of Troy, an enterprise that for the time being at least can get them nowhere. They are disconsolate over a setback. And even the much-admired attitude of Hector, when he declares: "Once will arrive that day when will sink our sacred Ilios" and still fights on at his lost post, is probably nothing more than spontaneous epic thoughtlessness on the part of the poet. The fact that Menelaus (IV, 164) first utters these words and Hector, later, only repeats them devalues the statement when it comes from his lips. Moreover, when he attacks the ships, his jubilation over the coming victory is not shadowed by any knowledge of certain doom, however secret. Whoever claims that it is, is reading tragic elements into the heroes of Homer; he or she is viewing Hector as Shakespeare presented him in *Troilus and Cressida*, and not as the warrior of the *Iliad*.

The collective exegesis of millennia weighs heavily on the Homeric epic. No one today can escape it completely, however acute his historic sense has become since the days of Herder. In general one can say that the simplest, "least interesting" interpretation is the most correct and reveals a more luminous beauty than do the "most interesting" products of the interpreter's imagination.

Yet it is not only the men but also the gods who fail to take the future seriously, even though it lies clearly before them and though it is from them alone that the seers themselves derive their wisdom. The gods show the same excitement displayed by the warriors at the changing of fate; they show displeasure or triumph, even though the downfall of Troy is certain and in the eyes of these eternal beings could already be regarded as a reality. This leads to those scenes that so delight us, as modern readers, because we, being human, keep the whole in view, whereas the gods, like children, cannot see beyond the most immediate future:

> Hera the wife, the white-armed goddess, looked upon them
>   with pity;
> Quickly she turned to Athena and spoke to her these
>   winged words:
> "O woe, daughter of Zeus, the thunderer, do we not yet
> Want to rescue the doomed Danai before time runs out?
> Now they must perish, thus bringing their adverse fate to an
>   end
> Under the power of one man. He rages quite unendurably,
> Hector, Priam's son, he who has wrought so much evil."
> Whereupon Zeus' blue-eyed daughter Athena gave this
>   reply:
> "He would already by now have lost his courage and
>   strength,
> Killed at the hands of the Argives, killed in his own native
>   land;
> But my father is raging, evil intent in his heart,
> Cruel and always unfair and thwarting all my decisions.
> Never does he consider how often I in the past,
> Rescued his son whenever Eurytheus' tasks proved too
>   much.
> Patiently suffering, Heracles cried to the heavens and Zeus
> Quickly sent me down from heavenly heights to aid and
>   abet him.

> Had I been able to see this in searching the depths of my
>   heart
> When he sent Heracles down to the bolted fortress of Hades
> There to abduct from the realm of darkness the death god's
>   hound
> Never could he have escaped from the Stygian stream of
>   horror!
> Zeus now detests me; but he follows the counsel of Thetis,
> For she embraced his knee, then stroked his chin with her
>   hand,
> Pleading with Zeus to grant fame to the city-destroying
>   Achilles.
> Yet I know that in time he will call me his dear blue-eyed
>   daughter!"

(VIII, 350–73)

Only Zeus is somewhat more farsighted: His equanimity is harder to shake, he has reservations, he makes plans and weighs the destinies of men on a grander scale. For this reason, his farsightedness is always spoken of with the greatest respect. He is called εὐρύοπα, "far-sight." His thinking, not attained by any other god and certainly not by any man, is exemplary in precisely the sense that Zeus is what man, just now, in Homer, at the end of the epic culture, is trying to become—now that writing has become known and the epic parataxis has begun to conform to an albeit loosely structured order of the whole. For man always reveres as divine the spirit that is just beginning to awaken in him and will then shape his life. The highest god is the future of man, expressed in this case by the *ratio* of Zeus. It is a goal of the history of the Greek people to fulfill this *ratio* on a human level.

But even the farsightedness of Zeus is limited. Even he is not completely free from worry and fear about what is occurring on earth. For above him there reigns an even higher being, on whom he is always dependent—Moira, in whose darkness everything comes together. But in the epic world Moira is the *deus absconditus*—unfathomable, impenetrable, the mystery that remains beyond all cognitive and intuitive powers, fate, which no one has yet thought to interpret as providence, and whose plan no one has yet attempted to fathom.

VI

Lyric poetry is unhistorical, has no foundation and no consequences. It speaks only to those who can empathize; its effects are of a fortuitous nature and pass, as a mood passes.

Epic poetry, on the other hand, finds in history its precisely assigned place. Here, the poet is not alone. He stands in a circle of listeners and tells them his stories. The way he presents events to himself is the way he presents them to his audience. And when he wanders on and his stories spread through the land his audience broadens, eventually encompassing the entire people.

The situation in which poet and audience come to face one another does not occur as a mere chance encounter. Were someone to come and present the saga of Gilgamesh in Greek, before a Greek audience, people would hardly listen to him, or if they did it would be with considerable lack of interest and without lasting appreciation. The audience appreciates Homer because he presents things as they themselves are accustomed to seeing them. And they are accustomed to seeing them thus because their ancestors were shown such images by a poet. The relationship between poet and audience is thus based on a tradition that loses itself in the darkness of prehistory, but that can be understood broadly as the legacy of a poet[42] who perceives and captures the slumbering rhythm and the idiom of this people and who, in his poetic creation, shows the people the foundations on which they might stand. The seeds of the language continue to have an effect and finally everything is established the way the Greeks perceive it, taken up and strung together in endless parataxis:

> But what remains is bequeathed by the poets.
> [Was bleibet aber, stiften die Dichter.]

This line is nowhere so appropriate as in its application to epic poetry. For the epos represents the most ancient bequest of the poets, and no other poetic creation is possible until, in a more or less definite manner, a foundation is laid, until a people can unite itself by means of an epic vision and see things the way the poet, himself obligated to the people, represents them. This is what is meant by Herodotus' statement that Homer and Hesiod invented the gods for the Greeks. That which remains, which is bequeathed by the poets, is most clearly visible in the gods, who indeed are born but never die, and in whose realm everything that ebbs and flows becomes perceptible.

We do not know Homer's predecessors. For us he is the most

---

42. See Martin Heidegger, *Hölderlin und das Wesen der Dichtung* (Munich, 1936); in English: "Hölderlin and the Essence of Poetry," in *Existence and Being* (Chicago, 1949), 293–315.

ancient poet in any European language and he stands for all those whose traces are still visible in his epics. To the extent that tradition binds the people of Europe together Homer can be considered the father of Europe. And to this extent Homer is the only poet in whom the essence of the epic appears more or less in its pure form. After Homer pure epic is no longer possible for the simple reason that the *Iliad* and the *Odyssey* and the entire epic cycle are already known and they in turn become the material for a new type of creative activity. Just as man cannot become a child again, mankind cannot return to the level of the epic via an uninterrupted tradition and be content with mere statement after having once begun to relate and to subordinate constituent parts. This subordinating process is unavoidable when the limit of parataxis is reached, making further paratactic stringing together of statements no longer feasible. Certainly the invention of writing furthered the relating and subordinating process. The ease of overview it affords invites us to gain a new perspective on things. Thus, Homer represents both the end of the oral and of the epic world. Only those peoples who know nothing of him when they step into the light of history succeed in creating epic poetry after Homer. We are not concerned with them at this point since all historical material serves here merely to elucidate systematic patterns. Neither can we be concerned with why the epic nowhere achieved such heights as in Greece. We shall focus on epic's greatest poet, who alone deserves the name of "father," and we shall only touch upon some main chapters in the history of the epos, chapters that are related to Homer and can be used to clarify the essence of his poetry.

It is clear from the foregoing discussions that we can properly speak of a history of the epic only if we use the term epic to refer to poetic works that, according to an external criterion, that is, the manner of delivery, are considered epic, that is to say, tales of considerable length that are in verse. Epics in this sense appear in great numbers even after Homer. We will not consider anything that constitutes simple imitation of Homeric poetic creation. And we consider a work to be an imitation and not a continuation of the epic tradition as soon as the naïveté of the epic world is destroyed. The most obvious documentation of such destruction is contained in the criticism of Xenophanes, who, writing in hexameters toward the end of the sixth century, and hence himself still a captive of Homer's language, declaimed against the teachings of the gods and the morality of Homeric poetry. In his *Silli* we find:

> Homer and Hesiod blame on the gods everything that really
> is only man's shame and disgrace: stealing and adultery and
> cheating on each other.[43]

Here "good" and "evil" have already been divorced from individual
figures. They have become abstract concepts that are merely tacked
on to such individually appearing figures. The carefree independence
of the individual has thus been destroyed.

> If the oxen and horses and lions had hands or could paint with
> their hands and create works of art like man, then the horses
> would create horse-like and the oxen ox-like divinities.[44]

Here the relationship between god and man becomes a problem of
which Homer was not yet aware. How Xenophanes solves it is of no
importance: As soon as the problem is even hinted at both gods and
men become problematic and are no longer possible in epic poetry. It
is enough for the epic poet to know that something exists, where it
originates, and that he can name it in his work.

> If god is the most powerful of all, then he can only be one; for
> if there were two or three then he would not be the most
> powerful or the best of all.[45]

Here Xenophanes arrives at a conclusion that completely destroys
Olympus. Homer draws no conclusions, speaks assertively of the
most powerful god, and lets the other gods who limit his power exist
alongside him. Of course, Homer is not logically consistent here. And
where logic does prevail he can perhaps still be honored as an artist,
but the beautiful that he proclaims is no longer, as it was before, also
the true.

And so, without contradicting the truth but also without the force
that provides a foundation for history, epic poetry continues to blossom among the Greeks, and among the Romans, who, as early as
Ennius but especially in Virgil, are indebted to the Greeks.

---

43. Hermann Diels, *Fragmente der Vorsokratiker*, 5th ed., ed. Walther Kranz (Berlin,
1934), 21 B 11 (1, 132, 2); in English: Kathleen Freeman, *Ancilla to "The Pre-Socratic
Philosophers": A Complete Translation of the Fragments in the Diels "Fragmente der Vorsokratiker."*

44. Ibid., 21 B 15 (1, 132, 19); in English: ibid.

45. Ibid., 21 A 28 (1, 117); in English: ibid.

In the Christian realm a truly epic epos seems no longer possible. Here the requirement of "independence for each part" has in every sense been lifted. Man becomes the object of a plan of salvation. He finds himself weighted down with Adam's Fall and in anticipation of the Day of Judgment. His existence is directed toward a momentous future, toward a beyond in the face of which the visible world becomes a mere passageway and the corporeal a thin veil. The epic poet of this world is Dante. The transparency of the realms and figures of paradise, God's overwhelming magnetic power, which pulls all beings upward, clearly show the new orientation according to which all lingering on earth, all self-glorification can only be a sin. Of course there also exists in Dante's *Divine Comedy* a realm that is divorced from God, that remains apart from this sacred tension and thus comes close to mirroring epic existence. But this realm is Hell. The quarrel about whether Dante achieved his finest work in the "Inferno" or in the "Paradiso" continues to rage. Whoever shares Dante's viewpoint must give preference to the "Paradiso." But whoever measures by the epic standard will find the "Inferno" more compelling. For here everything stands out more visibly. The individual characters stand there firmly, inscrutably, in a corporeality that offers substance to the eye. But the very traits that please the observer schooled in Homer mean damnation in the context of Dante's poem. Whoever is completely self-contained and whose body becomes all-important is damned; damned also whoever finds his goal in every moment of his activity and not in that glorious end toward which God created man. A momentous situation! The epic world has become Hell because it does not participate in the new movement upward that begins with Christianity. The situation is similar with Milton and Klopstock. In their works too, Hell is most successfully portrayed according to the standard of epic art. And since Klopstock closely imitates Homer in the technical, there need be no hesitation about the appraisal of his work: Only the descriptions of the godless spheres are stylistically uniform.

It is the task of historical research to investigate the change the epos undergoes in the Christian era, how for instance in the *Nibelungenlied*, or with Ariosto and Tasso, the dramatic or lyric predominates. In contrast, we should also point to the animal epos, to *Reinke de vos*, which of all the newer epics is certainly the most epic in character. The animals are not torn between the Fall and the Last Judgment. They undergo no development. A fox is a fox and a badger is a badger, irrevocably fixed in their nature by God. They can therefore be fitted with stereotypical epithets. The animal exists from day to day. It has its own environment. Each animal is a world in itself and as such it can even hold its own against the monarchy of the lion. Thus, Reineke the fox is truly a new, cunning Odysseus. And we should not be surprised that Odysseus celebrates his resurrection in animal form. It is mankind that has changed. The animals have remained what they were from the beginning.

Next to animals, children and fools must be mentioned, such as Till Eulenspiegel and all the other rogues playing their pranks in other epic works. They accept as little responsibility for acting according to generally valid principles as do the Homeric heroes, who live and act according to their own lights. But the recognition that the comic aspect of the naïve borders thus on the epic should not confuse us. Even Homer, when we read him with our modern awareness, often makes us smile. He does not of course smile himself when the gods are quarreling or when Zeus explains that his fondness for the Trojans began with the wine and incense offered to him by Priam. But we smile because it releases us from considering more strenuous questions about God, and because everywhere the Homeric epic frees us from the concerns of modern culture and the stresses of the spirit.

In the classical era of German literature the epos flowers once again, fostered by Voss's Homer translation. Voss's *Luise*, Goethe's *Hermann und Dorothea*, Hebbel's *Mutter und Kind* (Mother and Child), the *Idylle vom Bodensee* (The Idyll of the Bodensee) by Mörike are in first place. The narrative technique is modeled after Homer in every detail. But the objects are new. The poets choose idyllic themes. Only in the idyll can they still maintain to a certain extent the independence of the individual segments of life. If they were to move away from the idyll into the wide field of modern history, of the great political institutions, then their Homeric techniques would be thwarted by these very objects. Where everything is connected with everything else by the most precise organization, the individual citizen with the state, the state with the law and public morality, morality and law with religion, nothing can be captured by means of paratactical presentation anymore. Only the most careful abstraction from everything that cluttered the day of a person living in the last century makes it possible for a neoclassical epic to come into being. And only the incomparable Goethe knew how to overcome or hide these fearsome difficulties.

But in spite of Goethe's wise decision to limit the framework of *Hermann und Dorothea* to the idyll, this work deviates from the style of the Homeric epic. Goethe himself once declared a constant though gentle movement forward and an absence of retarding motifs to be unepic in character. When Schiller, in his letter of 26 December 1779, refers to its "limited place of action," to its "limited number of characters," and to its "brief course of action," and in such concentration finds a tendency toward tragedy; when in addition he points to its "intimate involvements of the heart" and to its "pathological interest"—by which, according to our concepts, only lyric qualities can be meant, we see that *Hermann und Dorothea* is situated in a very special way between the genres and that it—and not only in the general sense that applies to any work of art as such—partakes of the lyric as well as of the epic and the dramatic. The same is also true of *Achilleis*, however, where Goethe again chooses a purposeful course of action and where the love of the hero for Polyxena would have constituted such a distinctly lyric episode that it would hardly have been possible to do justice to it in Homeric verse and with Homeric techniques. By contrast, *Iphigenie auf Tauris* (Iphigenia in Tauris) tends toward the epic, as Schiller points out in the same letter. And when we consider that in Goethe's poems, even in many of his *lieder*, the motif—that which can be represented—plays a significant role, when we consider further that even "Wanderers Nachtlied" (Wanderer's Night Song) and "An den Mond" (To the Moon) end with a summarizing conclusion, then we realize that nature participates to an outstanding degree in all three genre concepts. This can only mean that his poetic genius creates organically. According to Kant's definition in his *Critique of Judgement*, an organism is a construct whose parts are ends in themselves and at the same time means to ends. The independence of the parts corresponds to the genre principle of the epic, the functionalism of the parts to the genre principle of the dramatic, the individual modification of the organic type to the lyric, which is always fortuitous and individual. It would be good, in the future, to use the term organic in this unambiguous sense and not to bandy it about indiscriminately as a designation of aesthetic value.

Finally, we come in this context to Spitteler, the writer who proved that his strength lay in the epic mode, and who with *Olympischer Frühling* (Olympian Spring) created a voluminous epic, which should not be overlooked even though it fills us with a strange feeling of unease. In spite of all misgivings and doubts pertaining in particular to Spitteler's language, it cannot be denied that epic traits of a clarity and purity not otherwise found in any recent poetic endeavor are visible in his work. A brilliant, overwhelming flood of images confronts us there. Everything is visible, not only countless objects and divine beings but also that world we look upon as the inner, invisible one; deep inner stirrings, passions—everything takes on a corporeal form here. And each thing, down to the most innocuous, maintains its own individual being. Legends of origin, prehistories, the most detailed responses to the ancient epic question "From where?" surprise the reader and become expansive, without regard for the goal toward which the story as a whole is moving. The work consists of episodes that could be deleted or multiplied at will. Here, too, the main action seems to be but a pretext for bringing in as many single elements as possible. The writer has not, as he himself admits, found a conclusion for his tale. In Schiller's words, the end moves in its "dignity" very close to the beginning, which, again, does not interest us as an exposition leading somewhere, but rather in and of itself.

The unintentional or even unwanted resemblance to Homer—which, as is true of everything pertaining to the genres, cannot form the basis for a value judgment—is of particular importance here. Thus, we might speak of a number of inconsistencies, of topographical contradictions, for instance, that make it impossible to put together all statements about Olympus and the realm of men into a single whole. We are forced to read with a sort of naïve unconcern, although on the other hand Spitteler feigns profundity by means of allegorical allusions and in so doing mars the impression of the work's epic fullness.

A strange poetic phenomenon! Perhaps it will be easier to understand when we consider that it belongs to an epoch that is already beginning to distance itself from the Christian tradition, that is not only forfeiting the Christian plan of salvation but also losing all secularized tension toward the future, the idea of progress, and eschatology in the sense of the Kantian and Hegelian dialectic spirals. The question "For what purpose?" remains unanswered, especially with Spitteler, who, like Nietzsche, emphasizes the complete purposelessness of existence at every opportunity. Does this not imply the return of a genuine epic style? Of course, the world the poet lives in will not give up its modern character. Hence, the new epos can have nothing to do with this modern world. In the starkest contrast to Homer, Spitteler constructs a thought-up, dreamt-up world of beauty and invents myths that are not concerned with any group, let alone any nation. In these myths, however, he remains dependent on the names and characters of the Greek gods, a fact that throws into the sharpest relief the utter impossibility of a truly epic work in our time.

It remains for future scholarship to enlarge properly upon these historic indications. Here they merely serve to elucidate Homer and to make clear that epic writing in the Homeric sense can never again be. Of course, the epic itself remains "stored up" in all poetic creation as an indispensable foundation. Even the lyric poet can only find words because the epic poet has spoken them before him (cf. page 179). And the dramatic in particular is built upon the firm foundation of the epic.

Dramatic Style: Tension

Teachers of poetics usually derive the nature of the dramatic style from the nature of the stage, and they hope to be able to advise and be of some benefit to the poet in the area of drama, especially since the theory of the epic and even more of the lyric promise little in the way of such practical application. Now, there is no doubt that every poet who plans to write a piece for the stage must acquire an exact knowledge of the possibilities of the stage and that the advice of those with experience can considerably shorten the path to his goal. However, the stage lends itself to greatly differing poetic modes. A modern social drama which is completely taken up by the dialogue is no less suited to the stage than a baroque magic opera [*Zauberoper*] in which the spoken word plays a subordinate part; a patriotic pageant with living tableaux unfolds in a space similar to that by a tragedy of Sophocles. Yet, no one would dare to call all this indiscriminately "dramatic" although its suitability for the stage cannot be doubted. On the other hand, there is a dramatic poetry of the highest order that is neither suited to nor even meant for the stage, for example, the novellas and also some of the dramas of Heinrich von Kleist, in which the action does not achieve the necessary visibleness. Hence, "suitability for the stage" and "dramatic" do not mean the same thing. Yet we would be going against all traditional terminology if we were to deny the very close connection between the two concepts. Might it be possible to discover this connection, not by deriving our understanding of the dramatic from the nature of the stage, but rather the reverse, by deriving the historical institution of the stage from the nature of the dramatic style? A phenomenological study permits only this interpretation. The spirit of dramatic writing gave birth to the stage as the only suitable instrument for a new poetry. But this instrument once it exists is also available for carrying out other poetic intentions, too, and in the course of the centuries has been used in many different ways. This will become clearer in what follows. Here, the foregoing statements merely serve to explain why the present discussion does not begin with the stage, but, though it stays in close touch with the drama, turns immediately to consider two types of the tension-creating style, types that are also possible and justified outside the realm of the stage, namely pathos and the problematic.

I

The language of pathos could easily be confused with lyric language. Like the person in a lyric mood, the person moved by pathos at times also stands all alone and expresses his or her emotions in spontaneous, often merely stammered utterances. Not infrequently in the drama the regular verse of the dialogue changes at the height of pathos into more complicated constructions that can hardly be distinguished externally from lyric stanzas, as in Sophocles' *commoi* [the lamentations recited by actors and chorus together—TRANS.] or in several monologues of Corneille. And as the lyric poet is able to dissolve the sentence into fragments, or even into single words, the poet of pathos is frequently able to destroy grammatical constructions and to jump as it were from one peak to the next in speaking.

> O, it broke over me, that day,
> More threatening than all of them to me!
> Night! Of unspeakable orgies
> And terrible sorrow!
> > (Sophocles, *Electra*, 201–4)

> Father, mistress, honor, love
> Noble and hard constraint, beloved tyranny . . .
> > (Corneille, *Cid*, I, 3)

"The girl is mine! I was once her god, now her demon! Wound for an eternity with her on a wheel of damnation—eye rooted in eye—hair standing on end against hair—our hollow whim-

> pering blending in one—and now I must repeat my tender
> words, and now chant for her the oaths she took—God! God!"
> (Schiller, *Kabale und Liebe* [Intrigue and Love], IV, 4)

Pathos has hence not infrequently been regarded as belonging to
the lyric genre. This can be justified from another standpoint as well,
since pathos and lyric poetry, as in the ode, readily blend into each
other and constitute a new unity held together by a particular tension.[46] However, now that we have worked out the idea of the lyric
as clearly as possible in a very definite sense, we are compelled to
recognize pathos as a separate genre. If the order of the whole makes
sense then this compulsion can only be welcomed as conducive to
clear concepts.

We shall begin by coming to grips with the terminology. Πάθος
is translated in the dictionaries by "experience, misfortune, sorrow,
passion," but also by many other expressions. Cicero[47] feels that,
strictly speaking, he should translate it as "morbus" [disease], but he
prefers the more appropriate expression "perturbatio" [disorder]. This
does not get us very far. We can of course see that a misfortune in the
drama can produce scenes of pathos and that passion is often expressed in pathos-laden words and gestures. But the great passion of
Goethe's Tasso is not characterized by pathos, and a misfortune like
the one befalling Hauptmann's Fuhrmann Henschel derives its effectiveness precisely from a quietude devoid of pathos.*

Aristotle, we believe, provides us with better information. In the
Nicomachean Ethics (B 4) the human soul is divided into πάθη, δυνάμεις,
and ἕξεις. Πάθη designates the "passions" in the most general sense
of the word. Man is moved by passions. Thus, in his *Rhetoric* (C 7),
Aristotle demands of a good speech that it be factual, suited to the
circumstances, and furthermore that it contain "pathos," that is to
say, it must affect man's passions and thus move him. The possibility
of empty pathos is also mentioned: "The listeners share the pathos
[συνομοιοπαθεῖν] of the pathos-inspired speaker, even when he says
nothing. Therefore many overwhelm their audience with mere noise."

It now becomes clear to us that our modern expression differs from
the Greek. By pathos we mean not so much passion itself as the

46. See Emil Staiger, *Meisterwerke deutscher Sprache* (Masterworks of the German
Language) (Zurich, 1943), 23–24.

47. Cicero, De finibus bonorum et malorum 3, 10.

* Since in modern-day usage the adjective "pathetic" is so far removed in its meaning
from the noun "pathos," we have translated the German adjective *pathetisch* using
circumscriptions with the noun "pathos."

pathos-filled speech that excites passions, πάθη. But we cannot be satisfied with this explanation either. Pathos-filled speech that moves us seems to bring us closer than ever to the lyric language that moves us. We can expect no further information from the Greeks on this subject. Everything that moves us, that throws us off-balance is, for them, "patho"-logical in the same way. They have no reason to distinguish between lyric poetry and pathos. But for us the question boils down to this: What is the distinction between the movement of pathos and that of the lyric?

The lyric, as has been stated, has a mellowing effect (page 87). We have already spoken about lyric mellowness, about its molten quality that is poured into us as a liquid substance, dissolving all that is solid and carrying us along in its flow. This effect goes unnoticed; it is internal. It presupposes the consent of someone in the same inner state. Where this consent is lacking it passes and comes to naught.

Pathos is not as discreet in its effect. It presupposes resistance, open enmity, or inertia, and it attempts more emphatically to destroy them. From this very different situation all its stylistic characteristics are comprehensible. Pathos is not poured into the listener, rather it is impressed upon or hammered into him. Its sentence structure does not dissolve, dreamlike, as in lyric poetry. Rather, the entire course of its utterance is concentrated in single words, as in the παρακοπά, παραφορά, φρενοπλανής of Aeschylus' *Eumenides* and also in Don Diego's monologue in the *Cid*, where a more modern spelling makes it possible, by exclamation marks, to assert the completely unlyric sense of the words:

> O rage! O despair! O hostile senility!
> (I, 4)

Similarly, repetition here does not mean absorbed listening to a single enchanting sound. The all-important word, which is to shatter the soul of the listener, is hurled out again and again with the greatest emotional exertion:

> Rome, the sole object of my resentment!
> Rome, to whom your arm will immolate my lover!
> Rome, who witnessed your birth and whom your heart adores!
> Rome, finally, whom I hate because she does you honor!
> (Corneille, *Horace*, VI, 5)

Finally, even a more complicated rhythm introduced at the height of pathos fails to create a mood. Like a thunderstorm the rhythm purifies the atmosphere by means of the strongest outbursts. Gryphius, who hardly ever succeeded in creating a fully lyric tone, sometimes accomplishes great things in this area, as in the monologue of despair held by the empress Julia in *Papinian*:

> Gods! Look at this!
> You see and can sit by silently?
> Is there no bolt that can strike?
> Do you merely arm yourselves in vain with the thunder-
>   heavy lightning bolts
> Or do you carry your arrows to the virtuous oaks?
> Or does the cry of murder not reach your ears?
>   O woe!
>   O alas!
>   Sacred Themis! Vengeance! O vengeance!
>   Sacred Themis, if you are not
>   Deaf and blind in the presence of crowned heads
>   If someone still utters the judgment;
>   If punishments still exist;
>   Hurl lightning! Devastate! Destroy! Burn!
>   Rage! Ruin! Ravage! Put asunder!
> Tear down all foundations upon which the murderer builds!
> Shatter what protects him! Destroy all he trusts!
>
>   (II, 311ff.)

No one can fail to recognize how purposeful the music of these verses is. There is perhaps hardly a reader capable of reproducing it fluently at first reading. He or she must see whether a line begins with or without a stressed syllable and must consciously make the transition from the trochees to the dactyls, from the dactyls to the iambs. This means that the poet is exerting force on the reader; and this exertion of force is intentional.

Thus the language of pathos—again in contrast to lyric language—presupposes an opposite. But unlike epic language, the language of pathos does not acknowledge this opposite; rather, it seeks to eliminate it, whether it is a case of the speaker's winning the listener over or the listener's being overwhelmed by the force of the speaker. As an example, let us cite Stauffacher's speech on the Rütli, from Schiller's *Wilhelm Tell*. His words incite "a great stirring among his countrymen," and finally all, aroused to the intensity of enthusiasm emanating from the speaker, strike their swords and repeat his last words: "We stand for our country, our children." A more perfect συνομοιοπαθεῖν could not occur anywhere!

Even when a single person, without addressing himself to anyone in particular, expresses himself with pathos—for example, the tragic hero in a monologue or the poet himself speaking in his own persona, like Gryphius or Schiller in their contemplative lyric—even in such instances the presence of the poet's vis-à-vis is still taken for granted, not only in the sense that such verses, too, require recitation before an audience, but also, and more important, in the sense that here the speaker addresses himself, and with a heightened power of expression he curses and cajoles the baseness of his existence.

The language of pathos coerces the listener, whoever he or she is. But when the pathos is genuine the speaker, too, experiences its force. I do not mean some perilous situation in which the speaker perhaps finds himself at the moment, not the danger to his homeland that oppresses Stauffacher, not the death of a son that overwhelms Julia in *Papinian*. Pathos need not necessarily arise from such afflictions. They could also affect people with melancholy. Furthermore, there is not only a pathos of pain but also a pathos of joy, like that of Fiesco gazing with intoxication on Genoa, or of Electra taking her revenge. The force that Stauffacher experiences as a speaker giving voice to pathos and that conveys itself to the gathering is freedom. The force Julia experiences is justice. And the force that inspires Fiesco to his speech of pathos is power.

It could seem strange that concepts used in this highly concrete sense are designed as forces. Love, hunger for power—to designate these in this way would be acceptable. But freedom, justice, and truth? We are more inclined to believe that these are thoughts that humans grasp rationally and can then espouse with passion. We think of force as something that must be added to thought from the realm of a human will. But there is no such thing as will, as an ability that exists without a goal at first, but that later can be directed. Will is itself the force of that which is to be realized. Only for this reason can it be effective even before the goal has been reached. It is possible that in the beginning only one thing is clear: That which exists is not to be. Instead, it ought to be different. But what should be different? For the present this remains uncertain. Only later is the goal recognized and a clearly outlined ideal set up in opposition to things as they are.

Thus, we can see that a great concept can inspire pathos. But pathos does not depend on the mediation of the concept. It is an unmediated movement which even in its origin and direction does not need to understand itself. In contrast to the lyric movement, however, it does have both an origin and a goal. Hence, we must put the matter this way: The man of pathos is moved by things as they should be and his movement is directed against things as they are.

It is neither possible nor is it necessary to examine all great scenes of pathos in this light. The pathos of the political speech fits here perfectly. The pathos of pain seems powerless. But what does belong here is the recognition of immense suffering on the part of the hero himself and all those surrounding him, of the height of consciousness that must grasp this suffering. Otherwise, what meaning could the impatience in the pathos of Antigone or the screams of Philoctetes have? The pretension to pathos is personified in the princes of baroque tragedies. They diminish the stature of those surrounding them and point beyond themselves to the divine origin of their power.

Things as they are always remain behind things that move in pathos. Or, viewed from the other side, pathos is elevated. Its elevation seems its essential characteristic. We therefore speak of "high" pathos. But though we can interchange the concepts "high" and "low" when, for instance, we say that something is beyond us when it is too deep, we can never speak of deep pathos. And the expression "low pathos" would be totally inappropriate. Instead, when we wish to speak critically of a speech characterized by pathos we say it is stilted. And with this term we are pointing to an illegitimate claim to elevation. Yet in dealing with pathos we can never get away from the concept of elevation.

Thus, the poet finds it to his advantage to elevate his characters socially, too. But this is not absolutely necessary. The laborer and the peasant would, for instance, in a drama about revolution, be capable of pathos. "Elevation" only means "to be ahead." Elevation, as yet empty and unlimited, constitutes the model for the space of the future, as the firm ground on which we stand constitutes that of the past. From this standpoint, the sharp criticism of pathos for being empty is in a certain sense justified. To the extent that its movement originates from what does not yet exist, pathos will always appear empty, especially in comparison to the lyric mood which is always replete.

But what does not yet exist shall come to exist. And it is toward this goal that the inspiring rhythm, vitalized by the tension between the present and the future aims. Towards this end, too, move the beats, shattering as inescapable demands, and the pauses in which the emptiness of that which does not yet exist is revealed so to speak as a vacuum. And into this vacuum, everything that exists at present, all lower being, is absorbed. Even the grammatical ellipses acquire their most precise meaning in this context. "Woe!" means Woe is! "O that day!" in Electra's cry of despair means: O that day was! "I shall be wound with her for an eternity on a wheel of damnation": This is what Ferdinand in Schiller's *Kabale und Liebe* (Intrigue and Love) wants to say when he envisages his fate and that of his beloved. What is missing grammatically, a form of the verb "to be," is intended in all pathos. It denotes truth viewed in the context of consciousness or of reality that, at the time of speaking, has not yet been achieved.

In addition to the spoken word, gesture also belongs to the expression of pathos. We are familiar with the gesture of arms outstretched to the sky, a gesture that points beyond man on earth toward heaven, affirming its existence as the visible place of origin of the movement—Stauffacher expresses the meaning of this gesture:

> When the burden becomes unbearable—he reaches up
> Confidently to the sky
> And summons down his eternal rights. . . .

So does Antigone, calling upon divine law. Medea does the same, as does Hecuba, who, racked with pain, stretches out her arms and wrings her hands seeking to summon down something: what, she does not know; she cannot find it. She cannot yet grasp what is to be. And yet she is moved by the power of what *must* occur, of what *must* transpire here below from out of the realm of the possible up above. Hence, this gesture resembles that of imploring prayer. Other gestures of pathos can be directed toward the listeners: the hand that describes a horizontal, demonstrative arch away from the speaker's breast, making room for the intention, the fingers, the closed fists, which seize the concept like an object and break in with it on the existing world.

But whoever speaks and acts in such a manner cannot remain among the listeners as a mere storyteller. He must be separated and differentiated from them in some way, must stand on an elevated or otherwise specially marked platform, must wear cothurn and mask, or move the mass of the audience from a stage. A stage in any form, even if only in the form of a speaker's dais, is inevitably required by the style of pathos. The first person who ever jumped onto a stone or a rise in order to address a few people to demonstrate that he was ahead of them is the person who invented the stage. When the speaker starts speaking, the ramp, platform, or whatever it might be does not give rise to the illusion that unity exists between him and his audience. It clearly shows what remains to be achieved and how high the sluggish listener must yet be elevated; it activates the force of pathos.

When modern dramatists want to do away with the conventional stage, then it simply means that they lack the necessary feeling for the language of pathos, that they expect something else of the theater, perhaps even lyric effects or epic pageants. Stageable plays can originate in the lyric and epic modes. Some things are possible in these modes that cannot be accomplished in the writing of pathos: fineness of psychological detail, for instance, in miming, in the voice; subtle allusions in the dialogue. Some of these effects can be lost on the stage, depending on the degree to which stage and audience are set apart. Goethe's *Torquato Tasso* and Ibsen's dramas are only possible on a smaller stage. Even though the stage remains in such cases, albeit only as a narrow demarcation between audience and drama, its stylistic value is changed. It separates the world of artistic illusion from that of reality, and for precisely this reason it must not be effaced. By contrast, the actor of pathos wants to efface the separation caused by the stage. The more it is permitted to fulfill its function of separating, and the greater the area of the profane, of the audience, becomes, the greater is the actor's triumph. He has nothing to lose. For the hero of pathos is not at all differentiated psychologically. The single emotion of pathos rules him completely. Pain, faith, hunger for power appear in grandiose unequivocalness and consume everything else that the soul could harbor. Pathos devours individuality. The person swept away by this emotion does not realize the particularity of his or her existence. Stauffacher on the Rütli leaves the good citizen of Steinen who is bemoaning his fate far behind. Polyeucte is not concerned with his house or his private existence and knows only one goal: to go to his death as a witness to the Christian faith. Sophocles unmistakably places a figure of pathos next to one who is emotionally unaffected: Ismene and Chrysothemis ponder their origins, their family, their vulnerability. In contrast, Electra and Antigone drive ruthlessly and single-mindedly toward their goal.

One might deem this improbable and feel the absence of the ever problematic, ambivalent depths of man. Yet we are not concerned with reality here, but rather with what is yet to be. If what is yet to be lays any claim to transforming things as they are, then it and all that is in its service will have to appear improbable—within limits, of course, limits within which the human potential can still be intuited. To the audience, to the other characters of the drama, even to themselves the heroes of pathos seem improbable. Antigone in her suffering does not compare herself to other young women of Thebes, but to Niobe, who in her sorrow turned to stone on the heights of Cipylos. Lessing's Marwood declares herself to be "a new Medea." Only the simple, great mythical figures of the παθη do justice to the height of their awareness.

The hero of pathos is absolute. The object world, his surroundings, his milieu, the general atmosphere do not concern him. They do not exist for him at all, thus they do not for the poet either. In the tragedy of antiquity and in the drama of French classicism there are no stage directions. There are of course historical reasons for this, but we can dispense with them in a purely aesthetic study. Only the blue sky above the scene or the splendid architecture are appropriate to the style of a Sophocles or a Corneille. Only in such unlimited spaces could the poet dare to reach out to those great yet simple events at the sight of which an entire people or an entire society has been lifted above itself.

Here pathos demonstrates its driving force. It achieves, in Schiller's words, a mighty "precipitation." Many an ancient tragedy could almost do without action and still precipitate irresistibly. In *Electra*, for instance, the single deed occurs at the very end. But Electra and Orestes are so moved by what is to be, and Clytemnestra fears it so, that the magnetic power of the conclusion is overwhelming. In *The Persians* the only action is the news of the defeat at Salamis. But the dread of the message and, when it does arrive, the effort of grasping its horror and of reaching the extreme of suffering—a Persian suffering, which to the audience is reason for the greatest jubilation—all this diminishes the present at every moment to such a degree and moves forward so relentlessly that this work in its degree of tension far surpasses any modern drama of intrigue. Then, when the depths of suffering have been plumbed, the Greek tragedians undoubtedly say "Ἅλις, ἀποπαύεσθε," "Cease, it is enough." The void of pathos has been filled. Nothing is lacking. The dramatist as well as his characters have reached their goal.

II

Through a study of pathos we thought we had found a way to an understanding of the stage. However, only certain possibilities of the stage became visible. There is, for example, also a tension-filled poetry that is devoid of pathos. The first examples we shall look at have nothing to do with the theater. However, after a rather long detour, a second access to the stage will open. I shall begin with an insignificant little verse narrative by Lessing:

Faustin
Faustin, who for fifteen whole years
Was far away from home and farm, wife and children,
Was brought home on his ship,
Having become rich through usury.
"Lord," sighed the good Faustin
when his hometown appeared in the far distance,
"Lord, do not punish me for my sins
and give me an undeserved reward!
Let me, because you are merciful, find daughter, wife and son
Healthy and happy."
Thus sighed Faustin and God heard the sinner.
He came and found his house in plenty and in peace.
He found his wife and his two children,
And—divine blessing!—two more.

                                                            (Faustin)

It is clear that the story of Faustin's voyage and return is only told for the sake of the final line. Without this punch line the whole thing would have no value. From the tale's very beginning we read with the expectation of a goal. We are forced to read this way because no single element holds us in thrall. Our impatience intensifies after the prayer, where the pronoun "he" at the beginning of the line is repeated, and it reaches its peak after "divine blessing." Only two words remain; they must rescue the whole thing. They are uttered; we are surprised, and look back with pleasure on the entire piece. Only now do we realize why Faustin must grow rich by means of usury. At the end, for laughter's sake we must not feel any pity, and God's clever mercy consists precisely in the fact that Faustin's wife, too, has practiced usury—with *her* "pound." All the details of the little poem are determined by its conclusion. The purpose of the poet does not, as in the epic, lie at every point of the story's progression, nor in the manner of movement, either, as in lyric poetry, but rather in its goal. Everything depends—in the truest sense of the word—on the end.

It was in keeping with Lessing's restless spirit for him to proceed in this manner. He is a master of the epigram, about which he states that it must be divided into "expectation" and "disclosure" and that the first part, the expectation, must be executed in precisely such a manner that the second, the disclosure, acquires the highest measure of clarity and emphasis. As a model he cites Martial:

Quod magni Thraseae consummatique Catonis
    dogmata sic sequeris salvus ut esse velis;
pectore nec nudo strictos incurris in enses,
    quod fecisse velim te, Deciane, facis.
nolo virum, facili redemit qui sanguine famam:
    hunc volo, laudari qui sine morte potest.

                   (I, 9)

In that you follow the maxims of great Thrasea and of Cato
the perfect, and yet are willing to live, and rush not with
unarmed breast upon drawn swords, you do, Decianus, what
I would have you do. No hero to me is the man who, by easy
shedding of his blood, purchases his fame; my hero is he who,
without death, can win praise.

Marital has no intention of telling about Thrasea or Cato. He only
brings up these names in order to say that a long industrious life
seems to him to have more merit than a quick heroic death. Everything
depends on this one thought.

    The old poetics assigns the epigram to the lyric category. There are,
of course, lyric epigrams, for instance the delicate landscape depictions
of Anyte of Tegea. But most epigrams do not convey any mood.
Rather, they are characterized by a strange, cold brightness and speak
not to the heart but to the mind.

    The same is true for the fable, which Lessing feels he can define:
"If I am to become aware of a moral truth by means of the fable, then
I must be able to read it over all at one time; and in order to be able
to do this it must be as brief as possible."[48]

    According to this principle he tells, for example, the fable of the
sparrows:

An old church which provided the sparrows with innumerable
nesting places was being repaired. And when it finally stood
there in its new glory, the sparrows returned to seek their old
homes. But they found them all walled up. Of what use, they
cried, is the great building now? Come, leave this useless pile
of stones.

48. Lessing, *Sämtliche Schriften*, ed. Karl Lachmann and Friedrich Muncker (Stuttgart,
1891), 7:470.

La Fontaine would certainly have provided this fable with nice little elaborations and would have delighted us with a description of the building and of the birds. Lessing is only interested in impressing upon us the reality of his purpose, or perhaps the difference between usefulness and beauty. Aesthetically, he omits everything that does not serve this purpose. La Fontaine's fables—with all their splendor—seem to him to be distorted in the direction of the epic.

We do not wish to make a value judgment here, and we only cite this example because it so perfectly illustrates stylistic differences. The type of poetic creation we have seen here cannot be called either characteristic of the epic, or of pathos, or of the lyric. And it cannot, in contrast to the ballad or the ode, be interpreted as a "mixed" type. We shall term it "problematic." We are using the term "problem" in its literal meaning, as referring to that which is "projected," the "projectile" that the person, having thrown it, must catch up to in its movement. The project in Lessing's fable is the concept of usefulness; the project in Martial's epigram is the maxim of virtue in life and in death; and in "Faustin" it is the line about the unwanted divine blessing. A point of departure for the movement must be assigned to this projectile. The poem traverses a straight line from its point of departure to its goal.

This is the way it is in the ideal case, for which we can most easily find examples among the epigrams. When we are dealing with narratives then, depending on the characteristics of the material and the opinion of the poet, all levels of representation are possible, from the more problematic to the more epic. We could even imagine the same object is being depicted in various ways. Thus, Goethe doubted whether his plan for "The Hunt" was suited to the epic genre, since everything here went in a straight line from beginning to end, whereupon Schiller reassured him by pointing out that not only the direction but also the manner of the action is up to the discretion of the poet.[49] If he chooses, the epic mode then will captivate us. However, if he proceeds in a more problematic manner, then he puts us in suspense. Suspense is brought about by the dependence of the parts on each other. No single segment is enough in itself or for the reader. It needs to be supplemented. Nor does the segment that follows it suffice; it merely poses a new question or demands a new supplement. Not until the end is the work of suspense complete and our impatience stilled.

But we also spoke about the lack of self-sufficiency of the segments

49. Schiller to Goethe, 15 April 1797; in English: See footnote 1 above; page 40.

in the lyric style. True, but in a different sense. The segments of lyric poetry are not self-sufficient; also, they are not related to each other. This is evident grammatically in the sentences, which even when complete, are often brief and only separated by commas (page 40). In works of suspense, however, dependent segments are related to each other. The beginning perhaps has the character of a premise; the end, of a conclusion. It is not necessary to express this relationship grammatically. The poet can string together one main clause after the other, and leave it to the reader to establish the correct connection. If the poet does express the connection, then conjunctions will play an important role in his or her language. "In order to, because, so that, in such a manner that, as a consequence, although, to be sure, if": The entire system of concessive, consecutive, and especially final junctures presses forward. Epic parataxis is displaced by the most extensive sort of hypotaxis. This is the case in Kleist's novellas. They risk being problematic in the extreme, and sometimes create the impression that the poet would prefer to tell the story in one sentence so that grammatically, too, the single segment does not merely hook onto the next, but fixes the positional value of every motif precisely in the logical order.[50] Lessing's prose is similar, with its stimulating interrogatory sentences and its colons, by which what has been said is, so to speak, dammed up, so that the sentence to come achieves the greatest possible concluding force. The same holds true for abundant punctuation wherever we find it—in Lessing, Schiller, Kleist, or Hebbel. It shows that single elements are not strung together but rather that a whole is divided into segments and that the order of the segments is very carefully considered.

In epic poetry, a work accumulates from details. In the problematic style, the whole must be clear before the poet can determine the type and the dimension of the segments. He ascertains the point toward which the whole is directed and then he considers how to order everything toward this point. Only thus is it possible to secure a relationship of all parts, to see to it that in the entire work there is no dead end or, as Schiller says, "nothing blind."[51] This creates little difficulty with fables, short narrative verse, or epigrams, by which we have until now, for practical reasons, explained the essence of problematic poetry. Such short pieces can easily be looked over in their entirety. In longer novellas, however, or even in novels such as those of Dostoevsky where the writer not only describes but also

---

50. See Staiger, *Meisterwerke deutscher Sprache*, 82ff.
51. Schiller to Goethe, 2 October 1797; in English: See footnote 1 above; page 40.

pursues an intricate problem through all its ramifications, he is forced into the greatest circumspection and concentration. He will endeavor to sketch external elements in a few lines and to bring out what is essential in important events, in "pregnant moments."[52] From time to time he will insert observations that summarize what has happened and relieve the burden on our memories. He will attempt in every way to make deliberation easier for himself and for the reader. He cannot permit himself "Homer's little nap." By the same token the audience cannot let its attention wander either. He who forgets one thing risks staying in the dark about everything.

But with the above, demands are again voiced that have been put on the dramatic writer from the beginning. The stage again becomes significant, though now not as a platform, as a means of elevating what lies ahead, but rather as a scenic framework within which a far-reaching action takes place. The audience gathers, perhaps around the ancient Greek orchestra, perhaps in front of a stage, which in more modern times has come to mean the world. The audience remains attentive for several hours and focuses on the one area in which the action takes place. Thus were the rules of the unity of place, time, and action born. In the newer drama the chorus, which with the Greeks remained on stage from beginning to end, is eliminated. Furthermore, it has now become possible to change the scene in any way desired with the help of stage sets. As a consequence, the more recent dramatists, relying in particular on the example of Shakespeare, believed they could dispense with the old rule. However, historic findings do not support this idea. Shakespeare was not familiar with stage sets. Yet he changes the scene at will and draws out the action over weeks or even months. The theater of the baroque develops sets of the most sumptuous splendor. The baroque's love of metamorphosis, mechanical devices, and stage effects of all types knows no limit and can be enjoyed to the fullest in the ballet and opera. Corneille and Racine, on the other hand, hold fast to the unity of place and time, and no one will believe that it was simply the example of the Greeks that caused them to do this. Even in the German Storm and Stress period, whose stage plays owe everything to the influence of Shakespeare, Schiller is remarkable in that he avoids fragmentation into short scenes. As early as *Kabale und Liebe* (Intrigue and Love), he presents us with a play that is very closed in place and time. The mature Ibsen chooses one house or room as the scene of the action, packs the action into a single day or even into a few hours, and is in

52. Schiller to Goethe, 2 October 1797; in English: See footnote 1 above; page 40.

this regard and without any external necessity as close to the Greek tragedians as Corneille and Racine.

This means that the need for compactness fulfilled by the theater of antiquity is also welcomed by a large group of more recent playwrights, by precisely those, apparently, who comprise the problematic writers. They do more or less avail themselves of the possibility of set changes, and fairly often they also allow themselves to extend the action beyond the classical twenty-four hours. No one any longer studies the old rules as painstakingly as Corneille. But they do not fail to recognize the deeper sense and value inherent in these rules. Of course, what Goethe wanted to express in *Goetz von Berlichingen,* or what Shakespeare states in *King Lear,* can be said better without regard to the rules of antiquity. But it is nonetheless characteristic of a number of writers (Corneille, Racine, Gryphius, Lessing, Schiller, Kleist, Hebbel, Ibsen) to decrease time, to diminish space, and to pick the pregnant moment from an extended action—a moment shortly before the end. From this point they bring the multiple elements together to form a unity that can be grasped by the senses, so that not the parts but the seams, not the single elements but the entire context, will become clear and nothing that the audience must remember will be forgotten. The framework of the stage encloses such a theatrical work in a significant manner. In a word: The stage has a concentrating effect.

Let us briefly cite some well-known dramaturgical rules confirming this characteristic. The exposition should be aesthetically fitting; that is to say, it should be woven into the mainstream of the action. Nowhere should there be a break in the action. Mere episodes are not permissible. These and similar rules are merely the practical consequences of the problematic style, in which the purpose of the movement is the conclusion, and consequently each segment can only be considered a function of the whole that reveals itself in this conclusion. If the genre being described here appears in more or less pure form, the individual acts will not be able to stand alone. We can, of course, regard the third act of Goethe's *Die natürliche Tochter* (The Natural Daughter), where the duke sorrows over Eugenia, whom he believes to be dead, as a unit more or less complete in itself. But this only means that this drama of Goethe's does not really "precipitate." It would make no sense to isolate an act from *Kabale und Liebe* (Intrigue and Love), or from *Prinz Friedrich von Homburg* (Prince Friedrich of Homburg), unless we presuppose a familiarity with the entire work. The pauses between the acts do not mean the same thing as the silence of the epic poet who will resume his tale the next day or whenever the audience wishes it. When the curtain falls the listeners must consider what they have heard and clarify in their minds the extent to which it has prepared the way for what is to follow, a function that in the Greek theater is in part assigned to the chorus. The division of the work into acts makes it easier to oversee the whole. They provide a sort of preliminary summary.

But similar summaries can also be found within the acts. The heroes and their counterparts, for example, occasionally summarize their opinions or their desires in a maxim. For a long time [in Schiller's *Wallenstein*—Trans.], we watch the confrontation between Max and Wallenstein without its becoming completely clear to us. But when Wallenstein begins: "Narrow is the world, and our mind is wide . . . ," he is summarizing the past and permitting us to view what is to follow as the conflict between idealism and realism. Visually impressive events can take on a similar significance. When Zawisch in Grillparzer's *König Ottokars Glück und Ende* (King Ottokar, His Rise and Fall) cuts through the tent ropes and reveals the kneeling king to the entire army, we know where we stand and what the situation is in connection with Ottokar, the vassals, and the power of the emperor. When Penthesilea lets her bow fall, it is an epoch-making event for the Amazon state and recalls to mind Penthesilea's crucial conversation with Achilles.

It is essential for these events and images to signify something. Purely epic images do not signify anything. They are to be looked at in and for themselves and speak only to the eye. By contrast, the falling tentwall and Penthesilea's bow clattering to the ground point to something. In a sudden flash they illuminate the terrain already covered and throw light on the path that lies ahead for the poet and the reader. We must think about this.

Here again, the stage performs a valuable service for the writer. Since it is not a question of depicting the bow and the tent as such— the way Homer describes the bow of Pandaros or the tent of Achilles— since these things are only there in order to reveal a broader context, the poet may consider himself lucky to be able to entrust their description to the set designer in a stage direction and turn immediately to a discussion or an interpretation of what is visible. This difference must be clearly noted. Whoever presents the Thirty Years' war in an epic manner has to describe Wallenstein's or Gustav Adolph's appearance. He has to describe the various scenes of action, the battlefields of Lützen, Pilsen, Eger. The dramatist need only draw up a list of characters and write "Eger" at the beginning of the scene. He might add more information about the scene, but he does not even take the

trouble to formulate pleasing sentences. And with all this, he lowers
the epic style to the level of a mere prerequisite. The audience interprets his doing so in the same manner. When the curtain goes up on
Ibsen's *Hedda Gabler* the audience knows that it is not meant to stare
at a beautiful room, but to think instead about why the stage is arranged the way it is. At first the audience does not know the answer.
Only gradually does it become clear: Ibsen is revealing this elegance
in order to make visible an expenditure that goes beyond Tesman's
means. The portrait of the general hangs on the wall to show the
audience that the heroine Hedda Gabler remains bound to her father
and his elegant life-style. The colorful autumn foliage shimmers
through the windows in order to trouble her with thoughts of with-
ering and dying. The playwright gives her rather thin hair in order to
put her at a disadvantage in relation to Frau Elvsted in at least one
respect, and to feed her jealousy. Everything is determined by a "for
this reason" and demands the question "for what reason?" It is this
way in the dialogues, too. Every sentence, as natural and spontaneous
as it may seem, has a very definite purpose. We are almost tempted
to say that not a single sentence of the play can be dispensed with if
we are to understand it completely and with certainty. The functional
value of the parts is carried through to the last detail. And if at first
we would like to assume that the play amounts to no more than an
interesting character study, we are finally convinced that Hedda herself is there for a reason, namely to bring up the question of the
value of the middle class, of the relationship between aristocratic
individuality and the everyday order, between sterile beauty and life-
sustaining tedium. The action points to a "problem"—in the usual
sense of the word, which, however, merely constitutes an enlarge-
ment on the "project" in the broader sense. The intellectual problem
is what it comes down to in the final analysis, which, from the vantage
point of the playwright, is the primary concern. And just as the
maxims in the dialogue constitute a sort of preliminary summary, final
maxims can summarize the whole or pass it on as a question. Schiller
decided on these in *Die Braut von Messina* (The Bride of Messina),
inspired by the example from antiquity where quite often the chorus,
in departing, fits the particular fate suffered individually into the
eternal laws of existence. In general, however, the playwright does
not proceed so deliberately, preferring to content himself with an all-
encompassing gesture that does not, in contrast to a maxim, risk
choking the life out of a work. This is true of Hebbel in *Die Nibelungen*,
where Dietrich takes the crowns from the king of the Huns and prom-

ises to rule mankind in the name of the Savior—a promise that the pagan world, on which the trilogy, and the mind and will of the hero, are built, is at an end and that the Christian world is beginning.

The whole structure and the ultimate meaning of the action only reveal themselves at the end. If the spectator is not to be left in uncertainty until the end, if he is somehow to get his bearings, the dramatist has to guide him carefully. The prologues of Euripides often provide this service. Lessing praised this procedure and pointed out that only the bungler believes the unexpected has the greatest effect in the drama. Still, a prologue from the mouth of an omniscient god is not really the best solution to an admittedly difficult assignment. It is not a question of revealing the whole course of the work ahead of time, but of providing an orientation, a signpost that would indicate whether we should keep to the right or the left. It is often said that great events project their shadows ahead of themselves. These projected shadows are what the writer wants to show if possible, in premonitions, in fearful anticipation, in signs that announce nothing definite but yet something ominous or joyous. Appiani's mood in *Emilia Galotti*, Adam's discomfort in the first scene of *Der zerbrochene Krug* (The Broken Jug) come to mind. Lessing and Kleist call out to the audience to be prepared for the worst, for the punishment of the rascal. There are countless means of anticipating the future without revealing it. The real artist knows how to make proper use of them; the dilettante goes astray. Only the most careful interpretation can distinguish the right from the wrong way.

Nevertheless, two reliable means can be singled out. The one is the oracle of antiquity. Its powerful poetic significance, which frequently makes itself felt in Sophocles, in its purest form in *Oedipus Rex* depends there on the fact that the god Apollo has long known the outcome of fate, but man cannot resist regarding the future as an uncertain result of his freedom. With the oracle both things are fully achieved. The spectator knows what lies ahead. He can now relate every word and every gesture to the final scene. But at the same time he still plans and hopes with the hero, and all the more passionately, since the infallibility of the oracle is not beyond all doubt—an ideal example, which combines the clearest anticipation of the future with the most vital suspense and radiates the powerful, exciting double light of "tragic irony."

The second means is conception and birth. The theme of the Gretchen tragedy, the theme of Hebbel's *Maria Magdalena,* or of Kleist's *Die Marquise von O.* (The Marquise of O.) is remarkably fruitful because the action is literally pregnant with the future, because conception forms the beginning for what, after a definite time, will reveal itself.

It will bring forth effects that cannot be clearly foreseen but that can be guessed at.

Ultimately, every resolution, every firm undertaking has the character of a conception. The man who plans, hopes, acts is always anticipating the future. And even though he can never be sure whether his plans, his hopes will be fulfilled in the future, even though he has to entrust his actions to the dark lap of fate, his desires still provide the spectator with an indication of how he or she should imagine the future. Herein lies the basis for the rule that the hero of a drama must be active, that a passive hero is supposedly undramatic. The point of this rule lies in the realization that the future must be anticipated. If this can come about some other way, then the hero may be passive—like Electra, Ajax, Bérénice, Maria Stuart, Hebbel's Klara, or Ibsen's John Gabriel Borkmann.

We are now at a point where we can understand why the two possibilities for the style of tension, the problematic style and that of pathos, can be successfully united. Pathos pushes forward, as does the problem. The former wills, the latter questions. But willing and questioning are one in a future existence which, depending on temperament and strength, opts more for the one side or the other. And if the questions inherent in a problem threaten to become so altogether abstract that only the shrewdest artistry can secure the public's participation in them, then pathos can inspire sympathy in the listener and awaken the questions, not in his mind, but in his heart. In the tragedy of antiquity, in the drama of French classicism, and in Schiller the unity of pathos and problem is perfect. In *Oedipus Rex* the pathos of the hero is even identical with the questioning. The Italian opera tends more toward pathos, whereas Kleist's dramas, as well as Grillparzer's, Hebbel's, and Ibsen's, concentrate on problems and know how to get and to hold an interest in the questions other than by means of pathos.

III

The possibility of writing characterized by problem or pathos or, bringing both together, the possibility of dramatic writing, is founded in the fact that man as such is always ahead of himself. I shall cite an example: Whoever recognizes something as being what it is, whoever even perceives it, already has at his disposal a context in which it can be articulated. The same object can belong to different contexts and thereby differ correspondingly. Thus, the peasant walks on his land

and with regard to its yield he views the earth as fertile, the slope of the hill as unsuitable for planting. The officer, with a view to its tactical purposes, sees the same land as a field of fire, as a dead angle, as a protective cover. The painter, with a view to painting a picture, sees large lines and color complexes. Without the "with a view to," which must be assumed in advance, no one sees anything. What the "with a view to" discloses in advance, *a priori*, albeit with the aid of objects, Heidegger terms "world."[53] Accordingly we speak of the world of the peasant, the officer, the painter, and we do not mean by this the sum of things with which each one is concerned, but rather the order, the κόσμος, in which something is able to reveal itself as something.

We speak in the same sense of the world of antiquity and of Christianity, the world of the Bible, Dante, Shakespeare. Here, too, the same being reveals itself differently in different worlds. The human body for Sophocles is not the same as for Dante, although in an anatomical, biological, or any other general sense the same object is being represented. The differences depending on different worlds are differences of style.[54] Thus we may without hesitation exchange the expression "world" in aesthetic scholarship with the expression "style." Every true writer has his style, that is, his own world.

But then are not the lyric and epic poets ahead of themselves? Do not they too create "with a view to" and does not everything become accessible to them only in a world that reveals and establishes itself in objects? Without a doubt! The lyric and the epic poet would otherwise not be human and would not speak a human language. As everyone who says a sentence must, at the first word, already have perceived the groove in which the word belongs, so everyone who notices something must know the context in which it belongs. Man does not deal with isolated things. He is the ζῷον λόγον ἔχον, the being who collects, summarizes.

But with this we are simply admitting again that every poetic creation as such must take part in all genres, just as in every expression of speech, be it ever so primitive, the essence of language is present, or at least its rudiments are there. In reality, we know only predominantly lyric or predominantly epic and dramatic poetry. But these

53. See Martin Heidegger, *Vom Wesen des Grundes*, 3d ed. (Frankfurt, 1949); in English: *The Essence of Reasons: A Bilingual Edition Incorporating the German of "Vom Wesen des Grundes,"* trans. Terrence Malick (Evanston, 1969). In *Being and Time* the world concept is not yet unambiguously determined.

54. See Emil Staiger, "Versuch über den Begriff des Schönen" (Attempt Concerning the Concept of the Beautiful), *Trivium* 3 (1945):189ff.

three possibilities are graduated precisely according to their relation to the world. The lyric poet *knows* nothing of "world." In this respect, too, he is "unworldly." Now this touches him, now that. Although nothing could affect him, although he could not perceive anything as affecting him if no world were open to him, yet he never inquires after the whole and is not concerned with how things fit together. We may compare the epic poet to the sailor or the wanderer. He sets out with his hero to see foreign lands and people. He travels over the entire face of the earth. Again and again his curiosity encounters new things. The old disappears like a town on the horizon. Yet because he views everything from a single, that is, from *his* viewpoint, he probably finds that everything in existence belongs to one and the same cosmos. Homer's enthronement of Zeus means that the world in which the poet encounters objects is beginning to awaken in his consciousness. But Zeus is the highest god more in name than in actuality. The other gods challenge him, and above him, in impenetrable darkness, Moira reigns. That means the world is still open, so to speak. Its outlines are not unequivocally fixed for Homer's conscious recognition. Instead of emerging clearly they lose themselves in the mist of his forgetfulness, which seeks only what is new and which is blithely unconcerned about discrepancies and contradictions.

The situation is quite different for the dramatist. He has no interest in always seeking something new. His interest is focused less on things themselves than on his reason for looking at them. He takes them as signs, as proofs or elucidations of his problem. We pointed out earlier that "problem" meant "project" in the literal sense of the word—what is projected, and what the projector is called upon to catch up with. It can be a clever concluding point, as in Lessing's "Faustin," or a moral maxim, as in Aesop's fables. In the highest sense we are dealing with an ideal problem. The "idea" about which there is so much discussion in dramatic writing must in no way be considered simply as a random project among other projects. It stands in first place in an ascending series. The question "for what purpose," which guides the dramatic writer, can, if weakly put, probably be answered in any way whatever, but if the question is put forcefully it pushes relentlessly on and rests only when a final existential reason is revealed. This final reason, this last "for what purpose" constellates that world which, as an uncomprehended order, has always determined desire, comprehension, feeling, and acting, but has now crystallized into an explicit worldview. Thus, the same world that is already darkly presented in Luther's language becomes a conscious idea in Goethe's

Faust.[55] The same world that is supported by Homer's hexameters comes to light in the concepts of pre-Socratic philosophy.

The dramatist orders all details of the drama with reference to the consciously grasped world and does not rest until everything coheres in a single idea, points toward it and by its light becomes completely clear and transparent. Whatever is unrelated to the idea is treated with indifference, left out. Therefore, his work, viewed externally, seems to be poorer than epic writing. His characters do not have that unconcerned multifacetedness that delights us in Homer's heroes. The many implements standing around in Homer, the weapons, the harnesses, the pitchers and cups, have disappeared, unless, of course, an implement becomes by chance the corpus delicti, like the broken jug in Kleist, or acquires significance in some other way. As a rule, no attention is paid anymore to eating and drinking. The dramatist looks beyond this as he does beyond everything that is not essential.

In this respect he resembles the judge who is presented a case for judgment. The judge will be intent on acquiring the most exact knowledge of the case. But he is not being exact if he thoroughly examines everything imaginable that has to do with the accused personally. He selects from the material only what will help him come to a just decision. He will likewise ask the lawyer arguing the case to omit from his speech anything that does not pertain to the crime. For his time is limited and deviations obscure the overall view of things. But he subjects everything that is pertinent to the closest scrutiny. He brings together the most remote elements. He spins a net of relationships, neatly prepares the premises, draws a chain of conclusions, and then passes judgment according to the law that has stood and been recognized from the beginning. And on this judgment according to the law that has stood from the beginning everything depends.

In this same manner, the two possibilities for the dramatic style, the style of pathos and the problematic style, come together to form a natural unity. The hero of pathos struggles for a decision, decides, and then acts. But judgment is passed on both decision and deed even if it should turn out that the deed atones for itself by its outcome. Even the alternating monologue and dialogue remind one of the courtroom. The monologue reveals the intention and secret motives of the action. It shows us how an act must be valued, what complicating or

---

55. See in this connection Hannes Maeder, *Versuch über den Zusammenhang von Sprachgeschichte und Geistesgeschichte* (Attempt Concerning the Connection between Language History and the History of Ideas) (Zurich, 1945), 35.

extenuating circumstances may be involved. In the dialogue, by means of longer exchanges and in brief stichomyths, pro and con are discussed. One character asks, the other must answer. One accuses, the other defends. Hence, in the drama, and in court, life is not presented, but judged.

Thus, owing to its inner nature, the drama tends toward the external form of the court, as is evidenced by a large number of plays of various eras. The *Oresteia* of Aeschylus reaches its climax in the powerful scene before the Athenian Areopagus. There gods and men are brought to court. There the pleading of the powers of night and day and especially Athena's verdict elucidate in retrospect the entire course of action from the departure for Troy to the deaths of Agamemnon and Clytemnestra. In *Oedipus Rex* Sophocles discovered the most significant possibility for dramatic creation: The hero appears as judge who is himself guilty. The passion of questioning, the pathos of justice finally destroys him. In *Antigone*, too, a trial takes place, first a human one with Creon, then the divine one, announced by Teiresias. In baroque tragedy the prince appears quite frequently in order to make peace. In *Der zerbrochene Krug* (The Broken Jug) Kleist took the old motif and rendered it comical, and in *Prince Friedrich of Homburg* he has taken the judgment of the rash young man out of the hands of those literal-minded, "owllike"judges, and put it before a higher court, the elector as voice of the Lord. And finally, Ibsen called his writing "holding court session." Though he hardly ever showed an actual trial on stage, he usually edited the action as one would the files of a trial.

Not the perfection (that is, the stylistic unity) of a drama, but its value, its deeper meaning, is determined in part by the highest level of appeal to which the case is taken. A Kotzebue, a Wildenbruch is satisfied with lower levels, with the state, the good of society. With the Greeks everything occurs in the presence of the gods. Sometimes, however, a question is put before one level after the other, the competence of each disputed over and over again, until finally an authority speaks beyond which one cannot go. Thus arises the most artful tension. From pillar to pillar the archway rises up to the dizzying heights of the dome.

The greatest example in the German language is provided by Schiller's *Wallenstein*. As the tragedy is now divided up, the soldiers voice their opinions on the plan and the personality of their commander in the first part, *Wallensteins Lager* (Wallenstein's Camp). They are not fully informed and they accept without hesitation assumptions and rumors. Their horizon, their world, is narrow. They are concerned only with the war. They want the gay soldiers' life to last. Whoever supports this life is their man. Word of other possibilities and values does reach the camp, for instance by way of the citizen who wants to hold back the recruit and by way of the Capuchin monk who preaches Christian virtue. But the citizen is laughed at. The monk is tolerated because even a priest is part of a military camp. But as soon as he acts on his beliefs and criticizes Wallenstein he loses his authority. The holy church is one thing, the unholy war another. The soldiers dispense with being consistent. For just this reason *Wallenstein's Camp* has a decidedly epic character. It is more a pageant than a drama. Isolated elements lie scattered about and become conspicuous, just as in the minds of the soldiers one thing comes and the other goes.

The second play, *Die Piccolomini* (The Piccolomini), takes place in the officers' sphere. A greater awareness of what they are doing is demanded of them. They have to integrate Wallenstein's plan and their own decision with their honor and the oath they have made to the emperor. Some think the matter through, others take it lightly, like Isolani, whose attitude is very close to that of the soldiers. Thus the second part constitutes a bridge between the camp and the commander. Its middle position becomes visible in the stage setting of the fourth act, where, in front, in the space that denotes responsibility, the document to be signed lies waiting; in the background a banquet is being held, and wine is dulling men's senses and drowning the great question "For what purpose." The officers are moving back and forth between foreground and background—just as man usually moves between serious concern and indifference.

In the third part, *Wallensteins Tod* (The Death of Wallenstein)—with the exception of a few scenes that summarize earlier situations and serve as a mere foil—indifference is gradually banned. Every scene, every word has its dramatic function. Wallenstein takes stock and tests his decision against all claimants that might possibly have a voice in the matter. One of the lowest is his pride. The emperor has insulted him. He is sorely tempted to avenge the insult. If he were to stop here, he would not even rise above Butler. But he goes on to make inquiries about justice. Countess Terzky convinces him of the need for equal justice on both sides. But the emperor has evidently done Wallenstein a public injustice, and has used his general to perform unjust deeds. Wallenstein is all the more ready to acknowledge Countess Terzky's point when in addition he consults an authority that in his hierarchy is even more highly placed, namely the good of the state, the salvation of humanity. The emperor is weak and cannot win peace for beleaguered Germany, whereas Wallenstein, with the support of the army, can hope to achieve just this. Finally, he looks beyond the present and

.tries to decipher the judgment of world history. It is the victor who writes history. Like Julius Caesar, Wallenstein, too, will stand covered with glory before posterity.

In this discussion the real world emerges more clearly and dark emotions brighten into sharply delineated concepts. Wallenstein's astrological belief crowns the ruling idea of his life. There seems to be nothing above this. But Max Piccolomini carries the question "for what purpose" even further and appeals to an authority that is valid beyond all that is earthly, to the judgment of the absolute person. Man does live to be active, to work and to assert himself. Yet when he is confronted with a choice and has to choose between the happiness of the senses and peace of the soul, even between self-preservation and duty, then he must choose duty. No further reasons need be given. The categorical imperative carries its justification within itself and pronounces itself unmistakably as the highest court.

The dramatist is on Max's side and would say with the prophet: "It has been told unto you, o man, what is good." Max's conversation with Wallenstein reveals the letter of the law to which all human actions, even Wallenstein's deed, are responsible. It reveals the idealistic world, upon which the entire action depends, Schiller's problem, upon which he has been focusing from the first scene on. What follows and what the dramatist, for technical reasons, draws out too long perhaps is solely the execution of the sentence.

This brief study shows that only by being relentlessly consistent do we arrive at the ultimate question, which basically is the first question. It is possible, at any time, to break off and be satisfied. The soldiery does not deal with any questions and likes it that way. Of course, for that reason it lacks dignity. But even Iocaste in *Oedipus Rex* exclaims to her husband: "O give up interpreting what they ask!"

If she were to succeed in suppressing the question, the question would turn into the fear that erodes life from within and scorns all would-be consideration. Iocaste shared Clytemnestra's fate. For whoever is fated to see the problem cannot escape it with impunity. He finds no peace until he has thought things through and has actively brought about order. This holds true for the hero of the drama whose movement is directed toward a goal, a final human goal if possible.

IV

But perhaps the movement goes even beyond the goal, so that the question "for what purpose" finally comes to nothing. Heinrich von

Kleist had already planned the idea of his life as a young man.[56] He saw truth and virtue as the highest goals. He described a path by which man could attain this goal with absolute certainty. Kleist's letters attest to the fact that with Prussian rigidity of purpose, with the "nordic acuteness of the hypochondriac"[57] he ordered his life according to his design on the large as well as on the small scale and related every hour, every deed, even every thought to the one encompassing idea. But soon it became evident that he could not take the seemingly sure path, not because he failed to exert the necessary effort, but, on the contrary, because he was unwilling to agree to the slightest compromise. The will to virtue is thus thwarted by inevitable conflicts of duty. He does not know whether he should behave as an officer or as a human being. His will to truth hits upon the realization provided by Kant that a truth independent of human existence is unthinkable. Thus, his struggle with this problem brings him to the realization that it is self-contradictory.

"My single, my highest goal has disappeared; I no longer have one at all."[58]

Die Familie Schroffenstein (The Feud of the Schroffensteins) reveals the inadequacy of the truth that God, a mysterious god, a *deus absconditus*, has provided.

But already in this first drama a higher world reveals itself, a world of "feeling," as Kleist expresses it, of love, for which happiness does not lie in quiet possession of virtue and not in discursive realization but in the union with what is loved. But the poet destroys this ideal, too, through his iron-clad rigidity. For him, the union has to be perfect. The "I in you and you in me" that the love songs speak of is to apply to the whole man. Kissing and embracing cannot be satisfied merely with bodily contact. Penthesilea hurls herself on Achilles and devours him in a loving endeavor to destroy her intolerable opposite. In the "fragile arrangement of the world" passion has driven itself *ad absurdum* and has proven that happiness in love is impossible. If this emotion had been milder, it would have contented itself with the happiness that is possible.

We call events such as the failure of the truth in *The Feud of the*

56. See Heinrich von Kleist, "Aufsatz, den sichern Weg des Glücks zu finden" (Essay: The Certain Way of Finding Happiness), in *Sämtliche Werke und Briefe*, ed. Helmut Sembdner (Munich, 1952), 2:301–15.

57. Goethe to Johannes Daniel Falk, about 1809.

58. Kleist to Wilhelmine von Zenge, 22 March 1801, in *Sämtliche Werke und Briefe*, 2, 652. In English: *An Abyss Deep Enough: Letters of Heinrich von Kleist, with a Selection of Essays and Anecdotes*, ed., trans., and intro. by Philip B. Miller (New York: Dutton, 1982).

Schroffensteins, the failure of love in *Penthesilea,* tragic. For Kleist the tragic occurs when that which constitutes an ultimate, all-encompassing meaning upon which a human existence depends falls apart. In the tragic, to put it another way, the framework of the world of a person or even of an entire people or class is destroyed.

However, this usage of the word needs justification. The word itself comes from the Greek and characterizes the poetry of the tragedians Aeschylus, Sophocles, and Euripides. But we must realize that many of these poets' plays, all of which are called tragedies, are without the tragic in the sense we have just described it. The *Oresteia* of Aeschylus, Sophocles' *Philoctetes, Iphigenia in Tauris* by Euripides do not end tragically. Rather, the relationship between man and the gods that is frequently endangered in the course of the action is definitely strengthened at the end so that no doubt remains and everyone knows where he stands. And the Aristotelian rule of the catharsis, no matter how it is interpreted, does not fit our explanation of the concept either. Our concept is related solely to the interpretation attempted by Goethe, Schelling, Hegel, and Hebbel, the interpretation of a certain extreme situation in which the idealistic worldview comes to face a crisis. But this interpretation concerns only a particular version of what we call tragic crisis, namely, specifically the sort of crisis that emerges from the insoluble contradiction between freedom and fate. The new terminology would like to free itself from such a limited view. Not the crisis of the idealistic world alone ought to be called tragic, but that of every possible world, that of antiquity as well as of the middle class, of the Christian as of the Germanic. And not only the crisis is meant but an irrevocable failure, a fatal desperation that knows no escape. We need a special word to designate this event. The only expression of similar intent is the one commonly used in German idealism, namely, tragic. In taking over the term we realize the contradiction with the older tradition, and we are aware that not every stage play that is called a "tragedy" can be designated as "tragic." This does not constitute a value judgment. Many nontragic, though painful and shattering, works of Shakespeare are without doubt more significant than the tragic *Feud of the Schroffensteins.* Schiller's later dramas, too, in which an ultimate significance is not placed in question, have their appreciable advantages over the tragic *Die Räuber* (The Robbers).

"Tragedy," taken in this sense, is in the first place not a term of dramaturgy, but belongs in the area of metaphysics. A skeptic who is destroyed by the truth, who takes his skepticism seriously, who in despair puts an end to his senseless life; a religious man whose struggle in the search for God is seemingly mocked by some horrible event, such as the earthquake of Lisbon in the eighteenth century, so that he can no longer get his bearings; a person in love who, like Werther, is convinced of the sole worth of passion and must see that his passion is destroying himself and the others: these are all tragic figures and find themselves in those extreme situations in which all orientation and thus, in essence, all human existence ceases to be. Their god is overthrown and without god man can no longer exist as man.

Thus, not just any misfortune is tragic, but only one that robs man of his hold, of his ultimate goal, upon which all else depends, so that from that point on he is out of his mind. The well-known maxim that chance is not tragic, that a tragic event must have a certain necessity, also points in this direction. This is true inasmuch as a single event can hardly shatter the foundations of faith. However, the tragic does not thwart just some wish or hope; rather, it destroys the foundations of all meaning, of the world. Of course, if the idea of an existence, for instance the world of rationalism, precludes demonic chance, if man feels secure in his belief that nothing can occur that would go counter to a mind akin to his, then chance is also tragic, and a tile falling from the roof and crushing the brain of a great talent will disturb the true rationalist no less than the discovery of the subjectivity of truth disturbed Kleist.

Before the tragic can occur as an actual "world"-catastrophe a world must be disclosed and understood as an all-encompassing order. If the tragic is to become effective and radiate its deadly force, it must afflict a person who consistently lives in the idea and who does not let himself be dissuaded in the slightest from his conviction of its validity. It is only the dramatic spirit that fulfills both possibilities. We have come to it as a force that holds individual elements firmly together and relates them to the ultimate, the problem. The epic writer is not consistent. His world is not rigidly set up. Therefore, it cannot crumble. His forgetfulness protects him from every recognition that might be fatal. If something collapses, it does not immediately bring the whole structure down along with it, because its parts are independent. The epic poet looks in astonishment at ominous fate and turns to what is close at hand. But more than anyone, the lyric poet is unable to achieve tragic insight: He sees absolutely nothing and he only speaks as long as he is at one with the object world. However, the dramatic spirit is always prey to the danger of the tragic. Not that this danger always has to occur as soon as he brings his work to its conclusion. It is of course possible that in the end everything of importance to him will be correct and will satisfy him through his awareness of it as an enduring structure. But the more consistent he is, and the more forcefully he pursues the question "for what purpose," the sooner he will arrive at the irreconcilable. For every idea, every world, is finite. And only in the presence of an unknown god does all life become harmonious. Thus, the tragic proves to be not a required result of dramatic style but one that is possible at any time.

The tragic ambushes the dramatic hero. He looks ahead to his problem, to his god, or to his idea. As was mentioned earlier, he puts aside whatever is not related to his idea and disregards it. However, it can happen that what he puts aside, though it has indeed nothing to do with his idea, is by no means immaterial, but is on the contrary hostile. Thus, the Prince of Homburg, obsessed as he is with his goal, disregards the field marshal's command, does not hear the elector's warning, does not clearly see the situation at the bridge head at the Rhyn. Similarly Wallenstein, placing his faith in the stars, disregards the questionable nature of his closest surroundings; with seeing eyes, as it says in the text, he is blind. The main danger arises precisely from what both these characters overlook. The elector's verdict destroys Homburg's idea of the harmony of existence, a harmony that seemed preestablished for his self; it also destroys his romantic world. Octavio's betrayal destroys the calculations Wallenstein has made with such great circumspection, thinking he has considered all factors, from the mood of the soldiers on up to Jupiter's radiant "Yes."

Homburg is overhasty. Everyone sees this. But Wallenstein, although he appears indecisive, is overhasty too. Overhastiness characterizes every human universal idea. The mind hurries on to the ultimate beyond the inexhaustible wealth of living possibilities. It blots out all but what is for it the one all-important meaning. Similarly, the theodicy expands to embrace the concept of the best of all possible worlds and does not take sorrow and evil seriously. Similarly, the man of passion places himself above the demands of society, whereas exactly the reverse is true of the good citizen, who does not recognize the language of an all-consuming passion. No god toward whom a man might direct his existence is so far-reaching and so great that exclusive allegiance to him would not exclude other gods, or betray them. The world of antiquity seals itself off by excluding inwardliness. In the world of ascetic Christianity the senses do not come into their own, and they avenge themselves through rebellion. It is everywhere this way: "If I serve one / I lack the other."[59]

And the more faithful man's service is, the more he gives of himself,

59. Friedrich Hölderlin, "Der Einzige"; in English: *Poems and Fragments*, tr. Michael Hamburger (London, 1966), 446–61.

the less he can escape the curse that he "lacks the other." But the one who waivers fares no better; he goes amiss everywhere and merely blurs his finiteness. Finiteness is the sin that is part and parcel of the nature of man and it is the basis for every real sin.[60]

The question of tragic guilt, as it is often posed in aesthetics, arouses the suspicion that this question itself is destined more to give reassurance about the tragic than to reveal the potential for the tragic inherent in man himself. The question of tragic guilt makes it seem that "innocent guilt" is merely the fate of those few isolated individuals who are afflicted by a particularly demonic misfortune. However, guilt is present before the deed itself and merely becomes evident through conscientious, decisive action. The visionary also runs ahead; in fact, he hesitates least of all. Still, his guilt does not reveal itself in obvious catastrophes. Who could be more rash than the romantic whose existence is personified by the Prince of Homburg in Act I? The Schlegel brothers, Tieck, and Novalis, are never prey to the tragic. For it to reveal itself the idea must be executed in the present. An Oedipus dreaming of justice with his hands folded in his lap would never divine the tragic contradictions between justice and the gods. But his pathos forces him to make the test. It is through action that he gains his dreadful insight, just as Homburg gains insight through the consequences of the battle of Fehrbellin. It is the actual deed that puts the preconception to the test. If the present declares itself against it, if something overlooked makes itself known, then dramatic action becomes tragic. Tragic man has the courage to assume the guilt that is inherent in the nature of man.

We must never forget that in all this the important question concerns the ultimate, the highest principles to which man as such is committed. Wallenstein, to whom the stars have lied, has ceased to be Wallenstein. He may still convince himself regarding Octavio's betrayal that this has happened "counter to stars' course and to fate." But his logical mind knows no peace ever again; when the murderer's lance gleams in front of him in the darkness, when he finally sees through the deception, he is destroyed before it strikes him. Meister Anton in Hebbel's *Maria Magdalena* is exactly the same—no longer himself when middle-class virtue is destroyed before his eyes. He "no longer understands the world." What is there left for him to think and do in the future?

With this I am alluding to the deadly nature of the tragic that Goethe

---

60. See Heidegger, *Sein und Zeit* (Halle, 1927), 280ff.; in English: *Being and Time*, 325ff.

sensed,[61] and that showed itself in Kleist's self-destruction. Only the relentlessly consistent mind experiences the tragic. But the tragic must destroy the relentlessly consistent mind. It drives this mind to madness or suicide if weariness does not place a merciful twilight over it. Hence, the tragic never finds pure and direct expression in poetry. The person who could express it has already moved out of the sphere of existence comprehensible to others. Comprehension is based on the communality of a limited world. But its framework is exploded in tragic despair.

Die Familie Schroffenstein (The Feud of the Schroffensteins) comes closest, perhaps, to the purely tragic with Johann's shrill laughter at the end, which immediately leads us to fear the outbreak of madness in the poet as well and which touches the spectator like a chill wind from deathly realms. For this reason Kleist's first drama is, from the aesthetic point of view, an almost unbearable work. Later Kleist depicted the catastrophe of truth or of love from a higher plane. In Alkmene, in the last gestures and words of Penthesilea, in the gleam of Homburg's second moonlit night, the possibility of a state of grace is expressed, which God's incomprehensible arbitrariness may on occasion accord man, a possibility that Kleist kept in view as long as he lived, and of which he personally despaired only in the final days of his life. In *Wallenstein* Schiller carries out the tragedy of realism. Here, however, he has himself already left the ground of realism upon which he had stood as a young writer, and he surveys the fate of his hero from the heights of Kantian freedom. When a writer does this, he is capable of exploding the framework of a world because life, for him, takes on its fullest meaning in the context of a larger world. This is what the process signifies that aesthetics has for a long time been calling "reconciliation." After having accepted the prospect of death—accepted it as a romantic—the Prince of Homburg is reconciled to the prospect of a world in which conflict between discursive knowledge and intuition no longer exists. Wallenstein himself is not reconciled but those who witness his fate are: The audience sees itself led by the writer to the standpoint of idealism as soon as the basis of earthly aspiration and plans disappears. With almost pedantic exactitude Hebbel showed the destruction of narrow and the construction of wider frameworks for existence when he dissolved the middle-class world in *Maria Magdalena*, the world of Oriental despotism in *Herodes und Marianne*, the Germanic world in *The Ninbelungs*—dissolved each of these into the Christian one. But in Sophocles' *Oedipus Rex* we gain

---

61. Goethe to Schiller, 9 December 1797; in English: See footnote 1 above; page 40.

the impression that the poet is rejecting the legitimate claim of man to justice, the new faith, and is clinging with rigid loyalty to the faith of his fathers.

In this reconciliation the playwright and the audience are appeased. But it is quite possible that here the drive to forge ahead could begin anew, that the larger world as well as the earlier one could again be put into question. There is no end in sight. For man, no matter how hard he tries, cannot go beyond the finite. Yet he is not satisfied with what is finite. Thus it is fortunate for him that his mental powers are limited too, that he grows weary and stops questioning, that he does not stay awake, but falls asleep and daily receives from nature the vital gift of forgetting.

V

But man is a tough creature and the same fate of finiteness that threatens him with tragic despair opens for him an unexpected escape into the delight of the comic. Regarding the tragic we explained that it bursts the framework of a world. Of the comic it is true that it falls out of the framework of a world and exists naturally and unproblematically outside of this framework.[62]

This falling out of the framework reveals itself most clearly perhaps in those conventions of comedy that have been maintained from Aristophanes to the present: All of a sudden a person speaks to the audience instead of to his companion or to an ideal witness; he calls on the audience for help against an enemy or anxiously confides his secret to the orchestra. This procedure is sanctioned in the *parabasis* of ancient Greek comedy and has already become such a matter of course that it is expected and no longer brings about spontaneous laughter.

But the phallus and belly in Aristophanes, the huge red nose or ear that stands out like a spoon: these fall out of the framework, too. The framework is made up here of the network of relationships within an organic whole of the type we have in mind when we look at a human body. When something fails to fit into the framework, an *a priori* expectation is thwarted, a sketch outline suddenly does not need to be carried out.

62. Compare to the following: Staiger, *Die Zeit als Einbildungskraft des Dichters* (Time as the Imagination of the Poet) (Zurich, 1939), 173ff.

The same is true of sounds in language that cause us to laugh. When we read these astonishing lines in Nestroy's *Judith*-parody:

> But Holofernes dines very frugally,
> Only chicken with salad and a cutlet, vealy . . .

our attention is drawn away from the meaning by the rhyme, which is farfetched and obtrusive beyond all measure. Instead of sustaining the tension that the anticipated end of the sentence would create there, we are sidetracked, so to speak, and are amused by the nonsensical play on sounds. We do not usually laugh at lyric rhymes, because the subtle harmony merely makes the meaning sway and resound, not fall out of the network of sense relationships altogether. For the same reason, a verse meter that unobtrusively orders the words in a line is not comical either; but a meter is comical that, as in Schiller's ballad "Der Gang nach der Eisenhammer" (Fridolin: or the Walk to the Iron Foundry), or in verses of Wilhelm Busch, draws attention to itself and spurns efforts to trace some meaning in it.

Whatever falls out of the framework must arouse laughter and be completely self-sufficient. An actor who does not master his or her part and who looks around for help is not funny, but rather irritating. A mature person will not laugh at a hunchback, because he or she can imagine the suffering caused by this deformity. But phallus, belly, and posterior are another matter. Regardless of what anomalous proportions they may assume, their overdevelopment seems merely to point to an excessive enjoyment of life. A person who consists mainly of belly, it seems to us, has an easier time of it than we and provides a highly impressive example. A linguistic error also easily distracts us from a sense of the whole. But it does not provoke any laughter, inasmuch as it does not, like too obtrusive rhyme or meter, lead to something that suffices in and of itself and gratifies nonreflective existence.

The theory of the ridiculous has tempted and wearied aesthetics for a long time. Skeptics enjoy pointing to the irreconcilability of the attempts at explanation. But examined closely, the situation is not that bad. Everyone can at least explain his own examples, and thus contributes something to the interpretation of the general phenomenon of the ridiculous. This is not the place to review the vast literature on the subject, since we are concerned here primarily with the relationship of the ridiculous to the dramatic style. To elucidate this all-too-concise thesis only a few suggestions shall be given.

Kant, in his *Critique of Judgement*, states: "Laughter is an effect caused by the sudden transformation of a suspense-filled expectation into nothing."[63]

What Kant calls "expectation" corresponds to the *a priori* of the "world," of the "project"; it corresponds to that in which man, in spite of all his intellectual insights and experience, is ahead of himself. But this expectation is not dissolved into nothing—that would be disappointment—rather, it collapses because something becomes visible that exists more spontaneously and with less cohesiveness. Sigmund Freud explained the delight of laughter as arising from an expenditure that has been spared us.[64]

Friedrich Theodor Vischer attempts to define this "expectation" more closely. Thus, he states that it is brought about "by a sublime element that announces itself and is caught up in an arc of movement characterized to a greater or lesser degree by pathos."[65] This expectation is dissipated by "the bagatelle of an element belonging solely to the lower world, previously hidden, which suddenly gets in the way of the sublime and causes its downfall."

But this apparently defines "expectation" too narrowly. It does elucidate the comic element in *Don Quixote* and similar comic instances. But with many of Eulenspiegel's pranks, for instance, expectation is not sublime; at best, it is merely clever. Thus, Vischer is only looking at the admittedly very fruitful possibility that laughter arises from the avoidance of a *sublime* project.

Schopenhauer sees laughter as "the apprehension of the incongruity between thought and perception." In the second part of *The World as Will and Idea* we read the following:

> In that suddenly emerging conflict between perception and thought, perception doubtless always is in the right: for it is not subject to error, needs no outside confirmation, but rather stands on its own. Its conflict with thought ultimately arises from the fact that thought with its abstract concepts cannot descend to the level of the endless variety and shading of the visible. This victory of perception over cognition delights us. For perception is the basic manner of knowledge, inseparable from animal nature in which everything which directly satisfies

63. Kant, *Kritik der Urteilskraft*, Inselausgabe (Leipzig, 1924), 213; in English: *The Critique of Judgement*, trans. James Creed Meredith (Oxford, 1952), 199.

64. Sigmund Freud, *Der Witz und seine Beziehung zum Unbewussten*, 4th ed. (Leipzig, 1925).

65. Vischer, *Über das Erhabene und das Komische* (On the Sublime and the Comical) (Stuttgart, 1837), 158.

the will is presented: it is the medium of the present, of enjoyment and of gaiety: this is not associated with any effort. The opposite is true of cognition: it is the second order of knowledge, the execution of which always demands some often significant effort; its concepts are so often in opposition to the gratification of our immediate desires because as the agent of the past, the future, and of serious purpose it constitutes the vehicle of our fears, our regrets, and all our concerns.[66]

Countless examples make this explanation even more convincing. The relation of the two levels between which laughter occurs, between which yawns the "height of the fall," so to speak, is superbly presented. Only the two concepts of thought and perception remain questionable. Not every plan is an act of cognition. Desire, sensual curiosity, the dull feeling of fear also make plans. When in *A Midsummer Night's Dream* Bottom's donkey head suddenly appears we think nothing at all; rather, the romantically eerie forest scene is unexpectedly confronted with the most compact corporeality. The view of the context of an organic whole for which belly and phallus are comical is a "projecting" perception. But laughter arises from any type of plan that proves to be inappropriate, in the sense that it contains too great a tension. Tension is relaxed by what, in a more general sense than Schopenhauer expresses it, constitutes the higher nature of man, by the synthetic exertion that, according to the pattern of "being ahead" and "returning to," makes possible all experience, all knowledge. But in so doing we do not always sink to the animal level. The everyday or prosaic occurrence, for example, falls outside the framework of the sublime and is ridiculous. We find examples for this in Keller's *Die mißbrauchten Liebesbriefe* (The Misused Love Letters): The postscript in Viggi Störteler's highfalutin love letters contains trivia about the store that in a simple business letter would not seem ridiculous. From the everyday it can descend further to the level of the naïve or coarse. The only important thing is that what is factual demands less of an expenditure of tension than what is projected, and that the same effort that seeks to realize a project may suddenly prove to be overtaxed. At the name John Kabys-Häuptle we immediately switch over from an Anglo-Saxon nimbus to a well-known, puffed-up product of our own garden. With Shakespeare's Pompey Bum of *Measure for Measure* we

66. Arthur Schopenhauer, *Sämtliche Werke*, ed. O. Weiss (Leipzig, 1919), 2:120; in English: *The World as Will and Idea*, trans. R. B. Haldane and J. Kemp, 2d ed. (London, 1957), 279–80.

move immediately from Roman greatness to that most undignified part of the human anatomy upon which everyone, no matter how he or she behaves, must sit.

It is not always easy to analyze the examples of comical effect, and often enough something in man rebels against the phenomenon and its interpretation. It is always important to ask from what laughter relaxes us and to what it releases us. The comedy of rationalism shows a modest fall height. The man with an imaginary illness, the hypochondriac, the miser, is the protagonist, that is to say a man who makes life unnecessarily difficult for himself and others. Tellheim's sublime concept of honor in *Minna von Barnhelm* constitutes a final, already very refined form of the comic. Here laughter begins with a somehow exaggerated seriousness and ends in the certainty of a mat-ter-of-fact reasonable life that requires no exertion to be right and pleasant. Thus, laughter does not end in low-lying areas, but on level ground where the gracious everyday life of a good society takes place. But the laughter in Goethe's farce *Götter, Helden und Wieland* (Gods, Heroes, and Wieland), for instance, begins on this level and ends in the coarse, unreflective world of Heracles' vitality. The fall height is not too great here either. True, it does reach into the depths of elemental sensuality (Goethe, of course, discloses these only discreetly), but at the same time it does not begin at a very high level. The distance from the heights of the most pompous pretension to the depths of the most bestial baseness is spanned by the German baroque comedy, *Horribilicribifax*, for instance, which almost frightens us today. But the comedy of antiquity spans the same distance, as in *Lysistrata*, for instance, where the answer to the most serious of questions: "War or peace?" and the safety of the polis depend in the end on sexual gratification. There the lecherous politician gladly sacrifices the con-cerns of the state to attain the nearest goal, to which his lust imperi-ously drives him.

The more fastidious reader will ask how such works are to be accorded the rank of great literature. But in the laughter that the comic provides lies an enormous triumph, an irrefutable truth. Again man is made aware of the limits of his finiteness, but only in such a way that he cannot get around affirming this finiteness. He plans, projects, debates, and creates relationships. He is always ahead of himself and tries to integrate the whole of life under a single point of view. But for just this reason he also always remains behind himself; and the comic lies in ambush for him, as does the tragic, yet not to destroy him but to bring him to a halt with the cry "Stop! What for?" Sosias in *Amphi-tryon* feels he can dispense with exacting inquiries into the essence of identity, and something in us agrees with him, a stubborness on the part of life, which refuses to be robbed of its immediate rights and happily spurns every justification.

It should now be clear how the comic belongs to the dramatic style. The comic writer creates tension in order to relax it. He acts as if he wanted to aim high, only to spare himself the effort just at the moment we ourselves are making the effort, at which time he displays something that can stand by itself. "What for?—What for indeed!"—this is the rhythm to which our understanding moves. The problems, the pathos eliminate themselves again and again. Of course, the unity of the dramatic work is thus endangered. Its purposefulness is interrupted. Aristophanes, in *The Frogs*, starts right out with a comic device. The audience expects a plot and gets ready to pay close attention. But instead Dionysus appears with the slave Xanthias, who asks him whether he should not, in the tradition of comedy, say something coarse. This vulgar talk and behavior immediately renders any prognostications of the future superfluous. Furthermore, it contains a polemic against the rivals of the poet. He falls out of the framework of illusion even before it has fully taken shape. Yet his doing so does not take us very far. With it we have reached an impasse and must again be led into the context of the plot. And so it goes over and over again in the antagonism between dramatic tension and comic release. More modern comic writers do the same thing. To cite only one example, there is the scene in Raimund's *Diamant des Geisterkönigs* (The Diamond of the Spirits' King). Eduard, the friendly protagonist, is hard-pressed. We anticipate a decision, be it for good or bad. Finally, by means of involved machinations, the spirit of his father is conjured up. The spirit appears and says: "I am your father Zephis and have no more to say than this . . ." and immediately disappears. Nothing comes of this event, or rather, what does come of it is a play on sounds at which our sense of play is so stimulated that for the time being we can dispense with the hoped-for decision. Hence, we end up countless times in conflict with the dramatic purpose that is essentially without purpose but that is without doubt highly satisfying.

The more a writer tends toward the comic the sooner he will be tempted to create dramatic tension merely as a starting point for laughter and to dissipate his energies in nothing but ridiculous details. Aristophanes, Plautus, Shakespeare in his coarsest works, Molière in his farces, Gryphius, Raimund—all these act without inhibitions here. But again and again comedy is reformed in the direction of the highly literary. Then that type prevails in which unified tension is maintained but in which the ridiculous has a tentative place only on the sidelines of the action, the type that is realized more purely in German by *Minna von Barnhelm*. However, Kleist's comedy *Der zerbrochene Krug* (The Broken Jug) is unique. The motif of the trial guarantees the work dramatic thrust from beginning to end. The judge himself is the guilty one and therefore zealously tries to steer attention away from the main issue. The comedy of his diversionary tactics and excuses becomes the resistance that Justice Walter has to break. This resistance increases the tension. The one plays into the hands of the other. It is the wittiest game ever conceived by the mind of a dramatist, as perfect in the realm of comedy as is *Oedipus Rex* in that of tragedy.

It is not surprising that Kleist, the most tragic of modern playwrights, is also the most comical. If the statement by Socrates, at the end of Plato's *Symposium*, that the tragedian must also be a writer of comedy really means something significant, then it must mean this: that the tragedian can only pursue his task to the destructive end when ultimately, instead of falling into the void of nothingness, he falls on the ground of the comic and incites the elemental laughter of the one who knows: The spirit may not become real without physical basis, but the physical basis can do without the spirit and suffices unto itself in elemental desire.

The Essence of the Poetic Genre Concepts

It has been the task of this book's first three sections to differentiate between the poetic genres and to determine the nature of each one. This task could only be fulfilled in the realm of unerring ideation, that is to say a realm in which lyric, epic, and dramatic characteristics were deduced from works of literature with regard to ideas grasped *a priori*. One could easily compare this procedure with Goethe's typology. In a letter to Sömmering of 28 August 1796 he writes: "An idea about objects of experience is, so to speak, a vehicle I use to grasp them, to make them mine."

The vehicle is not formed *from* experience, but rather *in* it and *through* it, just as the eye seems formed by light and for light, the eagle by air and for air. The concept of the original plant is a vehicle used to conceive of the multifaceted world of plants; the concept of the osteological type allows us to survey the animal world. The concept of the lyric, the epic, and the dramatic should be understood in the same *a priori* manner.

But the relationship of the individual literary work to the genre concept is different from that of the individual plant to the original plant, of the individual animal to the animal type. Of course, no individual plant is a perfect representation of the plant type. There really is no "original plant," just as there is no purely lyric, purely epic, or purely dramatic work. Yet in the case of the plant this only means that every single example is defined and qualified by a thousand fortuitous elements. Even under such conditions the plant remains nothing but a plant. The red color, the jagged leaves that, for the type, are not important, do not bring the plant any closer to the animal world or the realm of the anorganic; rather, they show the type individualized. In contrast, a lyric poem, precisely because it is a poem, cannot be just lyric. It participates to varying degrees and in different ways in all genre concepts and only a *predominance* of the lyric in them causes us to call the verses lyric.

We have often alluded to this fact. Now we must examine it more closely. Only then can we see what the genre concepts really are and what the old tripartition is based on.

It is no mere analogy when, in order to explain the relationship of lyric–epic–dramatic, we call to mind the relationship of syllable, word, and sentence. The syllable may be considered the actual lyric element of the language. It signifies nothing; it merely resounds and is thus capable of expression but not of a definite designation. In syllable sequences such as "eia popeia," "ach," "ἐλελεῦ," "αἴλινον," and "om," we came upon ultimate musical language phenomena. They do not determine any object. They lack intentionality. But they are immediately understandable as "cries of feeling" as Herder described them (cf. pages 75–76). Wherever the power of syllables emerges in language we can speak of the lyric effect.

In the epic style, by contrast, the individual word designating an object claims its full due (page 104). Already in the vocabulary of the Homeric epic, we felt we had to acknowledge the achievement of the epic writers. The fullness of words represents the fullness of ever-changing life, and we appreciate the epic writer because he places this fullness of life before us.

The functionalism of parts, which represents the essence of the dramatic style, is expressed in the whole sentence, where the subject is related to the predicate, the dependent clause to the main clause, and where a preview of the whole is needed to understand the individual parts.

But as in individual sentences, the dominant factor is either the relationship between their parts, or is their individual representations, or is their elements of sound, so in a literary work, either the dramatic, the epic, or the lyric comes to predominate. This does not mean that the other elements are missing or even that they could ever be missing completely in a literary work of art. The same sentence, in fact, depending on what meaning I assign to it, will sound predominantly lyric, epic, or dramatic. The line from Eichendorff's "Rückkehr" constitutes an example (cf. pages 63–64):

Then I heard fiddling, fluting . . . .

In the context of the poem these words resound in that rhythmic, melodically swaying tone that draws every syllable into the magic of the painful mood. The same sentence could appear in a more sober epic-verse narrative, in a hexameter for instance:

At dusk I came to a town. There I heard fiddling and fluting.

Here, not the mood but the image of music would be brought to life. And this image would in its turn become a function of a greater whole if, for instance, a wanderer, feeling threatened and going fearfully on his way, were to catch sight of something vague in the darkness, would listen tensely, and would later tell of this moment in the following words:

There I heard—fiddling and fluting! Happy people— and I felt safe.

It is, of course, difficult to make dramatic functionalism clear using such simple examples, just as it would be difficult in another context to glean lyric charm from hypotactic sentence structures. But this example does heighten our realization that stylistics is justified in considering the nondemonstrable tone in addition to the one that is externally perceivable.

The series syllable–word–sentence also explains why the genres were listed in the sequence lyric–epic–dramatic. The genres mentioned later are dependent on the earlier ones. I can and I do form syllables—as a child or in an emotional outburst—without saying a word or designating an object. But I cannot voice a word without at the same time forming a syllable; also, I cannot formulate a sentence without using individual words and with these words, syllables. In the same way, the dramatic genre is dependent on the epic genre. In the dramatic genre the world of objects is reduced to a mere precondition (page 155). But it must be present so that it can be placed in a context and be assessed. If its visibility is reduced the dramatic style becomes abstract, as sometimes in the novellas of Kleist, who, though he most meticulously relates the parts to each other, only sketchily executes the parts themselves. It is less obvious that the epic genre is dependent on the lyric. Yet whoever wants to present something must first have been one with it. Otherwise it will not involve him and us and his presentation will be "dry"—precisely because it lacks the lyric, that is, the fluid element. Original acts of presentation presuppose this interrelationship. They cannot use anything else as a point of departure.

Thus, the lyric is the ultimate attainable base of all creative writing (cf. page 73), the "sunder warumbe" [without asking why], the full-ness of the depths, from which it springs and then rises to the heights of dramatic poetry beyond which it cannot go except in extreme situa-tions of the tragic or the comic in which man as a spiritual or intellectual being destroys himself.

This sequence must not be viewed in the context of literary history; in other words, we are not saying that the poetic creativity of a single person or of an entire people begins with the lyric and ends with the dramatic. The lyric as lyric *writing*, the epic as epic *writing* emerges only at that moment when the language of poetry has already revealed itself more or less clearly in its broad outlines, in other words when man has already reached the level of the dramatic. Only at this point can the epic predominate. The literary historian does not consider this state of affairs because it eludes his methods of proof. He goes back to the oldest texts and even there he finds the sort of poetry that partakes of all genres. Although the problematics of his procedure may remain little worked out, and though functionalism in the sentence or in the narrative may be rudimentary, still even the naïvest of writers does not go to work without a plan or a creative tension of some sort. However, no philosophy of poetic creation can clarify why lyric or epic predominates in the beginning. Only a historical examination of the unique situation of a people, of a poet, can do so.

We are approaching the point where it must become evident what the essence of a genre really is and what its basis is. Precisely here, at the point where a systematic study of poetic creation fails, philosophy and history of the language come to our aid. The sequence lyric–epic–dramatic, syllable–word–sentence corresponds to the stages of language described by Cassirer: language in the phase of sentient expression, language in the phase of visible expression, language in the phase of conceptual thinking.[67] The first volume of Ernst Cassirer's *Philosophy of Symbolic Forms* pursues the course of language with such close attention that we have nothing to add; for page after page we can enjoy the clearest elucidation. Language develops in accordance with its nature from emotional to logical expression. Of course, in the written documents that have been handed down this is merely revealed and not proven in detail. For when a language becomes

67.Ernst Cassirer, *Philosophie der symbolischen Formen* (Berlin, 1923); in English: *Philoso-phy of Symbolic Forms* (New Haven, Conn., 1953), 1.

fixed in writing the process has already come a long way. Hence, the investigation, as it did in Wilhelm von Humboldt's case, goes back to preliterary stages and concerns itself extensively with primitive peoples.

There is a wealth of documents at our disposal. They corroborate each other to a great extent. Every language develops in the direction indicated in much the same way as every person develops from child to youth, from youth to man, and finally to old man. Thus Herder's fragment on the ages of language holds true in the light of modern thinking. And just as Herder refers to individuals as well as to entire nations, it is evident with Cassirer that every individual still takes the path that the preceding ages had to master. The young child remains for a long time at the level of emotional expression until his statements gradually acquire intentional meaning and designate concrete objects. To relate objects to one another, to create relationships, is a further achievement, which, as all parents will remember, is marked by the constant question "why." Of course, that which follows is always contained in what has preceded it, just as the young man lies dormant in the boy, the leaf already points to the blossom. And in the same way, what has been superseded is not lost at the higher levels. It is not past, it is "stored up." In a moment of surprise a grown man may suddenly utter a word that designates an object as though he were seeing it for the first time, with the joy and naturalness of a young boy. And the "cry of feeling" bursts out in a state of emotion, without signifying anything; it belongs to a not-yet-discursive possibility of communication.

Should it still seem strange that the sequence lyric–epic–dramatic is placed in this context? We have long understood that the genres refer to something that does not belong to literature alone. Now we can clearly see what the situation is. The concepts lyric, epic, and dramatic are designations of literary scholarship for fundamental possibilities of human existence in general. Lyric poetry, the epos, and the drama only exist because the areas of the emotional, the visual, and the logical constitute the essence of man, both as a unity and as a sequence where childhood, youth, and maturity are shared.

But this needs clarification. Cassirer sees the movement from the emotional to the visual and to the logical as a progressive objectification, a process in which for the first time something like a valid object world comes into being. We are prepared for this by the category of distance. In the lyric realm there is not yet any distance between subject and object. The "I" swims along in the transience of things. In the epic the subject-object dichotomy comes into being. With the act of looking the object becomes firm at the same time as does the "I" looking at this object. Yet subject and object are still bound to one another in the act of showing themselves and of looking. One comes into existence and substantiates itself in the other. But in dramatic existence on the other hand the object is put more or less *ad acta*. Here, we do not observe; rather, we judge. The measure, the meaning, the order that always revealed themselves to the observer in relation to objects and people during his epic wanderings is now in the drama separated from the object world and is grasped and asserted in itself, in the abstract. Thus, what is new acquires validity solely in regard to this "prejudgment." The world design has crystallized. The world, the spiritual self, becomes absolute; that means it becomes detached, and in detachment absolutely valid. From such a height the dramatist looks down upon changing life.

Feeling–showing–proving: In this sense the distance is widened. If we consider for a moment the abstract character of the dramatic concept of life and, on the other hand, the intimate, undemonstrably comprehensible aspect of the lyric mood, we will no longer hesitate to designate the dramatic essence as spirit, the lyric essence as soul, as has already been done without using these very words. Yet we must not regard spirit and soul as characteristics or abilities inherent in man. We also disclaim any theological interpretations of these concepts. What we call soul has nothing to do with that immortal part of man residing in his body. What we designate as spirit is not an inner, divinely kindled light. In both cases, rather, we are dealing with fundamental ontological possibilities that have no reality other than the "how" of being and of the world of objects and circumstances that reveal themselves to us. Soul is the fluidity of a landscape in memory; spirit is the functionality by means of which a greater whole is shown.

One could ask what justifies us in giving a new meaning to old, established words. We can easily show that the meanings are not at all new; they merely represent a certain selection from out of the multitude of things that have always been designated as "spirit" or "soul." Whoever praises a person for his spirit means that he can relate much that for others remains unrelated. Wit is an act of the spirit, albeit an "inappropriate" one because it relates what, objectively speaking, has no relation. Spirit is cold. Whatever reveals spirit and not also soul, spreads light but not warmth. The spirit's achievement is admired. The enchantment of the soul is loved. A soulful eye, a soulful voice engenders that irresistible sympathy that has been described in detail as lyric interpenetration (page 82). In this case, too, we do not deviate from our time-honored use of language, namely, that the soul, lyric existence, always seems to us to have more clearly feminine traits, while spirit, the dramatic existence, has harder, masculine traits. In Schiller's well-known epigram everything is grasped precisely in the manner described here:

> Why cannot the living spirit appear to the spirit?
> When the soul *speaks*, alas, the *soul* no longer speaks.

That the soul cannot speak without eliminating itself was made clear to us by the elucidating force of developed language (page 92), which is never merely musical but always also intentional, which means it produces an opposite. But does not Schiller use the concepts of spirit and sound synonymously? We could hardly expect him to do so in such a concise poem. The *living* spirit cannot appear to the spirit, but the spirit in and of itself can. The soul, however, bestows life. It is the fullness of life itself, its direct accessibility, a blessing that cannot be acquired, that is received as a gift from an essentially unknown and unnameable source. The thinking spirit must, of course, arise from out of this fullness of life and spread its sharp brilliance over everything that is given to it, just as in Hölderlin Jupiter raises himself above the dark realm of Saturn. But he "should not be ashamed of thanks." If he believes he is autonomous, then nothing remains for him when the flowing spring dries up but lifeless law, a plan that contains nothing planned.

At the same time he is also prey to deceit and error. Schelling says: "There is, to be sure, a witty but not a soulful error."[68] Here too the concepts "spirit" and "soul" are being used in our sense. The soul cannot err because it never takes up a position; rather, it is one with the flow of events. The spirit can err because it isolates the true from feeling and looking and captures it in signs, in words, and in writing. Error and deceit lie in the erroneous application of the sign. What makes this possible is the distance the spirit puts between itself and things. A warning voice calls it back. Man realizes why an immeasurable longing draws him to woman. Every gesture of love, the kiss, renunciation of his free upright position, sinking down and finally the union, in which he suddenly forgets all life that has become objective and thus his own self in order that he may gain life anew from the source: Every gesture attests to how much the spirit owes the soul. Remembering the earliest days of childhood constitutes a similar expe-

---

68. Friedrich Schelling, *Werke*, ed. Manfred Schröter (Munich, 1927), 4:361.

rience, when our spirit was powerless but the sound was all the more rich. Whoever is unable to draw from the depths of such memories and has never been able to experience love grows poor. But of course whoever remains locked in memories is incapable of finding himself and of communicating himself to others; a dullard, he is dependent on a few like-minded people and is not open to the claims of a securely established group. For a group is only firmly established in the dramatic spirit, in an explicitly graspable world where everyone *knows* what is at stake and words of faith and universally binding laws are clear. The Prince of Homburg knows the way from lyric to dramatic existence, from dreamy individuality to the self that is the bearer of the common spirit. If we disregard the moral basis of his orientation then we can say that Schiller, too, in the "Letters on Man's Aesthetic Education" is attempting to express the same thing. The polarity of person and condition is described there in such a way that anyone can readily discover the relationship between dramatic and lyric and can put together phenomenologically a Kantian doctrine. Just as no one can exist either solely as a condition or solely as a person, since the former remains dark and the latter empty, by the same token no one can exist solely as spirit or as soul, masculine or feminine, dramatic or lyric. As spirit he rigidifies, as soul he dissolves. In the dramatic realm he is threatened by fatal collapse, by the tragic failure of his world. In the lyric realm he faces dissolution—he can no longer maintain himself. Franz Baader was familiar with this phenomenon, when he designated the fluid and the rigid as most remote zones in which no life can flourish.[69] Hence a predominance of lyric or dramatic existence is pathological. At one extreme we find Brentano, who disintegrates before our eyes as a poet and as a person, at the other, Kleist, whose cruelty, abrasiveness, and harshness frighten us. In the middle we find the epic. In it the fluid element has just solidified; the fixed permanent self now discovers itself for the first time. We have no generally acceptable name for this "healthy" existence other than perhaps "body," or "corporeality" (cf. page 110), not in the sense of an object, but rather in the manner of its existence.

But such charts are questionable. Whoever sets them up must be aware of what they actually accomplish. In no way do they divide up man's emotional life the way the designations head, torso, and limbs do the human figure. Rather, one or the other phase is identified with reference to a whole that, like the color spectrum, goes unnoticed

69. Franz Baader, *Sämtliche Werke* (Leipzig, 1851–60), 3:269ff.

from one extreme to the other and is expressed as follows: Let this be
its name. Yet as Goethe remarks,

> . . . when we have made distinctions
> Then we must again give living gifts
> To the one living in isolation
> And be glad of a life to follow.[70]

The transition from the fluid to the rigid could be designated with
four and more names rather than with three. And it would be very
conceivable that a Swede, or a Russian, or a Spaniard, or a Turk who
has different experiences would divide the same whole in a different
way—just as the Greek word from the color spectrum isolates a segment that combines approximately half of our green with half of our
yellow.

Nonetheless, the tripartition lyric–epic–dramatic does in the end
acquire a special dignity, since we learn that it is founded on three-
dimensional time. In the flow of the lyric we hear the stream of
transience, which flows on unceasingly so that no one, according to
Heraclitus, can dive twice into the same river. Remembering, man
descends from the present into the river and swims along on the
gliding waves. No tarrying is possible. The river drives him on.

> O, if only one hour would
> Hold this timely blessing fast!
> But already the mild westwind
> Shakes out a full shower of blossoms.
> Should I be happy for the green
> To which I owe the shadows?
> Soon the storm will dissipate that, too,
> When, fallow, it has swayed in autumn.
>
> If you wish to grasp the fruit,
> Quickly take your share!
> They are beginning to ripen
> And the others are already sprouting;
> Right away with every rain shower
> Your charming valley changes,
> O, and in the same river
> You shall not swim a second time.[71]

70. Goethe, "Wohl zu merken" (Nota bene), in *Sämtliche Werke*, Inselausgabe (Leipzig, 1920), 15:283.

71. Goethe, "Dauer im Wechsel" (Permanence in Change), in *Sämtliche Werke*, Inselausgabe, 14:490.

And if we ever want to recall the same thing once again viewed from the outside, it bears no resemblance to itself in the lyric mood. The young man recalls his childhood differently from the man and the old man. Their memories are not congruent.

> Now you yourself! What
> Presented itself to you as rock solid—
> You now see walls and palaces
> With ever changing eyes.
> Gone are the lips
> Which used to heal with a kiss,
> That foot which at the cliff
> Matched itself with the mountain goat's temerity.
>
> That hand that moved willingly
> And gently to do good,
> This structured body,
> Everything is something different now.
> And what in that position
> Now gives itself your name
> Arrived here like a wave,
> And thus it hurries to the element.

But the final stanza says:

> Let the beginning combine with the end
> To form one!
> More quickly than the objects themselves
> Fly past yourself!
> Be thankful that the Muses' favor
> Promises something everlasting,
> Substance in your heart
> And form in your spirit.

We would not yet distinguish the "substance in the heart," which Goethe assumes to be already fixed, from the transitory. However, in the "form in the spirit," which gives permanence to the transitory, we recognize epic existence, which takes note of things as they are and, delivering them up to the memory, states: This is how they are made. Hence from the banks of the present man watches the flow of transience. And when we have assigned form, which is something corporeal, to the epic, then the "spirit" regards created life with a view to what is important. He asks "For what reason?" That is to say, lyric existence remembers, epic existence presents, dramatic existence projects. What is meant by remembering, presenting, and projecting should have become clear. But since we are now going to attempt the always confusing temporal interpretation no elucidation is superfluous.

The lyric poet, it has been said, can recall present and past, and even the future. But remembering obviously has preterit meaning. Nonetheless, there is no contradiction here. When we say that the lyric poet is able to recall present, past, and future, we are already taking these dimensions as time rendered present, just as it is made visible to us on our watches and on the pages remaining on the calendar. Lyric remembering, however, is return to the mother's womb in the sense that in such remembering everything reappears in that past state from which we have arisen. Of course, time is not yet actually contained in remembering, which dissolves in the moment. But viewed from the standpoint of the present, remembering is the past itself. That this is not mere theory is attested to by the feeling "I am sinking back!" that overcomes the person remembering, even if he is recalling the future, as does that grieving poet in "Wiederholung" [Repetition] by Kierkegaard.[72] He is immersed in that existence that was from the beginning, before a present arose, and with everything that moves him he returns to this earlier existence so that it is closest to him, even indistinguishably one with him, for in it he has lost himself and every temporal orientation.

What the lyric poet recalls, the epic poet presents. That is to say he holds life up to view, no matter when it is situated in time. Whether he is telling of Adam and Eve's Fall or of the Day of Judgment: He places everything before us as if he had seen this with his own eyes. Thus we do not say that he dwells on what is happening now. That is the case only when he decides to describe his own time, as Goethe did in *Hermann und Dorothea*. But he does render the present and he lays the foundation of present existence by showing where it comes from. His art is the easiest to understand because our daily existence usually moves in epic channels. We, too, render present what is generally past, and while doing this we imagine the future. But such an attitude toward the future has nothing to do with dramatic existence. Rather we could say:

72. Søren Kierkegaard, "Wiederholung," in *Gesammelte Werke*, 2d ed. (Jena, 1909), 3:122ff.; in English: *Repetition: An Essay in Experimental Psychology*, trans. Walter Lowrie (Princeton, 1941).

What the epic poet renders present the dramatic poet projects. He lives as little "in" the future as the epic writer does "in" the present. But his existence is directed, is aimed at its goal. He focuses in advance on his goal, on what is important. In the writing of problematic drama he knows from the beginning what it is that is important; in the writing of pathos he is still in the process of sorting and seeking a goal in the dark. Yet in both instances he throws himself, so to speak, toward a presupposed future. And his judgment is based on this presupposition. I can only judge inasmuch as I look at something with regard to a presupposed order. The expression "with regard to" comprises all possibilities of dramatic attitude, from the questioning to the passionately struggling.

Thus, the lyric, the epic, and the dramatic poets concern themselves with the same existence, with the stream of the transitory, which flows on endlessly. Yet each one interprets it differently. The various views are based in the "original time." But this time is the existence of man and is the existence of being that man, as a timebound creature, "lets be." Thus poetics ultimately leads to the problem of Martin Heidegger's *Being and Time*, a problem that reaches maturity in the works *On the Essential Basis, Kant and the Problem of Metaphysics, On the Essence of Truth,* and in the Hölderlin essays. To be sure, we do not find even a mention of the poetic genres in his works. But since the genre concepts have shown themselves to be literary scholarship's names for possibilities of human existence, it should no longer surprise us when something as general as a study of "existence and temporality" points to them. In the section of *Being and Time* that carries this title we read: "If the term 'understanding' is taken in a way which is primordially existential, it means *to be projecting towards a potentiality-for-Being for the sake of which any Dasein exists.*"[73]

Understanding in the sense of a fundamental existential element is expressed poetically in the dramatic style.

"State-of-mind is based primarily in having been . . . the existentially basic character of moods lies in *bringing* one *back to* something."[74] State-of-mind or mood is expressed poetically in the lyric style.

"Just as understanding is made possible primarily by the future, and moods are made possible by having been, the third constitutive item in the structure of care—namely, *falling*—has its existential mean-

---

73. Heidegger, *Sein und Zeit* 336; in English: *Being and Time*, 385.
74. Ibid., 340; in English: ibid., 390.

ing in the *Present*."[75] "Forgetting," and "curiosity,"both understood in a very particular sense here, belong in this category.

Falling corresponds to the epic style.

Projection, state-of-mind, and falling together constitute the "concern" with which in *Being and Time* the existence of man as time is designated.

These few remarks must suffice. It would be pointless to want to recapitulate Heidegger's ontology. It would perhaps even be misleading since *Being and Time*, at least in its mode of expression, is still burdened by a somber rigidity (already palpable in the concept of forfeiture) that hardly seems suitable in preparing our study of the essence of poetic creation. But the later writings, broader, brighter, and more open, deliberately restrain their analyses of time even though the main idea of being = time is still presupposed. Thus our task in this connection would consist in acquiring the hardwon insights of *Being and Time*, in the spirit of the Hölderlin studies and of the *Essence of Truth*, and then in building a bridge from ontological to aesthetic scholarship. But whoever would attempt to establish the basis of literature, and whoever accordingly starts from the experience of its confusing profusion and only "meets the idea halfway" (Goethe), soon sees himself forced to undertake this task in silence and to speak only of what is of actual concern to him. Poetics loses nothing by this process. For if it attempts to develop the three poetic genres from the thing itself, albeit taking into account constantly the idea of original time, then it must also be immediately convincing, and no philosophy could "from outside" secure a result that is founded empirically. At any rate we feel our case is strengthened when poetics bears out ontology and ontology poetics. We would hope to have worked out a section of that exact science of existence that is explained by ontology. Such a hope is all the more seductive as Heidegger was in no way the first to put time in the foreground of philosophical thinking. Since Kant's transcendental aesthetics the problem has arisen again and again. The philosophy of idealism circles around it more or less consciously. Kierkegaard and Nietzsche find themselves strangely drawn to it. Bergson succeeds in taking a big step, which in turn forces younger scholars like Minkowski[76] and Gaston Bachelard[77] to disagree

75. Ibid., 346; in English: ibid., 396–97.

76. Eugene Minkowski, *Le temps vécu* (Paris, 1936); in English: *Lived Time: Phenomenological and Psychopathological Studies*, trans. Nancy Metzel (Evanston, Ill., 1970).

77. Gaston Bachelard, *La dialectique de la durée* (The Dialectic of Duration) (Paris, 1935).

or to agree. Husserl's *Phenomenology of Internal Time Consciousness*[78] attacks with phenomenological methodology the "ancient cross of descriptive psychology and epistemology." We could list many more names. The question becomes more and more complex and in growing larger reveals how very enigmatic it is. We see in particular the difficulty of getting at time as "inner consciousness of time" or as "form of perception" by means of language. The three concepts past, present, future are far from adequate since they obviously contain a traditional prejudice against time. Laboriously, new perceptions must be brought to bear against this prejudice rooted in language, a task that has always been distasteful to the broader public.

However, time is still understood as one phenomenon amongst others. Martin Heidegger was the first to dare to postulate in it being itself, and he is devoting his entire philosophical existence to this one idea. His work is not yet complete. It seems that while working on *Being and Time* broader horizons opened up to him in which what he had achieved was to be modified and elevated to greater significance. Thus it is hardly to be recommended that one take over isolated results or even timidly adopt his not yet absolutely fixed, often violent language. More important than any result is the impact of the question itself. Just as in its time Kant's question "How are synthetic judgments *a priori* possible?" introduced a new era of humanistic scholarship, so the question of being as time might well be of historical impact. Whether or not it will be developed is decided by a fate whose meaning we cannot assess. Still, it is already clear today that we can acquire spiritual tradition in new ways in the light of Heidegger's question. Oriented toward time, that which is seemingly diverging grows brighter in unison. Intellectual history is no longer, as it was for Schopenhauer, a madhouse where no one listens to anyone else and no one understands another. Rather, we find that the great thinkers are all saying essentially the same thing.

In particular, the "monomania of German idealism," the triad, and the tripartite progression are legitimized by the nature of time. We have shown the dimensions, or as we would have to say in Heidegger's terms the three "ecstasies," of time in the poetic genres. And the fact cannot escape us that the triad makes its claims in aesthetics in other contexts, too. We distinguish three types of the ridiculous: wit, the comic, and humor. It would be easy to assume that humor repre-

---

78. Husserl, *Vorlesungen zur Phänomenologie des inneren Zeitbewusstseins*, ed. Martin Heidegger (Halle, 1928); in English: *The Phenomenology of Internal Time-Consciousness*, trans. James S. Churchill (Bloomington, Ind., 1964).

sents the lyric-ridiculous element, the comic the epic-ridiculous, and wit the dramatic-ridiculous. We could regard the triad music, plastic arts, and poetic creation in a similar way. Hegel's and Vischer's aesthetics already draw similar parallels without grasping the true basis for their potential, the reign of pure time.

But here a warning is appropriate. Nothing would be more noxious than a vague toying with temporal concepts. Whoever casually tries out the results of a particular study in some other area will achieve nothing. Only the most thorough knowledge of the matter gives value to scholarly presentation. But as a heuristic principle—and no scholar can do without it, no matter how free from any kind of presumption he believes himself to be—the temporal interpretation will probably assert itself again and again.

But even this is no arcanum assuring anyone holding its key immediate results. On the contrary! Like the Hegelian dialectics this method can only cause harm if it is not coupled with spontaneous feeling for artistic values. As we have seen: The dramatic spirit is nothing if it lacks its epic base and therewith the unfathomable depths of the lyric. Hence no scholarly judgment is of any use that is made up of fixed concepts from the start, instead of elucidating matters slowly from the darkness of within. In other words, the expert is vain and will spoil any insight he might have if he does not always remain an amateur, too. However, no one can want and learn love, least of all a happy love, the source of all living things.

Regarding the scholarship of poetic writing in particular, we must limit even further the significance of our results. We are convinced that we have discovered the foundation of lyric poetry, of the epos, and the drama. We have completely ignored the accidental nature of the outward appearance of a poem, whether it is presented as a tale, as a stage play or epigram, as ballad, hymn, or ode; we sought to elucidate the nature of the lyric, the epic, and the dramatic. If the concepts were correctly explained, in keeping with language usage, then a relation to poetry, the epos, and the drama should have been the result. Thus, we found the purest lyric style in the *lied*, and the purest epic style in the Homeric epic, whereas the stage, suitable for various purposes, became comprehensible first of all as a consequence of the dramatic style. From the standpoint of the German language no serious difficulties arise here. There are, of course, German playwrights who display no dramatic traits. But next to the great classic writers for the stage they hardly matter for a definition of the drama. Similarly, there are countless German poems that are not at all lyric. Still, the lyric *lied* constitutes the core of what is called lyric. However, in English, or in the Romance languages, everything looks very different. The Englishman finds it hard to understand that Shakespeare is not to be considered a purely dramatic writer. The Italian, when he says "lirica," thinks of Petrarch's *Canzoniere*. But for us, Petrarch's work is not a prototype of the lyric style.

Such differences are irritating and can hardly be eliminated. However, when we investigate them more closely, we find merely a technical problem here such as always arises when people who speak different languages begin to talk to each other. If we can impart to the Englishman what is meant by our genre definitions, he might accept an interpretation of Shakespeare's playwriting using our categories. It is not impossible that much could thus be grasped that had until now gone unsaid. By the same token we would, from the outset, not hesitate to interpret Calderón or Lope de Vega temporally. However, only in the process of interpretation itself would the strength of the ideas become visible.

There are other poets, however, whose words seem to preclude an attempt of this sort from the start. I shall just mention Horace. Everyone is, of course, free to interpret the Horatian ode with temporal categories. It would presumably be seen—and this is true of Hölderlin's odes, too—that we are dealing with a text that, according to our terminology, reveals a great tension between the lyric and the pathetic style. But what would be gained from this? If we say the same about Hölderlin's odes then in and of themselves the greatest of interrelations are revealed: The lyric element belongs to the area of innermost nature, the element of pathos to the realm of art, which prevents the poet from experiencing a self-forgetful dissolution and which forces him to conjure up the living spirit in his surroundings. Hölderlin lives between art and nature and interprets this position in terms of the period of transition described by Kant and Fichte as the fate of modern man. The ode here is in keeping with a spirit that recognizes no present and directs its scrutiny from the past to the future and back again to the past. Whoever would want to claim something similar about Horace would be thoroughly mistaken. For one thing, the meters of the ode presumably have a completely different meaning in ancient languages than in German. We do not know how the poet feels about the fixed rules of meter, for example whether—as in Hölderlin's case—an alcaic stanza is sometimes a rigid order and at other times carries the mood as if by itself. Moreover, the Horatian meters are not at all founded in the "essence," the "spirit," or the "soul" of the poet. Horace alludes to Alcaeus, Sappho, Anacreon, Asclepiades. He also alludes to the Greeks in his sentence structure and his motifs, and the charm of his poetry consists to a great extent in the artistic freedom and sovereign strength with which he renders foreign gestures and sounds and with which he moves, without being emotionally involved, in a sphere of art. Whoever wishes to interpret Horace must focus on this. Any other interpretation will inevitably lead to incorrect results. Whether this pertains to his work in its entirety or only in part need not concern us here where we are dealing with but a single example.

This example, however, stands for whole areas of poetic creation that the German literary historian, schooled on Goethe, easily overlooks, or, if he does see them, fails to appreciate. But these are areas that in world literature, particularly in the Romance languages, occupy such a prominent place and are so significant historically that anyone who overlooks them reveals the narrow confines of his education and of his literary insight. And is this education always so clearly separated from an "original" one? I need only mention Mörike, or Goethe's *Westöstlicher Divan* (West-Eastern Divan), to remind us how often, even in Goethe's time, allusion and artistic play are part of the essence and value of a poetic work. Fundamental poetics is not the proper tool for grasping such characteristics. Since fundamental poetics anchors poetic creation in pure time understood as the existential being of man it applies directly only to works that are created out of the foundations of this original being. We must emphasize the word *directly* here. For indirectly a way could be found from here to the purely artistic realm. For this to occur, however, a very subtle sense of history is needed, a sense of artistic nuances. Systematic research can indeed guide such a sense, but can never give rise to it. Thus let us emphasize once again that fundamental poetics merely paves the way for historical research, that even as propaedeutics it must always remain incomplete.

I would like to add one last point. A short while ago I used the term "value." But I have not yet specifically discussed the value of a poetic work. A poetics like the one here before us cannot be the foundation for an aesthetic judgment. Depending on one's viewpoint, one may consider this a decided disadvantage or an advantage. It is an advantage if no value judgment is possible except from a specific historical situation, a disadvantage if, as we feel compelled to believe, there exists an absolute hierarchy of values. I would not at this time wish to bring together what we believe and what literary scholarship can endorse. So this question must remain open.

Afterword

The *Basic Concepts of Poetics* has given rise to so much misunderstanding, the public has seemed so little prepared to relinquish the concepts of traditional poetics, that in the second edition an explanatory afterword seems called for. For this purpose I have selected the texts of lectures I gave as a guest lecturer at Oxford in the spring of 1948.

The word "poetics" is Greek in origin and is an abbreviation of the expression ποιητικὴ τέχνη. When we consider that this means "the art of poetic creation," that Horace translates the Greek phrase with "ars Poetica," that Boileau renders it with "art poétique," and that even Gottsched entitles his much maligned book *Kritische Dichtkunst*, [Critical Art of Poetry], we are left with the impression that poetics is only a question of such practical instructions as would accomplish for the poet what the doctrine of counterpoint and harmony does for the composer. Aristotle actually says in the very first sentence of his work that he wants to speak of ways in which a story must be put together if it is to be beautiful. And Gottsched expresses himself even more clearly: His book, he explains, enables beginners to make poems in an exemplary fashion.

Poetic creation is from this point of view faultless when it corresponds to available models. And there are various sorts of models. The poet can imitate Homer, Pindar, Sophocles, or Menander. Practical instruction thus presupposes a knowledge of all the possibilities of poetic creation. Poetics must take stock; must collect and organize the models; and must furnish an overview of the whole. Classifying the poetic creation thus becomes the second problem. But there is yet a third. Just as, according to the ethics of antiquity, virtuous behavior presupposes a precise knowledge of the nature of virtue, so the ancient doctrine of poetic creation and of all poetics based on the ancient presupposes knowledge of the nature of poetic creation in as general a sense as possible. Accordingly, poetics teaches what it is that constitutes the nature of poetic creation; poetics organizes the available models and in so doing poses the problem of genres; poetics instructs the inexperienced poet wanting to write.

Until Gottsched's time we can say that these three problems were one. Praxis is not possible without thorough theoretical knowledge; and thorough theoretical knowledge makes possible, or at least facilitates, the actual writing. Furthermore, to do justice to statements by many poets about the creative process, these poetics do mention an "ingenium," a θεία μανία, a divine madness, and are willing to acknowledge "inspiration," but this does not seriously detract from the singleness of purpose of their task. Only after Gottsched is faith in teachability of poetic creation shattered. To a great extent, such instruction in the craft of writing is still believed possible. But it is precisely the τέχνη, which originally belonged to the title *Poetics*, that is dropped. The lyric poet in particular expects nothing from theory. The dramatist is far more confident of being able to learn his art and to acquire a conscious mastery of it. However, he, too, is convinced that this will not help him at all if he is not a born writer.

This lack of confidence in being able to teach and learn poetic creation is usually understood as an expression of true recognition and reverence in the face of its mystery. Connected with this is the fact that, particularly in German idealism, the "queen of sciences," philosophy, lays claim to the doctrine of the nature of poetic creation. When poetic creation no longer imitates nature and the available models, as it did for Gottsched, but is a creative achievement expressing not a derived being but rather man's purest being, only the most fundamental thought can accommodate it.

However, after Hegel metaphysics became discredited. And to the extent that metaphysics is distrusted, all questions of "essence" are distrusted. People prefer to stick to the actual. This is why poetics has been content for some time now to collect the material, to classify it, and to describe the genres. Today poetics is generally seen as theory of the types and possibilities of poetic creation. Whoever announces a poetics promises to deal with these issues.

The task seems clear-cut. But it is questionable whether it can simply be detached from the other problems with which it was previously connected and be mastered by itself, and whether the concept of the model that is being repudiated might not still play a role, creating the most unpleasant confusion. Supposing poetics is attempting to define the lyric genre. Poems, it is said, are lyric, that is to say poems of limited dimensions. For an epos is also a poem and yet cannot be considered lyric. Thus poems of limited dimensions constitute the lyric genre—*lieder*, odes, hymns, sonnets, epigrams, and so on. C. F. Meyer, for example, has written such poems. But in the general consensus his poems are less lyric than, for instance, Eichendorff's *lieder*. What does this mean?—Stage plays, it is said, belong to the dramatic genre. What is written for the stage is designated as drama. But how many playwrights must put up with hearing critics say that their work is not markedly dramatic? Do such statements make any sense? A stage play, a drama is described as undramatic. A reader declares that a poem, a lyric piece, is not lyric. All this is evidently presupposing that there is some model according to which a stage play is judged and a different model according to which a lyric piece is judged. This is clearly the case in the following sentence I am taking from an essay that appeared a few years ago: "A drama is all the more perfect the more it is a drama, an epic poem the more it has epic character, a lyric poem the more it has lyric character."[79]

A drama can only be more of a drama if it corresponds more to model dramas, a lyric piece only more lyric if it comes closer to the models of lyric poetry. However, the reader, and even more the writer, oppose such a judgment by claiming the right to be original, the very idea that shattered the belief in models in the first place. I absolutely refuse to be in the least bothered in my love for C. F. Meyer's poetry by an ideal concept of lyric poetry. I am immediately ready to acknowledge Gerhart Hauptmann's *Florian Geyer* as a stage play of high merit although I can see that it is not what is generally called "dramatic." I do not consider its undramatic or unlyric aspect a disadvantage.

If poetics wants to take this sort of observation into account somehow, then it is still faced with the problem of distinguishing clearly between genre and model and of leaving the poet's freedom untouched by establishing the various genres. Poetics seeks to remedy this situation by arbitrarily increasing the number of genres. It recognized Hofmannsthal's work by accepting as valid a "lyric drama." Epistolary novels like *Werther* and *Hyperion* are viewed as epics in prose. And on and on goes the process until all phenomena have supposedly been covered. It creates for us a fanlike structure like the one Julius Petersen describes in his *Die Wissenschaft von der Dichtung*

---

79. Leonhard Beriger, *Die literarische Wertung* (Literary Evaluation) (Halle, 1938).

[The Science of Literature],[80] a wheel from whose axle, that is, the "original poetic creation," three main spokes, described as "epos," "poetry," and "drama," fan out. All mixed genres fall between the spokes, for instance, the monodrama and the dramatic monologue between the drama and the epos, and the prayer between the epos and lyric poetry. This does not mean, however, that we can put one of these labels on every existing literary work. The first part of *Werther*, for instance, is regarded as a lyric novel and thus belongs between the epos and lyric poetry, but the second part approaches the dramatic first-person narrative and stands between the epos and the drama. Dialogues in the *lied*, such as Goethe's "The Noble Boy and the Miller's Wife," combine elements of the ballad, the drama, and lyric poetry. These combinations are certainly not limitless but they are immense in number. This schema merely indicates that everything can be mixed with everything else. Of course, the three spokes "epos," "lyric poetry," and "drama" stand out strongly as basic genres. But why they are considered basic genres remains totally unclear. Perhaps because they are "simple" and the other genres "mixed"? That could be changed arbitrarily. We cannot understand why an epos should be simpler than a prayer, which appears here between lyric poetry and the epos, why a drama should be simpler than the ballad, which stands between a drama and the epos. Why, for instance, does not the drama appear as a mixture of epos and lyric poetry and thus correspond to the ancient precepts?—I could go on indefinitely. But it suffices if it is now clear that the wheel that Petersen constructed can be replaced by a list of all the poetic types, a list, however, that would leave a few blank pages at the end. For who could guarantee that new poets would not invent new poetic types? The situation seems hopeless. Admittedly, Petersen has escaped the danger of talking about models. But with his approach the principle of categorization becomes an illusion.

At this point it is understandable that a historically oriented approach rejects all poetics and confines itself, "without preconceptions," as the term goes, to the interpretation of the individual work. But before I commit myself to this approach I feel the need to clarify the terminological confusion that seems to be present here. Out of the noun "drama" we form the adjective "dramatic." A drama is dramatic—this, obviously, is a tautology. A drama is a stage play. Is every stage play dramatic? One would have to say no. There are, as we know, "lyric dramas." Bert Brecht claims the epic drama for him-

80. Julius Petersen, *Die Wissenschaft von der Dichtung* (The Science of Literature) (Berlin, 1939), 124.

self. How is it with the epos? A longer verse narrative is called an epos. Is every longer verse narrative epic? No. There are verse narratives that we are inclined to term lyric, for instance Eichendorff's *Julian*. On the other hand, we can also designate the novel an epic work although it is not a verse narrative and not really an epos, either. Here the situation becomes especially tricky. An epos is a narrative in verse form. Not every verse narrative is epic. A novel is no verse narrative; therefore it is no epos, yet it is still an epic work. The situation is no better with lyric poetry. Poems are termed lyric but there are poems that are not lyric. Epigrams, for instance, are put in the lyric category and they have always been included in lyric anthologies. Yet nobody thinks of calling the masterful, classic epigrams written by Schiller lyric.

A Babylonian confusion! I am showing it as it is and giving such a drastic picture because critics accuse my attempt at a poetics of confusing the terminology. Yet there is nothing left to confuse. The terms lie scattered, ruins of an old poetics that has lost its foundation. But scholarship presses for order, clarity, at least to the extent that it can say what a word means that it is compelled to use. When language usage is ambiguous but scholarship demands clarity, then scholarship should not be too particular regarding language usage. A straight stance is expected of wavering concepts, shimmering ones must show their true colors. On the other hand, scholarship also detests ambiguity in the area of terminology. It does not say "red" where everyone else says "green," not "brown" where everyone else says "purple." What is called "lyric" must be accepted by everyone as "lyric" even though everything is not called lyric that many are accustomed to calling "lyric."

Upon close examination that particular confusion of terms can easily be cleared up. The *nouns* epos, lyric poetry, and drama are, as a rule, used as names for the categories in which a literary piece as a whole belongs according to certain externally visible characteristics. The *Iliad* is a narrative in verse or, as Petersen says, "a report, in monologue form, of an action." Thus it belongs in the category "epos." Eichendorff's "Mondnacht" [Moon-Lit Night] is a poem or, as Petersen says, "a depiction, in monologue form, of a condition." Thus it belongs in the category of lyric poetry. However, I place C. F. Meyer's poems in this category, too. For at this point, I do not ask about the nature of these poems: whether they are more or less expressive of a mood, are musical, or are purely dynamic. Let it suffice to say that they are poems. They are categorized as lyric poetry.

The *adjectives* lyric, epic, and dramatic mean something different.

A lyric piece is not just any poem, just any presentation, in monologue form, of a situation. Rather, the adjective "lyric" clearly states that *this* particular presentation, in monologue form, of a situation is lyric in contrast to others that are not expressly lyric. A value judgment need not be attached to such characterizations. Rather, the example of C. F. Meyer leads us to suppose that the question of value has no direct bearing on these questions. On the other hand, there are "lyric dramas," that is, literary works that, as stage plays, belong in the category of "drama," but that still are lyric. What is meant by these adjectives? They do not correspond to their nouns as the adjectives "iron" and "wooden" do to the nouns "iron" and "wood" but rather as does the adjective "human" to the noun "human being." The human being belongs in a particular category of the higher vertebrates or, in respect to theology, in a category between "animal" and "angel." But not every human being is human. "Human" can refer to a virtue or a weakness. At any rate a particular trait, an essence, is expressed of which a person may but need not necessarily partake. Thus, lyric, epic, and dramatic are not names of categories under which literary works can be filed. The categories, the types, have increased tremendously in number since antiquity. The designations lyric poetry, epos, drama by no means suffice. In contrast, the adjectives remain constant as designations of simple qualities that a certain literary work can display or not. For that reason we can use them to designate a work from any category. We can speak of lyric ballads, dramatic novels, epic elegies and hymns. And in doing so we do not at all mean that this ballad is only lyric and this novel only dramatic. We only mean that the essence of the lyric or of the dramatic is more or less clear, is somehow expressed in these works.

What is the result of all this for poetics? It has become senseless to attempt to describe all categories in which literary works can be placed. Petersen's wheel showed us that. But it is not senseless to ask about the essence of the lyric, the epic, and the dramatic. For these qualities are simple and their stability is not disturbed by the shimmering and wavering character of particular literary works. Actually it is only from the vantage point of the simple, fixed designations that the character of a certain literary work shimmers and wavers, just as I can only observe and measure a movement when I myself stay fixed in relation to it. Whoever misassesses this situation does not know what it means to speak and think. For everything living is in motion and one thing merges with another. But man does not simply go along with this. He forms words and with words he retains something permanent in the phenomena by perceiving in one or the other a similarity and by his labeling it as such: "And whatever hovers in fleeting appearance / must be fixed with permanent thought."

These words tell the whole story. A detailed discussion of these lines belongs in the sphere of a philosophy of language.

But where should I begin if I wish to grasp the essence of the lyric, epic, dramatic? If I designate a novel as lyric, a novella as dramatic, if I feel a piece is essentially lyric, epic, or dramatic, then I must already know what the terms lyric, epic, dramatic mean. From the work lying before me at the moment I do not glean this. For I have yet to decide whether this work is dramatic, lyric, or epic; I cannot possibly derive the standard of measurement from what is to be measured. So first of all I come to the following conclusion:

"I know what is lyric from reading poetry that is generally considered lyric."

But what is generally considered lyric? Lyric poetry?

"No. I know now how thoroughly questionable the relationship of the adjective to the noun is."

But certain types of lyric poetry?

"Probably! For even though the relationship between adjective and noun is questionable the two probably cannot be completely separated from each other."

What kinds of lyric poetry then? The epigram?

"Not necessarily. Certain epigrams are lyric. Mörike wrote some. Others are granted a certain dramatic tension. At any rate I would not call epigrams of Schiller or Lessing lyric."

Now then: the hymn or the ode?

Hard-pressed, I would hazard the answer: To be sure, certain odes are lyric. Some of Hölderlin's odes doubtlessly have a lyric aspect. But then again it seems to me that the term "lyric" is connected with the idea of intimacy, an idea that does not characterize all odes. To the question "What is considered lyric?" I would prefer to answer: the *lied*. A *lied*, when I consult my feeling for the language, seems to be nothing but "lyric."

Yet I am still not satisfied. I would like to point out that Lessing too wrote *lieder*. I wonder whether my partner in discussion is prepared to recognize these *lieder* as being lyric. He surely would reply:

"No! But these poems assume the title of *'lieder'* without justification. They cannot be sung. They are pointedly witty and sometimes they are almost indistinguishable from Lessing's epigrams. As examples of true lyric I would suggest other *lieder*, for instance those of Eichendorff or Goethe, or the folk song. In these poems I believe the lyric element stands out most clearly. And when I am asked according to what criteria I would call a poem lyric I would say: according to that which has been elucidated for me through these poems."

Here I must interrupt the discussion. For someone could counter that I had conducted this little Socratic dialogue to suit myself. But I would protest this assertion. My partner is not a creature of my own caprice. He is the spokesman of our feeling for language, albeit, I readily concede, the spokesman of the feeling for the language of educated German-speaking people of our time. But this, to me, is the whole point. If I am to say, in a contemporary poetics written in German, what is lyric, then I must honor contemporary German usage. To what extent this detracts from the value of the poetics' results will be discussed later. One objection, however, should not be voiced, an objection that is raised again and again, but that becomes no more valid through constant repetition, namely: If the nature of the lyric is defined according to the *lied* of romanticism and of Goethe, then what is the situation with Keats, Petrarch, Baudelaire, Góngora, Hölderlin? Do they not deserve to be considered lyric poets every bit as much as Eichendorff? Are they not even greater lyric poets than the balladeers of bourgeois romanticism? In this objection there hides a whole rat's nest of misconceptions. I shall examine these in order.

The term "lyric poet," cropping up unexpectedly here, is risky. Who is a lyric poet? A creative writer who has created lyric works or one who has created lyric poetry? Here the answer is clear: the one who has created lyric poetry. Hofmannsthal would be included not as the creator of his lyric dramas but as creator of his poetry. But then the objection runs as follows: Do not poems of Keats and Baudelaire belong just as much to lyric poetry as the *lied* of Eichendorff or Goethe? And with that the objection already breaks down. For here again lyric poetry designates the category into which poems can be put, a large, very roomy category: All poems belong here, albeit in various subcategories. By contrast the expression "lyric" does not serve as a collective term. And when I say that the lyric is most perceivable in the romantic *lied* this does not mean that I have reduced the large category of lyric poetry to the dimensions of the romantic *lied*; rather, I have merely explained that the romantic *lied* participates most fully and unambiguously in the nature of the lyric, μετέχει, in the Platonic sense.

This brings me to the second misconception that the objection implies. The partner in my fictitious discussion did not deny that a lyric element is also to be found in odes and hymns. But when it is a question of extracting the essence of the lyric, in as pure a form as possible, he would rather not restrict himself to examples that are permeated with other elements. He would indeed not deny that Keats and Hölderlin are eminently lyric. He would merely point out that the individuality of their poems does not exhaust itself in the essence of the lyric, that something else is involved, whereas romantic *lieder* can most readily be interpreted as purely lyric pieces.

"Pure"—with this term we touch upon the third misconception. Romantic lyric poetry is "purely" lyric or at least comes closest to being "purely" lyric. But by this token it could be said that Hölderlin is less pure. And "less pure" means "more clouded," mixed with an impure element, less perfect. One's good taste opposes this view, as do all those who believe they must defend Keats and Petrarch and Hölderlin as great poets. But they are running into doors that are wide open. I myself would be the last to say that Eichendorff is a greater poet than Hölderlin. What is the misunderstanding based on? The purity of the genre appears here again, unexpectedly, as a predicate of value, as it did in the old model poetics. We have expressly rejected this and want to reject it once again. For this prejudice seems to be rooted far too deeply in our minds. "Not purely lyric" does not at all mean that the lyric element is mixed with mud and refuse; rather it means that in addition to the lyric element other characteristic traits can also be perceived. And could it not be that a poetic work is all the more perfect the more the lyric, the epic, and the dramatic merge in it? *The Basic Concepts of Poetics* makes this assumption plausible. But I shall leave the question open for now. I shall merely point out one thing, namely, that a poetic work that is nothing but lyric, epic, or dramatic is inconceivable; that every work partakes more or less of all genres; and that only a judgment of whether it does so to a greater or lesser degree determines whether we call it lyric, epic, or dramatic. This claim can be substantiated by the full nature of language. It also applies to the romantic *lied* and to the *lieder* of Goethe, although we believe that the lyric element can be found here in more or less pure form. We merely find it most clearly revealed there, but not altogether purely. This means in other words: Even the determination of the essence of the lyric element does not completely exhaust a romantic *lied*.

At any rate we hope to hear the most exhaustive answer here. Let me summarize the results: From romantic *lieder*, written by Goethe, and four others that resemble his, we glean the essence of the lyric. This seems to be the best way of putting it. Thus I do not say that we intend to interpret Eichendorff or Goethe in an exhaustive way. We shall conduct the interpretation with a view toward the lyric. We shall retain only that which according to our personal feeling seems to be contained in the term "lyric." Whatever else these poems contain we shall let be or mention in passing in order to show that they do contain something else as well.

At this point a final objection will probably be voiced. Is it not sinfully subjective if we trust our feeling to such a degree? We must keep to what is before us and our feelings must remain silent. Where, otherwise, would scholarship be? I do not know on what concept of scholarship such an objection is based. Presumably it is a concept that derives from the natural sciences. But literary scholarship has no choice but to proceed in this manner. Let us take an example that does not belong in the realm of systematic research, an example in which it is a question of explaining a single real work of art, present in the here and now, for instance a poem by Goethe. I do not at present wish to interpret this poem with respect to the lyric. It is my goal to interpret the text in every regard, or at least in every regard conceivable to me. If I am not satisfied merely to compile what has already been said about the text, if I believe that I have something new to say about it, then I really have no choice but to use feeling as a point of departure. I shall clarify this feeling, a vague hunch, obscure even to me, and I shall render it in exact terms. If my feeling has been wrong the object itself will protest. It will become obvious that my various statements will not mesh, that the meaning I give a line will contradict the meaning inherent in the sentence structure perhaps, or that my feeling is based on false biographical assumptions. But if my feeling has been correct, then I shall experience that delicious pleasure that can belong to the interpreter: that every observation, all knowledge I acquire about the text substantiates that first obscure hunch. But then could one just as well begin without such a feeling? No! This is precisely what we cannot do. For without that first feeling I could not perceive anything in the text. I do not know what is essential or vital and what is conventional. Whoever wants to understand explicitly must always already have understood obscurely. Here, I am describing the situation that the methodology of humanistic scholarship calls the "hermeneutic circle." But it is not a vicious circle; rather it is the path to knowledge that alone is open to our research.[81]

The situation is the same when I want to grasp the essence of the lyric. Having grown up in modern times, with the German language, fleetingly and vaguely acquainted with the expression "lyric," filled with the feeling that a simple word designated a simple essence, I begin to point to the essentially lyric wherever I encounter it, in

81. See in this connection Staiger, *Die Kunst der Interpretation* (The Art of Interpretation) (Zurich, 1955).

sounds, rhymes, sentences, stanzas, motifs—wherever it might be. If I am always guided by a true feeling, always one and the same feeling, then everything I say must ultimately be in agreement; and a phenomenon that is clear and unequivocal must reveal itself to me. But if I am further confronted with the objection that I have merely described what a modern German-speaking person is in the habit of calling "lyric," then I can only answer: "Of course!" Language usage may change. But the phenomenon itself remains the same, constituting an objective context that is fixed in its nature. The terminological question of how it will be designated in the future and among other peoples does not interest me.

Does an investigation based on such a foundation have a claim to validity in connection with world literature? Is it only valid for the German language? Or is it perhaps only valid for the German language of Goethe's time? I have taken most of my examples from German literature, more specifically from the classic and romantic periods. In addition I have taken into consideration Homer in the section on the epic. Occasionally I quote Sappho, the Greek tragedians, classical French drama, Gryphius, rarely ever French poetry, never Italian, English, Spanish, or Russian literature. I have already given the simple reason. I am most familiar with German and Greek literature. I cannot read Spanish and Russian literature in the original. I love and revere Spanish and English literature but I do not know them well enough to interpret them. Does not such a confession of my weaknesses and limitations also mean a relinquishing of universal literary scope? I acknowledge the possibility that everything is of interest only from the German perspective. The possibility of worldwide significance seems, however, still to be open. For if, in the end, the genre concepts are anchored in the nature of language and not specifically the German language, then the same claim is raised here that Ernst Cassirer makes in his *Philosophy of Symbolic Forms*, namely, the claim that the subject under discussion is man in general. I am aware of how questionable such a universal claim is and I know that it is always only *my* world, *my* universe, or the universe of a certain circle, a certain tradition about which I can speak. Needless to say, I must do the latter if I am to say how the matter presents itself to me.

There is a large and widespread body of poetic works, particularly in the area of Romance languages, about which even the question of the validity of the *basic concepts* seems to make no real sense. As an example I cite Horace and call to mind with his name creative writers in whose work the artistic element, allusion, quotation, preoccupation with older literature comes to the fore. Whoever wants to understand Horace must remember that his language does not create the closed world that poetics seeks to describe, that not only does it vibrate within itself but it also remains tied to something that lies outside it. Only to the extent that what lies outside—in Horace's case Greek poetry—represents a pure poetic world can an investigation in the sense of poetics be possible. But this says nothing about the originality of Horatian poetry.

However, as neat as it now appears, an artistic writing can only rarely be divorced from a more original one. With a poet like Mörike, for instance, how insufficient would be an examination limited to pointing up the fundamental character of his work! Costume, mask, pose, a subtle stylistic playacting is clearly present in almost every word Mörike writes down. Only ignorant pedantry would condemn such work as false. We owe the happiest miracles of language to such playacting. The layperson accepts it innocently; the amateur savors the allusion; and neither can do without it.

Here the limitations of my poetics seem to me to be much more clearly visible than where they are usually sought with such great zeal; for instance in Shakespeare, Calderón, Petrarch, or in connection with the novel, the "epic" art form of the modern period. And in fact no one will deny that in these poets the epic, lyric, and the dramatic intermingle as in the poets of Goethe's time. It is a commonplace to speak of the epic feature of Shakespeare's histories. And who has not made the distinctions between Tolstoy's more epic narrative art and Dostoevski's more dramatic one? The consternation to which my poetics has given rise here is of an entirely different sort. Critics are annoyed that Shakespeare is not seen as primarily dramatic and many novels not as primarily epic. Now I willingly concede that the terminology is more problematic here than when applied to the writing of Goethe's time, where the essence of the lyric can still be gleaned more purely from lyric poetry, that of the dramatic in its purest form from stage plays. Basically, however, we have here the old misconception that with respect to the poetic genre concepts we are dealing with categories into which poetic works must be placed. Not only is this not at all the case, but the whole point of my poetics lies in the opposite direction: It intends to fix the concepts "lyric, epic, and dramatic," used for a long time in a stylistic sense, in their meaning as such and to divorce them from "epos, lyric poetry, and drama." It should prevent Tasso, for instance, from being considered a flawed writer because he is not as purely epic as Homer, or C. F. Meyer from being put behind Eichendorff because his poems are less lyric. My poetics remains explicitly neutral toward all attempts at categorizations and no longer wants to regard the genre as a model at all, at least for now.

I say "for now" cautiously. For if I were to be asked whether there is no connection at all between the epos and the epic, between lyric poetry and the lyric, I would not dare answer with an unqualified "no, there is absolutely no relationship." Let us replace the nouns with terms that in this context, too, protect us from confusion, thus for epos "longer verse narrative," for drama "stage play," for lyric poetry "shorter poems." The question would then be: Can a longer verse narrative be something completely other than epic? I would hardly concede that. I am thinking for instance of Klopstock's *Messias*. The enormous talent of its creator is hardly in doubt. His work, however, is not pleasing. Why? Because it is not possible to sustain the same mood of extreme pathos for thousands upon thousands of verses. Here it seems to me the limits permissible to a longer verse narrative have been far overstepped. Milton's work, too, has tones of lyricism and pathos. But it always retains the foundation of a monumental imagery. Thus we stay with it and are captivated long after Klopstock has tired us.—Another example: Keller's poems. Here, too, our pleasure is not unqualified. For it often seems to us that, considering the brevity of many of his poems, Keller's epic imagination that is at work does not have time to develop correctly. In such few lines a different, more magical lyric or more concise art is needed. Again the limits permissible to a poem are not observed. And so, with the concept of limits it seems thoroughly admissible to append to the basic concepts a lengthy model poetics containing the questions: What is possible within the limits of the ode, the elegy, the novel, the comedy? But I refuse to undertake this task myself. For relationships seem to me to be so complex and difficult in this area, and so great is my faith in new, completely unexpected possibilities on the part of creative writers, that I prefer going from the basic concepts directly over to the interpretation of individual works.

But what does poetics contribute to the individual interpretation? The fear has been expressed that in this instance something like a school was being founded that would busily go about interpreting all poetic works according to one and the same prescription. I object to this and would rather see my book destroyed than accept this nonsense. Whoever sees the situation simply as one of examining all poems with a view to the essence of the lyric is still confusing "lyric poetry" and "lyric" and deserves no further answer. But by the same token, whoever examines essentially lyric pieces for their lyric element may not claim to have interpreted a single work. He has merely enriched my collection of examples with a new one and furnished supplemental material for my poetics; he has not made an individual, historical study. Let us look at "Wanderers Nachtlied" (Wanderer's Night Song) by Goethe. Very many lyric characteristics are unmistakably visible here. The mood clearly predominates. The musicality of the words and their meaning cannot be separated from each other. Form and content are so completely one that the one particular, inimitable feeling has created its particular inimitable stanza. But where in this interpretation geared to the lyric do we find the path—traced in the poem—ranging through the whole of nature from the mineral world on up to man? Where in this interpretation is the last line, which constitutes the whole point of the poem? It could be made up of certain epic or dramatic elements. I hardly dare say this because now the following impression arises: Interpretations, if not based on one chapter of the poetics, could at least be based on *all* chapters of the poetics. One would only need to examine how every poetic work partakes of the three genres we have described. That would of course conform to the spirit of the present poetics, at least insofar as it claims that the triad is founded in the language; thus in the triad the essence of the literary work of art is exhausted. Yet that is bare theory, which is useless in real life. How a poetic work vibrates in the epic, the lyric, and the dramatic, what course its tension takes and how it balances itself out is so very delicate that any simple application of fixed concepts fails from the outset. The interpreter, now as then, will have to prove himself by displaying that characteristic that since Herder's day has been indispensable in our profession: a direct feeling for a work's individual historical quality.

Then, of course, assuming this, poetics can perhaps be of help. But the moment when direct feeling is to develop into clear concepts is always problematic There lurk the well-known dangers: the dangers of equivocation, namely that our language designates two different things with a *single* word, so that the second meaning suddenly intrudes on our thoughts instead of the first. There is also the danger of logical deceit, namely that an argument will look solid from all sides, yet somewhere at an unnoticed point an error will occur because thought divorced from feeling went its own way. Here perhaps schooling by basic concepts could be helpful. The basic concepts attempt to free frequently used words from their ambiguity, and they point to the ambiguity of many phenomena, for instance music, rhyme, repetition, the paratactic sentence, the image as dream and fantasy, the sensual in the two spheres of the human body and of the sculptured body, remembering and commemorating, the suspenseful and the captivating, and whatever else of this sort there may be.

This achievement, however, is more one of a prophylactic nature. Yet now other possibilities present themselves. Certain connections that until now were not clearly visible are revealed by the basic concepts, for instance, the connection between motive and sentence structure, between problem and hypotactic language, between vocal magic and improvisation, between imagery and ancient meter. Such findings present themselves to us as an essential unity. It is not that one can be derived from the other. All are phenomena of "style"—to designate with this word the one thing in which various expressions of an artistic individuality or of an epoch are identical. Looked at this way, "poetics" prepares the way for a stylistics. And such a stylistics would perhaps benefit all of modern anthropological science.

What does modern anthropology want? Let me point out the great attempts of German idealism to present human existence as a cosmos: Today we stand respectfully but also with great skepticism before such attempts. These systems are all too obviously determined by a certain worldview. We can prove that Schiller distorts his terminology. Schelling and Hegel cling to arbitrary statements made merely for the sake of the whole, distorted just so that individual elements will fit into the grand preconceived plan. And so we get to the point of regarding idealist philosophy as something of the past and of permitting a preoccupation with its teachings only in the realm of the history of philosophy. The history of philosophy, Schopenhauer says, resembles an insane asylum where everyone contradicts everyone else. Only a collector of human oddities could take pleasure in it. And indeed, the historian often seems to see himself as such a collector. He stacks his materials, piles one on top of another, and starts an archive of mankind in which the files lie peacefully in arbitrarily arranged drawers. However, we have no reason to belittle this historical research. It has accomplished a great amount of work that, were it not already done, would first have to be done by all of us—from the editions of our classics to the patient inventory of every detail that ever was.

Yet today the flowering of a *solely* historical orientation is probably over. Again the all-encompassing question presents itself: What is man? Anthropology attempts to provide an answer, at first by describing isolated phenomena without a firm view of an order, for instance the nature and forms of empathy, will, imagination. But Max Scheler has already protested against what he called "a mere picture book phenomenology," that is, against research that is satisfied with the description of arbitrarily selected, widely scattered phenomena that are merely strung together. Since then a *structure* of human existence is becoming clearer and clearer. Terms such as levels, points of juncture, fundamental relations, modes of human nature are used—all this without ideological bias. But in this perspective tradition suddenly becomes fruitful in a new way. Let the philosophers, inasmuch as they are claiming an ideology, contradict each other. Many of their concepts still retain an objective validity. Great passages of their works are pure descriptions of humankind; they contain insights that no change in belief, or in ideas about the Divinity, or in opinions about the highest values can overthrow. Nicolai Hartmann has shown this particularly well in connection with Hegel's logic, Heidegger in connection with Kant's critique of reason. But we are only at the beginning. The goal is inspiring, for the more we assure ourselves of a spiritual heritage the better we realize that man in the course of his long history is not wildly floundering in possibilities, that the observers of human existence are not raising a Babylonian hue and cry but rather, if we understand correctly, that they are saying, within the historical constraints of their time, more or less the same thing.

Here I would hope that my poetics could be helpful. It calls itself a contribution of literary scholarship to the problem of general anthropology; that is, it strives to show how man appears in the realm of poetic creation. For this very reason it does not deny but stresses emphatically that the validity of the genre concepts is not confined to literature, that it is a question here of terms in literary scholarship for general human possibilities. The entire investigation is directed toward the question: "What is man?" And whoever reads this poetics with this anthropological question in view certainly fares better than one who asks himself how such a poetics could be of use in studies in literary history.

It only seems as though the posing of such a question were hybris. Man is not an object about which wrong or right or even final pronouncements can be made. Man's essence is formed, arises in what he thinks of himself, in the unfolding of his self-consciousness. By giving specific answers to the question: "What is man?" we commit ourselves to specific possibilities. We become aware of ourselves, become conscious of ourselves in a specific way. Thus, one can say: In every system, in the worldview of every writer something of what man is capable of being is realized. The truth of such a worldview cannot be measured by what man actually is in the depth of his being. For this actual person, this person in and of itself, does not exist. Or he exists only for a spirit we would have to call divine. Here, too, the truth can only be measured by the degree to which it can be fruitful, to which it is capable of elucidating our present and our past. Thus, it is fundamentally not out of the question that all phenomena in the realm of poetic creation could prove to be coherent within such a system, that an objective order of all extant writing could become visible in such a system: creative writing, language, man in general. Still, it remains a universal order as imagined by a historically determined, tradition-bound mind. It is everyone's privilege to say: This type of order does not interest me. But he or she cannot go so far as to say: This order is not objective. One person looks at a landscape with the eyes of a tactician and is capable of evaluating every hill, every tree, and every house from a tactical perspective. Another looks at the same landscape with the eyes of a farmer and again, everything, hill, tree, and house, forms a whole. The perspective may be different but the perception remains objective and can be verified according to the particulars. It seems to me that my attempt at a new poetics should be viewed in the same way. I should not want to defend myself if someone were to say that I was telling him nothing. I would be contradicting myself.

One last word on the problem of value. The *Basic Concepts of Poetics* does not explicitly raise the question of value. This seems to me to be an obvious prerequisite of such an undertaking. But others are of a different opinion. They say: Of what use is a poetics if it does not show me what I am to regard as ugly or beautiful? Now of course, we could reply that although not within the framework of this poetics but nonetheless in precise presentation of literary scholarship *one* condition of the beautiful can be shown: the pure stylistic harmony of every single part of the work of art. But this does not accomplish much because this is precisely the question we are asking, namely, is the stylistic harmony, achieved for instance in Gothic art, of greater value than the stylistic harmony in antiquity, that of romanticism greater than that of the classical period. I know of no definite answer. We are left at this point with a personal decision. But one thing is given by poetics here, too, namely the possibility of understanding ourselves in the context of our own evaluation, if not better, then at least in larger contexts. It would be easy to say: Obviously, a work is more perfect if it keeps more to the middle and does not go to the two extremes, to the lyric, which threatens to dissolve, or to the dramatic, which becomes rigid. Or: A work is more perfect when the three genres all have as strong a part as possible in it and are completely in harmony. I would be more inclined to agree with the latter. Yet someone else could reply that in so doing I am holding man to the center of his being. But man, he says, is something that should be overcome as soon as possible, be it that he returns to the inwardliness of his speechless origins or that he fails tragically in a last overextension of the dramatic element. Certain romantics have demonstrated the former, Heinrich von Kleist the latter. That I agree with one and disagree with the other says nothing about the thing itself but does say something about me. But I am able to place my decision within the context of the whole. And this is a human need, as is the wish for knowledge.

Index